Written and Compiled by

Patrick Sebranek, *Former English Chairman, Union H*
School, Union Grove, Wisconsin

Dave Kemper, *Parkview Junior High, Mukwonago, Wiscor*

Illustrated by Chris Krenzke

The Write Source   **Burlington, Wisconsin**

To the Teacher

The Write Source handbook is suitable for use in grades 4 through 9. The handbook stresses the fundamental principles of writing—the writing process, the paragraph, poetry, usage and mixed pairs, punctuation, spelling, capitalization, and so on. The handbook also contains sections on reading, speaking, thinking and writing, the book review, literary terms, the classroom report, vocabulary skills, and a complete glossary of prefixes, suffixes, and roots.

The Write Source can be used in the English classroom as a reference book or with any of three coordinating workbooks. The workbooks provide numerous opportunities for students to practice their writing, revising, and proofreading skills.

The Write Source handbook can help students throughout the school day—and even later at home—whenever they have a question about punctuation, usage, or writing. The handbook is truly an all-school handbook: It includes a very helpful math section, a glossary of computer terms, a study skills and test-taking unit, and an 8-page full-color map section. The handbook has been designed with the student in mind and contains interesting examples, plenty of white space, and numerous full-color illustrations.

Acknowledgments

The Write Source is a reality because of the help, advice, and rstanding given by our families: Judy, Julie, and Janae; ne and Tim; and Katie. Also, three of our students allowed us their papers as samples in the handbook: Mike Evans, Lynn ki, and Lisa Servais.

are grateful for the help and advice of a number of educa-nice Vanderlaan, Lois Krenzke, Barb Scherrer, Judy s, Kay Droster-Pockat, Joan Hafemeister, and Linda e also want to thank John Janty, head of the math de-t Waunakee High School, for his help with "Improving Skills," and Verne Meyer, Dordt College, for his contri-e "Words and Sentences" and "Mechanics of Writing" nally, we must thank Amy and Rita whose dedicated l us through many rough spots.

gh

sin

1st Edition

ISBN 939045-02-8 (Hard Cover)
ISBN 939045-03-6 (Soft Cover)

Using the Handbook

The **Table of Contents** near the front of your handbook gives you a list of the major units and the page number on which each unit begins.

The **Index** at the back of the handbook is one of its most useful parts. The index contains much more information than the table of contents. It is arranged in alphabetical order and includes every topic covered in the handbook. The numbers after each word in the index refer to the **topic numbers**, not the page numbers. (The topic numbers are the numbers which appear to the left of each new topic in the handbook.) Since there are often many topics on one page, these topic numbers will help you to find information more quickly.

Let's say, for example, you were asked to find information on *collective nouns*. If the index of the handbook listed only page numbers, it would tell you to go to page 2. (Go to page 2 and look for information on collective nouns. Did it take you a while to find this information?)

Now look at the sample index to the left and locate *collective noun*. You will find two numbers: 5 (which you found on page 2) and 396. Go to 396 and locate this additional information about collective nouns. Was it easier and quicker to find this time? It should have been. That is the advantage of using topic numbers in an index rather than page numbers. It saves time.

To the Student

Words are a very important part of our lives. We use them for reading, writing, speaking—and even thinking. It's hard to imagine a world without words. Our language is made up of thousands of words, each one with its own special *meaning, feeling,* and *sound.* We begin using these words very early in life and continue to use more and more words as we grow older.

We use some words every day. These words seem to come to us naturally. We probably don't remember ever "learning" them. We use them with ease and usually quite effectively. We don't need any language lessons to tell us how to ask our mother what's for supper, or how to ask our teacher if we can get a drink of water, or how to ask our friends what they plan to do this weekend. Somehow, we always find the words we need to let people know what we want or need.

But there are times when the words are a little harder to find—especially when you, the student, are in school searching for a clear and correct way to say something in a writing assignment. Finding the right words to express your thoughts in writing is not always easy. It takes practice. As you practice, it is important for you to write freely and naturally. This will make it easier for you to express your thoughts in a way other people will understand. You can, however, also make your thoughts clearer and easier to understand by following certain helpful hints.

Learning to write well is a little bit like learning to play baseball. Some people can hit the ball well without much help; others can benefit greatly from simply knowing how to hold the bat properly or how to shift their weight as they swing. In both writing and baseball, it is important to understand some of the helpful hints and then to practice using them.

So what are some of the helpful hints of writing? Well, one of the most basic is to choose words which say exactly what you want to say. Another is to choose words which your readers will understand. A third rule is to choose words which are lively and colorful, words which your readers will like and remember.

But these hints are quite general, you say, and don't really "show" you how to improve your writing. You're right. And that's why we have written *The Write Source* for you. We plan to show you in the pages which follow exactly what you can do to improve your writing. We will give you some specific hints, rules, and guidelines which we think you will find helpful. But remember, no matter how many hints, rules, and guidelines you know, you won't become a better writer unless you practice.

Table of Contents

Words and Sentences

Parts of Speech

1 To make it easier to understand words and how to use them, all words in the English language have been put into one of eight groups. These groups are called the **parts of speech**. Each part of speech contains words which are used in basically the same way in sentences. Because words can be used in eight different ways, there are eight parts of speech: *noun, pronoun, verb, adjective, adverb, preposition, conjunction, interjection.*

Noun

2 A **noun** is a word which is the name of something: a person, place, thing, or idea.

> Grandma Ulferts, uncle; Lake Michigan, river;
> John Deere tractor, carburetor; Labor Day, sympathy

3 Nouns are grouped in certain classes: *proper, common, concrete, abstract,* and *collective.* The two main classes of nouns are **proper** and **common**. A **proper noun** is the name of a specific person, place, thing, or idea. Proper nouns are always capitalized.

> Sandra Day O'Connor, Grand Ole Opry, Corvette,
> *Call of the Wild*, Fido, Friday, February

A **common noun** is any noun which does not name a specific person, place, thing, or idea. Common nouns are not capitalized.

> child, country, rainbow, blockhead, winter, happiness, love

4 Nouns are also grouped according to the kind of thing they name: **concrete** or **abstract**.

A **concrete noun** names a thing that is tangible or physical (can be touched or seen). Concrete nouns are either proper or common.

> Chevrolet, White House, car, guitar, drums, book, author

An **abstract noun** names something you can think about but which you cannot see or touch. Abstract nouns are either common or proper.

> Christianity, Judaism, satisfaction, poverty, illness, love, excellence, creation, evolution

5　Another type of noun is the **collective noun**. A collective noun names a *collection* of persons, animals, places, or things.

> persons .... tribe, congregation, class, team
> animals ....flock, herd, gaggle, clutch, litter
> places ....United States, United Nations
> things .... batch, cluster, bunch

6　Nouns are also grouped according to their **number**. Number of a noun tells us whether the noun is singular or plural.

A **singular noun** names one person, place, thing, or idea.

> boy, stage, rock festival, fear

A **plural noun** names more than one person, place, thing, or idea.

> boys, stages, rock festivals, fears

7　A **compound noun** is a noun made up of two or more words. Some compound nouns are written as one word *(football)*, some as two words *(high school)*, and some as hyphenated words *(brother-in-law)*.

8　Nouns have **gender**. That is, they are grouped according to sex: feminine, masculine, neuter, and indefinite.

> feminine .... mother, hostess, women, cow, hen
> 　　　　　　　　　　 *(female)*
> masculine .... uncle, brother, men, bull, rooster
> 　　　　　　　　　　 *(male)*
> neuter............. tree, cobweb, closet (*without sex*)
> indefinite .... president, teacher, doctor, child, lawyer, baby, duckling, clerk, assistant *(male or female)*

9　Nouns are also grouped into one of three cases. The **case** of a noun tells us how it is related to the other words in the sentence. There are three cases: **nominative, possessive,** and **objective**.

A noun is in the **nominative case** when it is used as the subject of the verb.

> The guidance *counselor* looked the eighth-grade student in the eye and warned him, "The high school *principal* won't allow you to take more than one study hall."

A noun is also in the nominative case when it is used as a predicate noun (or predicate nominative). A predicate noun follows a form of the *be* verb *(is, are, was, were, been)* and repeats or renames the subject. In the examples below, *place* renames *study hall* and *waste* renames *hours.*

> "A *study hall* is a good *place* to work on your assignments, but two *hours* of study hall is a *waste* of your valuable time."

A noun is in the **possessive case** when it shows possession or ownership.

> The *student's* face showed concern. "But I need an *hour's* rest every day in order to do well in my classes."

A noun is in the **objective case** when it is used as the direct object, the indirect object, or the object of the preposition.

> "Don't worry. You'll enjoy *high school* with only one study hall." (*High school* is a direct object.)

> "High school teachers give every *student* plenty of time to finish his or her assignments." (*Student* is an indirect object.)

> "The goal of every *student* should be to learn as much as possible while in high school." (*Student* is the object of the preposition *of.*)

Pronoun

10 A **pronoun** is a word used in place of a noun (*him, it, which, they, whom, that, themselves, herself*). Pronouns appear in different forms:

> Simple .... I, you, he, she, it, we, you, they
> Compound ...... myself, yourself, himself, herself, ourselves
> Phrasal .... one another, each other

There are five different types of pronouns: **personal, relative, indefinite, interrogative,** and **demonstrative.**

11 All pronouns have antecedents. An **antecedent** is the noun which the pronoun refers to or replaces.

> The *speaker* coughed and reached for the glass of water. When the glass reached his lips, he noticed a *fly* which was "swimming" in the water. (*Speaker* is the antecedent of *his* and *he; fly* is the antecedent of *which.*)

12 Some of the most common **personal pronouns** are these: *I, you, he, she, it, we, they.* These pronouns have other forms including the following: *his, hers, her, its, me, myself, us, yours,* and so on.

13 There are three forms of personal pronouns. The form of a personal pronoun shows whether the pronoun is singular or plural in **number;** first, second, or third in **person;** nominative, possessive,

3

or objective in **case**.

14   **Singular** personal pronouns are these: *I, you, he, she, it.* **Plural** personal pronouns are these: *we, you, they.* Notice that the pronoun *you* can be singular or plural.

15   The **person** of a pronoun tells us whether the pronoun is speaking, is spoken to, or is spoken about.

A **first person** pronoun is used in place of the name of the speaker.

> *I* am speaking.
> *We* like snakes.

A **second person** pronoun is used to name the person or thing spoken to.

> Eliza, will *you* please stop complaining.
> *You* dogs stop growling right now!

A **third person** pronoun is used to name the person or thing spoken about.

> *She* said that garbage is good fertilizer.
> *He* always uses *it*.

16   Like nouns, pronouns fall into one of three cases. Their **case** tells how pronouns are related to the other words used with them. There are three cases: **nominative, possessive,** and **objective**.

17   A pronoun is in the **nominative case** when it is used as the subject of the verb. The following are nominative forms: *I, you, he, she, it, we, they.*

> *I* like myself when things go well.
> *You* must live life in order to love life.

18   A pronoun is also in the **nominative case** when it is used as a **predicate nominative.** A predicate nominative follows a form of the *be* verb (*am, is, are, was, were, been*), and it repeats the subject.

> "It is *I*," growled the big wolf from under Grandmother's bonnet.
> "It is *he*!" shrieked Little Red as she twisted his snout into a corkscrew.

19   A pronoun is in the **possessive case** when it shows *possession* or ownership. (*Note*: You do not use an apostrophe with a personal pronoun to show possession.)

> my, mine, our, ours, his, her, hers, their, its, yours

20   A pronoun is in the **objective case** when it is used as the direct object, indirect object, or object of a preposition.

> Nathaniel hugged *me*. (*Me* is the direct object of the verb, *hugged*.)
> Benji told *me* a story. (*Me* is the indirect object of the verb, *told*.)

4

Teddy Snappers listened because the story was about *him.* (*Him* is the object of the preposition, *about.*)

21

Singular			
	Nominative Case	**Possessive Case**	**Objective Case**
1st Person	I	my, mine	me
2nd Person	you	your, yours	you
3rd Person	he	his	him
	she	her, hers	her
	it	its	it
Plural			
	Nominative Case	**Possessive Case**	**Objective Case**
1st Person	we	our, ours	us
2nd Person	you	your, yours	you
3rd Person	they	their, theirs	them

22 When a *personal pronoun* throws the action back upon the subject of a sentence, it is called a **reflexive pronoun.**

Soapy cut *himself.*
He was giving *himself* a haircut.

Note: The sentence would not be complete without its reflexive pronoun.

23 When a *personal pronoun* calls special attention to a noun or pronoun, giving it special emphasis, it is called an **intensive pronoun.**

Soapy *himself* picked the bowl he used as a pattern for his haircut.

Note: The sentence *would be complete without* its intensive pronoun.

24 A **relative pronoun** relates one part of a sentence to a noun or pronoun in another part of the sentence. The relative pronoun stands at the beginning of that part of the sentence it relates to a noun or pronoun.

Candid Camera once showed a horse *that appeared to be able to talk.* (*that* relates to *horse*)

An actor, *who was hidden in the horse's stall,* did the talking. (*who* relates to *actor*)

A woman, *who stopped to reply to the horse's greeting,* solemnly wrote down the betting tips *that he gave her.* (*who* relates to *woman*; *that* relates to *tips*)

Relative pronouns are **simple** (*who, what, which, that*) or **compound** (*whoever, whosoever, whatever, whatsoever, whichever*).

5

25 An **indefinite pronoun** is one that does not specifically name its antecedent (the noun or pronoun it replaces). Common indefinite pronouns are: *all, any, many, most, each, either, neither, one, everybody, another, anybody, everyone, nobody, everything, somebody,* and *some.*

> While we were fishing, *somebody* made me a sardine sandwich.
>
> The "sardines" wiggled in my sandwich, and *anybody* could see there were fewer minnows in the minnow pail.

26 An **interrogative pronoun** asks a question.

> *Who* is knocking on the door, and *what* do you want?

27 A **demonstrative pronoun** points out a noun. *This* and *these* designate a noun nearby. *That* and *those* designate a noun far away.

> *This* was a wonderful experience for her.
> All of *that* seemed so long ago when she thought about it now.

Caution: To add *here* or *there* to a demonstrative pronoun is incorrect.

> This *here* is a dumb dog.
> That *there* is an even dumber cat.

It is also incorrect to use *them* in place of *these* or *those.*

> *Them* are both dumb animals.

28

Kinds of Pronouns				
Relative				
who, whose, whom, which, what, that				
Demonstrative				
this, that, these, those				
Interrogative				
who, whose, whom, which, what				
Intensive and Reflexive				
myself, himself, herself, yourself, themselves, ourselves				
Indefinite Pronouns				
all	both	everything	nobody	several
another	each	few	none	some
any	each one	many	no one	somebody
anybody	either	most	nothing	someone
anyone	everybody	much	one	something
anything	everyone	neither	other	such

Verb

29   A **verb** is a word which expresses action or existence.

> Stevie Wonder *hosted* the show.   (action)
> Many famous people *joined* him on stage.   (action)
> They *were* present to honor Dr. Martin Luther King,
> Jr.   (existence)

30   Verbs have **number.**   They are **singular** or **plural.**   If the verb is
singular, its subject must be singular.   Likewise, a plural verb must
have a plural subject.

> Because it was raining, *he was* in town for the
> day.   (Singular subject and verb)
> Country *people plan* their shopping days around
> the weather.   (Plural subject and verb)

31   Verbs fall into one of **three points of view: first person** *(I)*,
second person *(you)*, and **third person** *(he, she, it)*.

Point of View	Singular	Plural
1st Person	I sniff	we sniff
2nd Person	you sniff	you sniff
3rd Person	he/she/it *sniffs*	they sniff

32   A verb is in the **active voice** if the subject is doing the action in a
sentence.

> The *baseball hit* the batter.

33   A verb is in the **passive voice** if the subject is receiving the action
or not doing the action himself.

> The *batter was hit* by the baseball.

34

Tense	Active Voice		Passive Voice	
	Singular	Plural	Singular	Plural
Present Tense	I find	we find	I am found	we are found
	you find	you find	you are found	you are found
	he/she/it finds	they find	he/she/it is found	they are found
Past Tense	I found	we found	I was found	we were found
	you found	you found	you were found	you were found
	he found	they found	he was found	they were found
Future Tense	I shall find	we shall find	I shall be found	we shall be found
	you will find	you will find	you will be found	you will be found
	he will find	they will find	he will be found	they will be found
Present Perfect	I have found	we have found	I have been found	we have been found
	you have found	you have found	you have been found	you have been found
	he has found	they have found	he has been found	they have been found
Past Perfect	I had found	we had found	I had been found	we had been found
	you had found	you had found	you had been found	you had been found
	he had found	they had found	he had been found	they had been found
Future Perfect	I shall have found	we shall have found	I shall have been found	we shall have been found
	you will have found	you will have found	you will have been found	you will have been found
	he will have found	they will have found	he will have been found	they will have been found

35 A verb has three principal parts: the **present, past,** and **past participle.** All six of the tenses are formed from these principal parts. The past and past participle of regular verbs are formed by adding *ed* to the present form. The past and past participle of irregular verbs are usually different words; however, some irregular verbs remain the same in all three principal parts.

36 A verb is in the **present tense** when it expresses action (or existence) which is happening *now* or which happens *continually, regularly.*

> I *hear* the boy's voice as he *calls* from his tree house that *sits* near the top of a tall maple.

37 A verb is in the **past tense** when it expresses action (or existence) which is completed at a *particular* time in the past.

> I *heard* him this morning, and it *reminded* me of the summer I *stayed* with my grandmother.

38 A verb is in the **future tense** when it expresses action that *will* take place.

> Sarah *will try out* for the play tomorrow.

39 Common Irregular Verbs and Their Principal Parts

Present Tense	Past Tense	Past Participle	Present Tense	Past Tense	Past Participle	Present Tense	Past Tense	Past Participle
am, be	was, were	been	fly	flew	flown	shine		
begin	began	begun	forsake	forsook	forsaken	(light)	shone	shone
bid (offer)	bid	bid	freeze	froze	frozen	(polish)	shined	shined
bid (order)	bade	bidden	give	gave	given	shrink	shrank	shrunk
bite	bit	bitten	go	went	gone	sing	sang, sung	sung
blow	blew	blown	grow	grew	grown	sink	sank, sunk	sunk
break	broke	broken	hang			sit	sat	sat
bring	brought	brought	(execute)	hanged	hanged	slay	slew	slain
burst	burst	burst	(dangle)	hung	hung	speak	spoke	spoken
catch	caught	caught	hide	hid	hidden,	spring	sprang,	sprung
choose	chose	chosen			hid		sprung	
come	came	come	know	knew	known	steal	stole	stolen
dive	dived	dived	lay	laid	laid	strive	strove	striven
do	did	done	lead	led	led	swear	swore	sworn
drag	dragged	dragged	lie (recline)	lay	lain	swim	swam	swum
draw	drew	drawn	lie (deceive)	lied	lied	swing	swung	swung
drink	drank	drunk	raise	raised	raised	take	took	taken
drown	drowned	drowned	ride	rode	ridden	tear	tore	torn
drive	drove	driven	ring	rang	rung	throw	threw	thrown
eat	ate	eaten	rise	rose	risen	wake	woke, waked	waked
fall	fell	fallen	run	ran	run	wear	wore	worn
fight	fought	fought	see	saw	seen	weave	wove	woven
flee	fled	fled	set	set	set	wring	wrung	wrung
flow	flowed	flowed	shake	shook	shaken	write	wrote	written

40 A verb is in the **present perfect tense** when it expresses action which *began in the past* but *continues in the present* or *is completed in the present.* (To form the present perfect tense, add *has* or *have* to the past participle.)

> She *has practiced* singing for many days.

41 A verb is in the **past perfect tense** when it expresses action which *began in the past* and *was completed in the past.* (To form the past perfect tense, add *had* to the past participle.)

She *had forgotten* the words the last time she tried out for the play.

42 A verb is in the **future perfect tense** when it expresses action or existence which *will begin in the future* and *will be completed by a specific time in the future.* (To form the future perfect tense, add *shall have* or *will have* to the past participle.)

Sarah *will have returned* to her house before she finds out if she got a part in the play.

43 **Helping verbs** *help* to form some of the tenses and voice of the main verb. (Helping verbs are also called *auxiliary verbs.*)

In the following examples the **main verbs** are in boldface, and the *helping verbs* are italicized.

Elmer *was* **using** super-strength, slow-drying glue.

For ten minutes he *had been* **holding** the two broken parts together.

He *should have* **bought** a C-clamp for a glue job like this.

While Elmer's hands *were* thus **engaged**, his friends *had been* **rolling** his pants cuffs up and his socks down.

Common helping verbs are these: *shall, will, would, should, must, can, may, have, had, has, do, did,* and the forms of the *be* verb—*is, are, was, were, am, been.*

44 Verbs are **transitive** or **intransitive**.

Transitive verbs *transfer* their action to an object. An object must receive the action of a transitive verb for the meaning of the verb to be complete.

Squeaky *rides* his *horse.* (*Rides* transfers its action to *horse*; therefore, *horse* receives this action. Without the word *horse* the meaning of the verb *rides* would be incomplete.)

That beautiful *horse is ridden* by Squeaky. (The subject of the sentence, *horse*, receives the action of the verb, *is ridden.*)

45 A transitive verb throws the action directly to a **direct object** and indirectly to an **indirect object**. For a sentence to have an indirect object, it must have a direct object. A sentence can, however, have only a direct object. Direct objects and indirect objects are always nouns or pronouns.

Bif scribbled his *girlfriend* a **note.**
(direct object: **note**
indirect object: *girlfriend*)

Mr. Land faithfully taught his *students* **geography.**
(direct object: **geography**
indirect object: *students*)

Many students today can program **computers.**
(direct object: **computers**)

46   The object of a transitive verb is called the **direct object** if it receives the action *directly* from the subject.   (The direct object answers the question *what* or *whom?*)

Rita sent a *telegram.*
(*Telegram* is the direct object; it answers the question, "Rita sent a *what?*")

47   An **indirect object** receives the action of a transitive verb, *indirectly.*   An indirect object names the person *to whom* or *for whom* something is done.

Rita sent *me* a telegram.
(*Me* is the indirect object.)

Note: When the word naming the indirect receiver of the action is contained in a prepositional phrase, it is no longer considered an indirect object.

Rita sent a telegram *to me.*
(*Me* is the object of the preposition *to.*)

48   An **intransitive verb** completes its action without an object.

The pitcher *fell* from my hands.
Milk *spilled* over the floor.

49   Many verbs can be either **transitive** or **intransitive.**

I *drove* my car.   (transitive)
I *drove* over a skunk.   (intransitive)

50   A **linking verb** is an intransitive verb.   The most common linking verbs are forms of the *to be* verb (existence):   *is, are, were, was, been, am,* and verbs such as *smell, look, taste, remain, feel, appear, sound, seem, become, grow, stand, turn.*

51   A linking verb *links* a subject to a noun or adjective in the predicate.

She *is* a competent attorney.
The court case *was* successful.

In the first example above, *attorney* is linked by the verb *is* to the subject *she.*   *Attorney* repeats or renames the subject; it is called a *predicate noun* or *predicate nominative.*

In the second example above, *successful* is linked by the verb *was* to the subject *case.*   Because *successful* describes the subject, it is called a *predicate adjective.*

52   A **verbal** is a word which is made from a verb, has the power of a verb, but acts as another part of speech. There are three types of verbals: **gerunds, infinitives,** and **participles.**

53   A **gerund** is a verb form which ends in *ing* and is used as a noun.

Smoking rots your lungs.

54   An **infinitive** is a verb form which is usually introduced by *to;* an infinitive may be used as a *noun*, as an *adjective*, or as an *adverb*.

> *To scream* in class is her secret wish. (*To scream* is a noun.)
> The first student *to giggle* will be in trouble. (*To giggle* is an adjective.)
> Joe turned *to laugh*. (*To laugh* is an adverb.)

55   A **participle** is a verb form ending in *-ing* or *-ed*. A participle functions as an adjective because it can modify a noun or pronoun.

> Those kids *digging* for China are already tired.
> Those *tired* kids will probably lose interest before they make it.
>
> (*Digging* modifies kids in the first sentence above. *Tired* modifies kids in the second sentence.)

Adjective

56   An **adjective** is a word used to describe a noun or pronoun.

> Why did *ancient* dinosaurs become *an extinct* species?
> Perhaps *other small* animals preyed on *their* eggs.
> Maybe *a deadly* epidemic wiped them out.

57   The articles *a, an,* and *the* are adjectives.

> In return for *a* piece of land, he offered me *an* old house and *the* remains of his crumbling barn.

58   Adjectives can be **proper** or **common.**

A **proper adjective** is formed from a proper noun, and it is always capitalized.

> Lake Bella was created by a dam which flooded farmland in the *Bigelow* area. Old farm wells and springs feed the *Lake Bella* bottom.

A **common adjective** is any adjective which is not proper, and it is not capitalized (unless it is the first word in a sentence).

> The *old farm* wells feed the *sandy lake* bottom.

11

59 Adjectives can be **simple** or **compound.**

A **simple adjective** is one word: *many, nice, sick, intelligent.*

A **compound adjective** is made up of more than one word. (Sometimes it is hyphenated.)

> The *freshwater* springs feed the *mile-deep* lake bottom.

60 A **demonstrative adjective** is one which points out a particular noun. Common demonstrative adjectives are *this, these* (designate something nearby) and *that, those* (designate something at a distance).

> *This* hockey stick is better than *that* one.

Take note: When a noun does not follow *this, these, that,* or *those,* they are pronouns, not adjectives.

Caution: Do not use *here* or *there* after a demonstrative adjective.

Incorrect: This *here* car is fast. That *there* horse is faster.
Correct: *This* car is fast. *That* horse is faster.

61 An **indefinite adjective** is one which gives us an *approximate* number or quantity. It does not tell *exactly* how many or how much. (See *indefinite pronoun,* 25.)

> *Some* students protested what they thought was a policy unfair to *many* female athletes. They felt the girls had put in as *much* serious practice time as the boys.

62 A **predicate adjective** follows a form of the *be* verb (*linking verb*), is part of the predicate, and describes the subject.

Jose's cats are *lazy.* (*lazy* cats)
They are also *fat* and *chunky.* (*fat* and *chunky*)

12

63 Adjectives have three forms: **positive, comparative,** and **super-lative**.

The **positive form** describes a noun or pronoun without comparing it to anyone or anything else.

Superman is *tough*. Superman is *wonderful*.

The **comparative form** (*-er*) compares two persons, places, things, or ideas.

Tarzan is *tougher* than Superman.
Tarzan is *more wonderful* than Superman.

The **superlative form** (*-est*) compares three or more persons, places, things, or ideas.

But I, Big Bird, am the *toughest* of all!
But I, Big Bird, am the *most wonderful* of all!

64 Some adjectives that are *two syllables long* can either use *er/est* endings or add *more/most, less/least* to express comparison.

For example, you can say, "*clumsy, clumsier, clumsiest*."
But, you can also say, "*clumsy, more clumsy, most clumsy*."

65 When adjectives are *three or more syllables long*, they usually require the words *more/most, less/least* to express comparison.

The **correct** forms of wonderful are *wonderful, more wonderful, most wonderful.*
You would **not** say, "*wonderful, wonderfuller, wonderfullest*."
The **correct** forms of ridiculous are *ridiculous, less ridiculous, least ridiculous.*
Likewise, you would **not** say, "*ridiculous, ridiculousless, ridiculousleast*."

66 Other adjectives use completely different words to express comparison.

good, better, best
bad, worse, worst

Adverb

67 An **adverb** modifies a verb, an adjective, or another adverb. An adverb tells *how, when, where, why, how often,* and *how much.*

Dad snores *loudly*. (*Loudly* modifies the verb *snores*.)
His snoring is *really* annoying. (*Really* modifies the adjective *annoying*.)
My brother also snores *very* loudly. (*Very* modifies the adverb *loudly*.)

68   Adverbs often end in *-ly*, but not always. Words like *very, quite,* and *always* modify adverbs or adjectives, making them adverbs. (*Note:* Not all words ending in *-ly* are adverbs. A word like "lovely," for example, is an adjective.)

69   Adverbs can be grouped by **time, place, manner,** or **degree.**

- Adverbs of **time** tell *when, how often,* and *how long.*

annually	tomorrow	often	daily

- Adverbs of **place** tell *where, to where,* or *from where.*

here	there	backward	outside

- Adverbs of **manner** often end in *-ly* and tell *how* something is done.

unkindly	gently	well	regularly

Note: Some adverbs can be written with or without the *-ly* ending. When in doubt, use the *-ly* form. (**Examples:** *slow, slowly; deep, deeply; quick, quickly*)

- Adverbs of **degree** tell *how much* or *how little.*

scarcely	too	entirely	generally

70   Adverbs, like adjectives, have three forms: **positive, comparative,** and **superlative.**

Positive	Comparative	Superlative
well	better	best
badly	worse	worst
fast	faster	fastest
loudly	more loudly	most loudly
dramatically	less dramatically	least dramatically

Preposition

71   A **preposition** is a word (or group of words) which shows how two words or ideas are related to each other. Specifically, a preposition shows the relationship between its object (a noun or a pronoun that follows the preposition) and some other word in the sentence.

> The caterpillar hung *under* Natasha's nose. (*Under* shows the relationship between the verb, *hung,* and the object of the preposition, *nose.*)

There are three basic kinds of prepositions: **simple** (*at, in, of, on, with*), **compound** (*within, outside, underneath*), and **phrasal** (*on account of, on top of*).

72   A **prepositional phrase** includes the *preposition,* the *object* of the preposition, and the *modifiers* of the object.

> Little kids often run *away from big caterpillars.*

(preposition: *away from*   object: *caterpillars*   modifier: *big*)

Note: A prepositional phrase may function as an adjective or as an adverb.

> But little kids *with curious minds* enjoy their company. (The prepositional phrase, *with curious minds*, acts as an adjective and modifies *kids*.)

73 A **preposition** never appears alone. To be a preposition, it needs an object. If a word found in the list of prepositions appears in a sentence, but has no object, it is not a preposition. It is probably an adverb.

> Natasha never played with caterpillars *before*.

(*Before* is used as an adverb in this sentence because it modifies *played*, a verb.)

74	**List of Prepositions**				
aboard	at	despite	in regard to	opposite	through
about	away from	down	in spite of	out	throughout
above	back of	down from	inside	out of	till
according to	because of	during	inside of	outside	to
across	before	except	instead of	outside of	together with
across from	behind	except for	into	over	toward
after	below	excepting	like	over to	under
against	beneath	for	near	owing to	underneath
along	beside	from	near to	past	until
alongside	besides	from among	notwithstanding	prior to	unto
alongside of	between	from between	of	regarding	up
along with	beyond	from under	off	round	up to
amid	but	in	on	round about	upon
among	by	in addition to	on account of	save	with
apart from	by means of	in behalf of	on behalf of	since	within
around	concerning	in front of	on top of	subsequent to	without
aside from	considering	in place of	onto		

Conjunction

75 A **conjunction** connects individual words or groups of words.

> A puffer fish is short *and* fat. (The conjunction *and* connects the word *short* to the word *fat*.)
>
> The puffer puts his lips on a snail *and* sucks out the flesh. (The conjunction *and* connects the phrase *puts his lips on a snail* to the phrase *sucks out the flesh*.)

76 A **coordinate conjunction** connects a word to a word, a phrase to a phrase, or a clause to a clause. The words, phrases, or clauses joined by a coordinate conjunction must be *equal* or of the *same type*. Common coordinate conjunctions are these: *and, but, or, nor, for, yet, so.*

> *Air* and *plane* combine to make the compound word *airplane*. (*And* connects two equal words.)
>
> Airplanes take off in good weather *and* in bad weather. (*And* connects two equal phrases.)

15

> The airplanes took off in the bright sunshine, *but* they landed in total darkness. (Two equal clauses are connected by the coordinate conjunction *but*.)

77 **Correlative conjunctions** are coordinate conjunctions used in pairs. (See chart.)

> *Neither* pickles *nor* sauerkraut should be put on a chocolate sundae.

78 A **subordinate conjunction** is a word or group of words that connects, and shows the relationship between, two clauses which are *not* equally important. A subordinate conjunction connects a dependent clause to an independent clause in order to complete the meaning of the dependent clause.

> A chocolate sundae tastes best *when* it is topped with chopped nuts. (The clause *when it is topped with chopped nuts* is dependent. It depends on the rest of the sentence to complete its meaning.)

79

Kinds of Conjunctions	
Coordinate:	and, but, or, nor, for, yet
Correlative:	either, or; neither, nor; not only, but also; both, and; whether, or; just, as; just, so; as, so
Subordinate:	after, although, as, as if, as long as, as though, because, before, if, in order that, provided that, since, so, so that, that, though, till, unless, until, when, where, whereas, while

Note: Relative pronouns and conjunctive adverbs can also connect clauses.

Interjection

80 An **interjection** is a word or short phrase included in a sentence in order to communicate strong emotion or surprise. Punctuation (usually an exclamation point) is used to separate an interjection from the rest of the sentence.

Wow! Would you look at that!

Oh, no! He actually did it!

Man! Duke painted his horse!

Yikes! I don't think Old Paint is too crazy about the paint job!

Parts of a Sentence

81 A **sentence** is made up of one or more words which express a complete thought. (*Note:* A sentence begins with a capital letter; it ends with a period, question mark, or exclamation point.)

> This book should help you write. It explains many things. How do you plan to use it? I hope you find it helpful!

82 A **modifier** is a word or a group of words which changes or adds to the meaning of another word.

> *The priceless* picture slipped.
> (*The* and *priceless* modify picture.)
>
> *The old* painting smacked *noisily* on *the concrete* floor. (*The* and *old* modify painting; *noisily* modifies smacked; *the* and *concrete* modify floor.)

83 A sentence must have a **subject** and **predicate** in order to express a complete thought. Either the subject or the predicate (or both) may *not* be stated, but both must be clearly understood.

> (*You*) Feed your dog.
> (*You* is the understood subject.)
> Who took my shoe? Fido. (*did*)
> (*Did* is the understood predicate.)
> Whose mutt is this? (*It is*) Mine.
> (*It* is the understood subject, and *is* is the understood verb.)

84 A **subject** is the part of a sentence which is doing something or about which something is said.

> My *dog* licks my toes.   *Licking* is one thing dogs do well.

85 A **simple subject** is the subject without the words which describe or modify it.

> Many large *dogs* behave like little puppies.

86 A **complete subject** is the simple subject and all the words which modify it.

> *Many large dogs* behave like little puppies. (*Many* and *large* modify *dogs*. The three words—*many large dogs*—make up the complete subject.)

87 A **compound subject** is made up of two or more simple subjects.

> *Students* and *teachers* need school.

88 A **predicate** is the part of the sentence which says something about the subject.

> Principals *remember*.

89 A **simple predicate** is the predicate (verb) without the words which describe or modify it.

> Little people *can talk* faster than big people. (*Can talk* is the simple predicate; *faster than big people* describes how little people *can talk*.)

90 A **complete predicate** is the simple predicate and all the words which modify or explain it.

> Little people *can talk faster than big people*.

91 A **compound predicate** is composed of two or more simple predicates.

> Big people *talk* slowly but *eat* fast.

92 A sentence may have a **compound subject** and a **compound predicate**.

> Sturdy *tongues* and thick *teeth say* sentences slowly but *chew* food quickly.

93 Whatever receives the action of the simple predicate is the **direct object**.

> Picasso painted *pictures*.   His pictures express *feeling*.

(*Note: Pictures* receives the action of the verb *painted*. It answers the question *Picasso painted what?*)

94 The **direct object** may be **compound**.

> Chickens eat *oyster shells* and *grit*.

95 A **phrase** is a group of related words which lacks either a subject or a predicate (or both).

> *ran very fast*   (The predicate lacks a subject.)
> *the young colt*   (The subject lacks a predicate.)
> *down the steep slope*   (The phrase lacks both a subject and a predicate.)
> *The young colt ran very fast down the steep slope.* (Together, the three phrases present a complete thought.)

Phrases usually take their names from the main words which introduce them (prepositional phrase, verb phrase, etc.). They can also be named for the function they serve in a sentence (adverb phrase, adjective phrase, etc.).

> The ancient oak *tree* ....noun phrase
> *with* crooked old limbs .... prepositional phrase
> *has stood* its guard, ... verb phrase
> *very* determined, ... adverb phrase
> *protecting* the little house. .... verbal phrase

96 A **clause** is a group of related words which has both a subject and a predicate.

18

97 An **independent clause** presents a complete thought and can stand as a sentence; a **dependent clause** does not present a complete thought and cannot stand as a sentence.

In the following sentences, the dependent clauses are in *italics* and the independent clauses are in **boldface.**

> **A small pony can attack a large horse** *if it kicks its heels in the horse's belly.*
>
> **Sparrows make nests in cattle barns** *so they can stay warm during the winter.*

Types of Sentences

98 A **sentence** is classified according to the way it is put together (structure) and according to the type of message it contains. The structure of a sentence may be **simple, compound, complex,** or **compound-complex.** A sentence may communicate a message which is **declarative, interrogative, imperative,** or **exclamatory.**

99 A **simple sentence** is a sentence with only one independent clause (one complete thought). It may have either a simple subject or a compound subject. It may also have either a simple predicate or a compound predicate. A simple sentence may contain one or more phrases, but no dependent clauses.

> My *back aches.* (simple subject; simple predicate)
> My *teeth* and my *eyes hurt.* (compound subject; simple predicate)
> My *cheeks* and my *forehead look pale* and *feel warm.* (compound subject; compound predicate)
> *I must be getting a case of the flu.* (simple subject: *I;* simple predicate: *must be getting;* phrase: *a case of the flu)*

100 A **compound sentence** is made up of two or more simple sentences. These simple sentences (also called independent clauses) must be joined by a coordinate conjunction, by punctuation, or by both.

> The flu made me feel horrible, *but* the feeling didn't last long.
> The flu only lasts a few days; a cold can last for a week.

101 A **complex sentence** contains one independent clause (in **boldface**) and one or more dependent clauses (in *italics*).

> **People sleep a lot** *when they have the flu.*
> (**independent clause;** *dependent clause*)
>
> **We often sneeze a lot** *when we have a cold because our nose is out of whack.* (**independent clause;** *two dependent clauses*)

19

102 A **compound-complex sentence** contains two or more independent clauses (in **boldface**) and one or more dependent clauses (in *italics*).

> **My throat feels raw,** and **my nose turns red and sore** *whenever I catch a cold.*

103 **Declarative sentences** make statements. They tell us something about a person, place, thing, or idea.

> The Statue of Liberty stands in New York harbor. For nearly a century, it has greeted immigrants and visitors to America.
>
> The statue was given to the American people by France in 1886 to celebrate America's first one hundred years of independence.

104 **Interrogative sentences** ask questions.

> Did you know that the Statue of Liberty is made of copper and stands over 150 feet tall?
>
> Would you know what it meant if someone said that the statue symbolizes *liberty?*
>
> Do you know the official name of the statue?

105 **Imperative sentences** make commands. They often contain an understood subject (you).

> If you don't know the official name, go to the library and look it up.
>
> Then share your answer with the class the next time the topic comes up.

106 **Exclamatory sentences** communicate strong emotion or surprise.

> What! I can't believe you think I can find the official name!
>
> What do you think I am, a genius!

(*Note:* Use only one exclamation point after an exclamatory sentence.)

The Mechanics of Writing

Capitalization

107 Capitalize all proper nouns and all proper adjectives. A proper noun is the name of a particular person, place, thing, or idea. A proper adjective is an adjective formed from a proper noun.

> Common Noun ....country
> Proper Noun .... Egypt
> Proper Adjective .... Egyptian

108 Capitalize the names of people and also the initials or abbreviations that stand for those names.

> Mark Twain, John F. Kennedy, Samantha Smith,
> William J. Franklin, Jr., Laura Ingalls Wilder, Reggie Jackson

109 Capitalize geographical names.

> Planets and heavenly bodies .... Earth, Jupiter, Milky Way
> Continents .... North America, Africa
> Countries .... United States, Canada, Ireland
> States .... New York, Missouri, North Dakota
> Counties .... Westchester, Juneau
> Cities .... Sleepyside, Juneau
> Bodies of water .... Mississippi River, Pacific Ocean, Lake Michigan
> Landforms .... the Alps, the Rocky Mountains
> Public areas .... Mount Rushmore, the Statue of Liberty, the Eiffel Tower
> Roads and highways ..... the Ohio Turnpike, Park Avenue, Route 447, Interstate 80

110 Capitalize words which indicate particular sections of the country; words which simply indicate direction are not capitalized.

> Cotton was once king of the *South*.
> The candidate was not popular on the *West Coast*.
> We spent our vacation up *north*.

21

Note: Also capitalize proper adjectives formed from names of specific sections of a country. Do not capitalize adjectives formed from words which simply indicate direction.

> I attended an *Eastern* college.
> The plane flew a *southerly* course.

111   Capitalize the names of languages, races, nationalities, and religions, as well as the proper adjectives formed from them.

> Mexican, Methodist, Japanese, Judaism,
> African art, Irish linen, Swedish meatballs

112   Capitalize the name of an organization, association, or a team and its members.

> New York State Historical Society, the Red Cross, General Motors Corporation, the Honolulu Academy of the Arts, the Miami Dolphins, a Republican, the Democratic Party, the Freemont High Drama Club

113   Capitalize abbreviations of titles and organizations.

> U.S.A., M.D., FBI, B.C., NATO (North Atlantic Treaty Organization)

114   Capitalize titles used with names of persons and abbreviations standing for those titles.

> Mayor Franklin, Senator Johnson,
> President Ronald Reagan, Prof. Andrew McLean,
> Dr. Benjamin Spock, Lieutenant Perez

115   Capitalize words such as *mother, father, aunt,* and *uncle* when these words are used as names.

> My *aunt,* Lucille, visits every summer.
> (*Aunt* is not part of the name.)
> *Aunt* Lucille called this morning.
> (*Aunt* is part of the name.)
> *Mom, Dad* is on the phone.
> My *mom* will pick me up this evening.

Note: These words are usually not capitalized if they follow a possessive (*my, his, our,* etc.). See the last sample sentence above.

116   Capitalize the first word of a title, the last word, and every word in between except articles (*a, an, the*), short prepositions, and short conjunctions. Follow this rule for titles of books, newspapers, magazines, poems, plays, songs, articles, films, works of art, pictures, and stories.

> *Gone With the Wind, Much Ado About Nothing,* the *Boston Globe, National Geographic, Ode to a Nightingale,* the *Mona Lisa*

117 Capitalize the names of days of the week, months of the year, and special holidays.

> Thursday, July, Independence Day,
> Labor Day, New Year's Day, Arbor Day

118 Capitalize the names of historical events, documents, and periods of time.

> World War I, the Bill of Rights, the Magna Carta, the
> Middle Ages, the Paleozoic Era

119 Capitalize the names of businesses and the official names of their products. (These are called trade names.) Do not, however, capitalize a general descriptive word like *toothpaste* when it follows the product name.

> Post Toasties, Memorex tape, Buick Apollo,
> Colgate toothpaste, Kellogg's Frosted Flakes

120 Capitalize the names of subjects taught in school when they name particular courses.

> I took American History 101 this semester.
> Early Math was a difficult course.
> Jake turned in his history paper late.

121 Capitalize the first word of every sentence and the first word in a direct quotation.

> My sister plays the trombone. She's very good.
> Ms. Jackson yelled, "Close that door before any
> more of that smoke blows in here."

122

Capitalize	Do Not Capitalize
American . . . . *un*-American
January, February . . . . *winter, spring*
Lakes Erie and Michigan . . . . Missouri and Ohio *rivers*
The South is quite conservative. . . . . Turn *south* at the stop sign.
We praise God each day. . . . . The *god* Zeus is honored in mythology.
Duluth Central High School . . . . a Duluth *high school*
Governor Tony Earl . . . . Tony Earl, our *governor*
President Ronald Reagan . . . . Ronald Reagan, our *president*
The planet Earth is egg shaped. . . . . The *earth* we live on is good.
I'm taking History 101. . . . . I'm taking *history*.

Plurals

123 The plurals of most nouns are formed by adding *s* to the singular.

> cheerleader—cheerleader*s*;   wheel—wheel*s*

The plural form of nouns ending in *sh, ch, x, s,* and *z* are made by adding *es* to the singular.

> lunch—lunch*es*; dish—dish*es*; mess—mess*es*;
> fox—fox*es*; buzz—buzz*es*

124 The plurals of common nouns which end in *y* (with a consonant letter just before the *y*) are formed by changing the *y* to *i* and adding *es*.

> fly—fl*ies*; jalopy—jalop*ies*

The plurals of nouns which end in *y* (with a vowel just before the *y*) are formed by adding only *s*.

> donkey—donkey*s*; monkey—monkey*s*

Note: The plurals of proper nouns ending in *y* are formed by adding *s*: Two new Open Pantry*s* are being built in our town.

125 The plurals of words ending in *o* (with a vowel just before the *o*) are formed by adding *s*.

> radio—radio*s*; rodeo—rodeo*s*; studio—studio*s*

The plurals of most nouns ending in *o* (with a consonant letter just before the *o*) are formed by adding *es*.

> echo—echo*es*; hero—hero*es*; tomato—tomato*es*

Exception: Musical terms always form plurals by adding *s*; consult a dictionary for other words of this type.

> alto—alto*s*; banjo—banjo*s*; solo—solo*s*; piano—piano*s*

126 The plurals of nouns that end in *f* or *fe* are formed in one of two ways: if the final *f* sound is still heard in the plural form of the word, simply add *s;* if the final sound is a *v* sound, change the *f* to *ve* and add *s*. (*Note:* Several words are correct with either ending.)

> Plural ends with *f* sound: roof—roof*s*; chief—chief*s*
> Plural ends with *v* sound: wife—wi*ves*; loaf—loa*ves*

127 Some words (including many foreign words) form a plural by taking on an *irregular* spelling; others are now acceptable with the commonly used *s* or *es* ending.

> child—children; goose—geese; datum—data

128 The plurals of symbols, letters, figures, and words discussed as words are formed by adding an *apostrophe* and an *s*.

> He wrote three *x's* in place of his name.
> "*Hello's*" and "*Hi there's*" were screamed at my dad.

Note: Some writers omit the apostrophe when the omission does not make the sentence confusing. The examples above must have apostrophes; the example below need not.

> Give me four 5'*s* (5*s*) for a twenty.

129 The plurals of nouns which end with *ful* are formed by adding an *s* at the end of the word.

24

three pailfuls; two tankfuls

130 The plurals of compound nouns are usually formed by adding *s* or *es* to the important word in the compound.

brothers-in-law; maids of honor; Secretaries of State

Abbreviations

131 An **abbreviation** is the shortened form of a word or phrase. The following abbreviations are always acceptable in both formal and informal writing:

Mr., Mrs., Miss, Ms., Messrs., Dr., a.m., p.m. (A.M., P.M.), A.D., B.C.

Note: Do not abbreviate the names of states, countries, months, days, units of measure, or courses of study in formal writing. Do not abbreviate the words *Street, Road, Avenue, Company,* and similar words when they are part of a proper name. Also, do not use signs or symbols (%, &, $, #, @) in place of words. The dollar sign is, however, acceptable when writing a number containing both dollars and cents.

132

State Abbreviations

	Standard	Postal
Alabama	Ala.	AL
Alaska	Alaska	AK
Arizona	Ariz.	AZ
Arkansas	Ark.	AR
California	Calif.	CA
Colorado	Colo.	CO
Connecticut	Conn.	CT
Delaware	Del.	DE
District of Columbia	D.C.	DC
Florida	Fla.	FL
Georgia	Ga.	GA
Guam	Guam	GU
Hawaii	Hawaii	HI
Idaho	Idaho	ID
Illinois	Ill.	IL
Indiana	Ind.	IN
Iowa	Iowa	IA
Kansas	Kan.	KS
Kentucky	Ky.	KY
Louisiana	La.	LA
Maine	Maine	ME
Maryland	Md.	MD
Massachusetts	Mass.	MA
Michigan	Mich.	MI
Minnesota	Minn.	MN
Mississippi	Miss.	MS
Missouri	Mo.	MO
Montana	Mont.	MT
Nebraska	Neb.	NE
Nevada	Nev.	NV
New Hampshire	N.H.	NH
New Jersey	N.J.	NJ
New Mexico	N.M.	NM
New York	N.Y.	NY
North Carolina	N.C.	NC
North Dakota	N.D.	ND
Ohio	Ohio	OH
Oklahoma	Okla.	OK
Oregon	Ore.	OR
Pennsylvania	Pa.	PA
Puerto Rico	P.R.	PR
Rhode Island	R.I.	RI
South Carolina	S.C.	SC
South Dakota	S.D.	SD
Tennessee	Tenn.	TN
Texas	Texas	TX
Utah	Utah	UT
Vermont	Vt.	VT
Virginia	Va.	VA
Virgin Islands	V.I.	VI
Washington	Wash.	WA
West Virginia	W.Va.	WV
Wisconsin	Wis.	WI
Wyoming	Wyo.	WY

Address Abbreviations

	Standard	Postal
Avenue	Ave.	AVE
Boulevard	Blvd.	BLVD
Court	Ct.	CT
Drive	Dr.	DR
East	E.	E
Expressway	Expy.	EXPY
Heights	Hts.	HTS
Highway	Hwy.	HWY
Hospital	Hosp.	HOSP
Junction	Junc.	JCT
Lake	L.	LK
Lakes	Ls.	LKS
Lane	Ln.	LN
Meadows	Mdws.	MDWS
North	N.	N
Palms	Palms	PLMS
Park	Pk.	PK
Parkway	Pky.	PKY
Place	Pl.	PL
Plaza	Plaza	PLZ
Ridge	Rdg.	RDG
River	R.	RV
Road	Rd.	RD
Rural	R.	R
Shore	Sh.	SH
South	S.	S
Square	Sq.	SQ
Station	Sta.	STA
Terrace	Ter.	TER
Turnpike	Tpke.	TPKE
Union	Un.	UN
View	View	VW
Village	Vil.	VLG
West	W.	W

133 Most abbreviations are followed by a period. **Acronyms** are exceptions. An acronym is a word formed from the first (or first few) letters of words in a phrase.

radar (**r**adio **d**etecting **and r**anging), CARE (**Co**operative for **American R**elief **E**verywhere), VISTA (**V**olunteers **in S**ervice **to A**merica), UNICEF (**U**nited **N**ations International **C**hildren's **E**mergency **F**und)

134 An **initialism** is similar to an acronym except that the initials used to form this abbreviation cannot be pronounced as a word. Initialisms are not usually followed by periods.

Initialism: CIA—Central Intelligence Agency

Numbers

135 **Numbers** from one to nine are usually written as words; all numbers 10 and over are usually written as numerals.

two; seven; nine; 10; 25; 106; 1,079

Note: Numbers being compared or contrasted should be kept in the same style.

3½ to 4 years old   *or*   three-and-a-half to four years old

136 You may spell out large numbers that can be written as two words.

two thousand; but 2001

137 You may also use a combination of numbers and words for very large numbers.

1.3 million, 17 million

138 Use numerals for any numbers in the following forms: money, decimal, percentage, chapter, page, address, telephone, ZIP code, dates, time, identification numbers, and statistics.

$2.39; 26.2; 8 percent; chapter 7; pages 287-89; 2125 Cairn Road; July 6, 1945; 44 B.C.; A.D. 79; 4:30 P.M.; Highway 36; a vote of 23 to 4; 34 mph

139 Use words, not numerals, to begin a sentence.

Fourteen students "forgot" their assignments.

140 Numbers which come before a compound modifier which includes a figure should be written as words.

The girl walked on *two* 8-foot wooden stilts.
The basket was woven from *sixty-two* 11½ inch ropes.

Spelling

Spelling Rules

141 **Rule 1:** Write *i* before *e* except after *c*, or when sounded like *a* as in *neighbor* and *weigh*.

Exceptions: Eight of the **exceptions** are in this sentence:

> *Neither sheik* dared *leisurely seize either weird species* of *financiers.*

Note: Other exceptions to the *ie* rule are *their, height, counterfeit, foreign,* and *heir.*

Rule 2: When a one-syllable word (bat) ends in a consonant (bat) preceded by one vowel (b**a**t), double the final consonant before adding a suffix which begins with a vowel (batting).

When a multi-syllable word (con trol) ends in a consonant (**l**) preceded by one vowel (**o**), the accent is on the last syllable (con **trol**), and the suffix begins with a vowel (ing)—the same rule holds true: double the final consonant (controlling).

> sum—summary; god—goddess; prefer—preferred
> begin—beginning; forget—forgettable; admit—admittance

Rule 3: If a word ends with a silent *e*, drop the *e* before adding a suffix which begins with a vowel.

> state—stating—statement; like—liking—likeness
> use—using—useful; nine—ninety—nineteen

(Notice that you do *not* drop the *e* when the suffix begins with a consonant. Exceptions include *truly, argument,* and *ninth.*)

Rule 4: When *y* is the last letter in a word and the *y* comes just after a consonant, change the *y* to *i* before adding any suffix except those beginning with *i*.

> fry—fries; hurry—hurried; lady—ladies
> ply—pliable; happy—happiness; beauty—beautiful

When forming the plural of a word which ends with a *y* that comes just after a vowel, add *s*.

> toy—toys; play—plays; monkey—monkeys

142 ## A List of Commonly Misspelled Words

Note: The words in the list below are divided into syllables to help you pro-
nounce them as well as remember how to spell them. You can also use the list
as a guide for dividing words at the ends of lines. Remember, though, you
should never leave a single letter on a line (*a*-board) by itself.

A

ab-bre-vi-ate	ad-ver-tis-ing	an-a-lyze	ap-pli-ance
a-board	a-fraid	an-cient	ap-pli-ca-tion
a-bout	af-ter	an-gel	ap-point-ment
a-bove	af-ter-noon	an-ger	ap-pre-ci-ate
ab-sence	af-ter-ward	an-gle	ap-proach
ab-sent	a-gain	an-gry	ap-pro-pri-ate
ab-so-lute (-ly)	a-gainst	an-i-mal	ap-prov-al
a-bun-dance	a-gree-able	an-ni-ver-sa-ry	ap-prox-i-mate
ac-cel-er-ate	a-gree (-ment)	an-nounce	ar-chi-tect
ac-ci-dent	ah	an-noy-ance	arc-tic
ac-ci-den-tal (-ly)	aid	an-nu-al	aren't
ac-com-pa-ny	air-y	a-non-y-mous	ar-gu-ment
ac-com-plice	aisle	an-oth-er	a-rith-me-tic
ac-com-plish	a-larm	an-swer	a-round
ac-cord-ing	al-co-hol	ant-arc-tic	a-rouse
ac-count	a-like	an-tic-i-pate	ar-range (-ment)
ac-cu-rate	a-live	anx-i-ety	ar-riv-al
ac-cus-tom (ed)	al-ley	anx-ious	ar-ti-cle
ache	al-low-ance	any-body	ar-ti-fi-cial
a-chieve (-ment)	all right	any-how	a-sleep
a-cre	al-most	any-one	as-sas-sin
a-cross	al-ready	any-thing	as-sign (-ment)
ac-tu-al	al-though	any-way	as-sis-tance
a-dapt	al-to-geth-er	any-where	as-so-ci-ate
ad-di-tion (-al)	a-lu-mi-num	a-part-ment	as-so-ci-a-tion
ad-dress	al-ways	a-piece	as-sume
ad-e-quate	am-a-teur	a-pol-o-gize	ath-lete
ad-just (-ment)	am-bu-lance	ap-par-ent (-ly)	ath-let-ic
ad-mire	a-mend-ment	ap-peal	at-tach
ad-ven-ture	a-mong	ap-pear-ance	at-tack (ed)
ad-ver-tise (-ment)	a-mount	ap-pe-tite	at-tempt

at-ten-dance	bliz-zard	care-less	com-mit
at-ten-tion	both-er	car-pen-ter	com-mit-ment
at-ti-tude	bot-tle	car-riage	com-mit-ted
at-tor-ney	bot-tom	car-rot	com-mit-tee
at-trac-tive	bough	cash-ier	com-mu-ni-cate
au-di-ence	bought	cas-se-role	com-mu-ni-ty
Au-gust	bounce	cas-u-al-ty	com-pan-y
au-thor	bound-a-ry	cat-a-log	com-par-i-son
au-thor-i-ty	break-fast	ca-tas-tro-phe	com-pe-ti-tion
au-to-mo-bile	breast	catch-er	com-pet-i-tive (-ly)
au-tumn	breath (n.)	cat-er-pil-lar	com-plain
a-vail-a-ble	breathe (v.)	cat-sup	com-plete (-ly)
av-e-nue	breeze	ceil-ing	com-plex-ion
av-er-age	bridge	cel-e-bra-tion	com-pro-mise
aw-ful (-ly)	brief	cem-e-ter-y	con-ceive
awk-ward	bright	cen-sus	con-cern-ing
B bag-gage	bril-liant	cen-tu-ry	con-cert
bak-ing	broth-er	cer-tain	con-ces-sion
bal-ance	brought	cer-tain (-ly)	con-crete
bal-loon	bruise	cer-tif-i-cate	con-demn
bal-lot	bub-ble	chal-lenge	con-di-tion
ba-nan-a	buck-et	cham-pi-on	con-duc-tor
ban-dage	buck-le	change-a-ble	con-fer-ence
bank-rupt	bud-get	char-ac-ter (-is-tic)	con-fi-dence
bar-ber	build-ing	chief	con-grat-u-late
bar-gain	bul-le-tin	chil-dren	con-nect
bar-rel	buoy-ant	chim-ney	con-science
base-ment	bu-reau	choc-o-late	con-scious
ba-sis	bur-glar	choice	con-ser-va-tive
bas-ket	bury	cho-rus	con-sti-tu-tion
bat-tery	busi-ness	cir-cum-stance	con-tin-ue
beau-ti-ful	busy	cit-i-zen	con-tin-u-ous
beau-ty	but-ton	civ-i-li-za-tion	con-trol
be-cause	C cab-bage	class-mates	con-tro-ver-sy
be-come	caf-e-te-ria	class-room	con-ve-nience
be-com-ing	cal-en-dar	cli-mate	con-vince
be-fore	cam-paign	climb	cool-ly
be-gan	ca-nal	clos-et	co-op-er-ate
beg-gar	can-celed	cloth-ing	cor-po-ra-tion
be-gin-ning	can-di-date	coach	cor-re-spond
be-have	can-dle	co-coa	cough
be-hav-ior	can-is-ter	co-coon	couldn't
be-ing	can-non	cof-fee	coun-ter-feit
be-lief	can-not	col-lar	coun-ter
be-lieve	ca-noe	col-lege	coun-try
be-long	can't	colo-nel	coun-ty
be-neath	can-yon	col-or	cour-age
ben-e-fit (-ed)	ca-pac-i-ty	co-los-sal	cou-ra-geous
be-tween	cap-tain	col-umn	court
bi-cy-cle	car-bu-re-tor	com-e-dy	cour-te-ous
bis-cuit	card-board	com-ing	cour-te-sy
black-board	ca-reer	com-mer-cial	cous-in
blan-ket	care-ful	com-mis-sion	cov-er-age

29

co-zy
crack-er
crank-y
crawl
cred-i-tor
cried
crit-i-cize
cru-el
crumb
crum-ble
cup-board
cu-ri-os-i-ty
cu-ri-ous
cur-rent
cus-tom
cus-tom-er
cyl-in-der

D dai-ly
dair-y
dam-age
dan-ger (-ous)
daugh-ter
dealt
de-ceive
de-cided
de-ci-sion
dec-la-ra-tion
dec-o-rate
de-fense
def-i-nite (-ly)
def-i-ni-tion
de-li-cious
de-pen-dent
de-pot
de-scribe
de-scrip-tion
de-sert
de-serve
de-sign
de-sir-able
de-spair
des-sert
de-te-ri-o-rate
de-ter-mine
de-vel-op
de-vel-op-ment
de-vice
de-vise
di-a-mond
di-a-phragm
di-a-ry
dic-tio-nary
dif-fer-ence

dif-fer-ent
dif-fi-cul-ty
din-ing
di-plo-ma
di-rec-tor
dis-agree-able
dis-ap-pear
dis-ap-point
dis-ap-prove
dis-as-trous
dis-ci-pline
dis-cov-er
dis-cuss
dis-cus-sion
dis-ease
dis-sat-is-fied
dis-tin-guish
dis-trib-ute
di-vide
di-vine
di-vis-i-ble
di-vi-sion
doc-tor
doesn't
dol-lar
dor-mi-to-ry
doubt
dough
du-al
du-pli-cate

E ea-ger (-ly)
econ-o-my
edge
e-di-tion
ef-fi-cien-cy
eight
eighth
ei-ther
e-lab-o-rate
e-lec-tric-i-ty
el-e-phant
el-i-gi-ble
el-lipse
em-bar-rass
e-mer-gen-cy
em-pha-size
em-ploy-ee
em-ploy-ment
en-close
en-cour-age
en-gi-neer
e-nor-mous
e-nough

en-ter-tain
en-thu-si-as-tic
en-tire-ly
en-trance
en-vel-op (v.)
en-ve-lope (n.)
en-vi-ron-ment
equip-ment
equipped
e-quiv-a-lent
es-cape
es-pe-cial-ly
es-sen-tial
es-tab-lish
ev-ery
ev-i-dence
ex-ag-ger-ate
ex-ceed
ex-cel-lent
ex-cept
ex-cep-tion-al (-ly)
ex-cite
ex-er-cise
ex-haust (-ed)
ex-hi-bi-tion
ex-is-tence
ex-pect
ex-pen-sive
ex-pe-ri-ence
ex-plain
ex-pla-na-tion
ex-pres-sion
ex-ten-sion
ex-tinct
ex-traor-di-nar-y
ex-treme (-ly)

F fa-cil-i-ties
fa-mil-iar
fam-i-ly
fa-mous
fas-ci-nate
fash-ion
fa-tigue (d)
fau-cet
fa-vor-ite
fea-ture
Feb-ru-ar-y
fed-er-al
fer-tile
field
fierce
fi-ery
fif-ty

fi-nal-ly
fi-nan-cial (-ly)
fo-li-age
for-ci-ble
for-eign
for-feit
for-mal (-ly)
for-mer (-ly)
forth
for-tu-nate
for-ty
for-ward
foun-tain
fourth
frag-ile
freight
friend (-ly)
fright-en
ful-fill
fun-da-men-tal
fur-ther
fur-ther-more

G gad-get
gauge
gen-er-al-ly
gen-er-ous
ge-nius
gen-tle
gen-u-ine
ge-og-ra-phy
ghet-to
ghost
gnaw
gov-ern-ment
gov-er-nor
grad-u-a-tion
gram-mar
grate-ful
grease
grief
gro-cery
grudge
grue-some
guar-an-tee
guard
guard-i-an
guess
guide
guid-ance
guilt-y
gym-na-si-um

H ham-mer
han-dle (d)

hand-ker-chief	in-flu-en-tial	light-ning	nec-es-sary
hand-some	in-i-tial	lik-able	ne-go-ti-ate
hap-haz-ard	ini-ti-a-tion	like-ly	neigh-bor (-hood)
hap-pen	in-no-cence	li-quid	nei-ther
hap-pi-ness	in-no-cent	lis-ten	nick-el
ha-rass	in-stal-la-tion	lit-er-a-ture	niece
hast-i-ly	in-stance	liv-ing	nine-teen
hav-ing	in-stead	loaves	nine-teenth
haz-ard-ous	in-sur-ance	lone-li-ness	nine-ty
head-ache	in-tel-li-gence	loose	nois-y
height	in-ten-tion	lose (r)	no-tice-able
hem-or-rhage	in-ter-est-ed	los-ing	nu-cle-ar
hes-i-tate	in-ter-est-ing	lov-able	nui-sance
his-to-ry	in-ter-fere	love-ly	**O** o-be-di-ence
hoarse	in-ter-pret	**M** ma-chin-er-y	o-bey
hol-i-day	in-ter-rupt	mag-a-zine	ob-sta-cle
hon-or	in-ter-view	mag-nif-i-cent	oc-ca-sion
hop-ing	in-ves-ti-gate	main-tain	oc-ca-sion-al (-ly)
hop-ping	in-vi-ta-tion	ma-jor-i-ty	oc-cur
hor-ri-ble	ir-ri-gate	mak-ing	oc-curred
hos-pi-tal	is-land	man-u-al	of-fense
hu-mor-ous	is-sue	man-u-fac-ture	of-fi-cial
hur-ried-ly	**J** jeal-ous (-y)	mar-riage	of-ten
hy-drau-lic	jew-el-ry	ma-te-ri-al	o-mis-sion
hy-giene	jour-nal	math-e-mat-ics	o-mit-ted
hymn	jour-ney	max-i-mum	o-pin-ion
I i-ci-cle	judg-ment	may-or	op-er-ate
i-den-ti-cal	juic-y	meant	op-por-tu-ni-ty
il-leg-i-ble	**K** kitch-en	mea-sure	op-po-nent
il-lit-er-ate	knew	med-i-cine	op-po-site
il-lus-trate	knife	me-di-um	or-di-nar-i-ly
im-ag-i-nary	knives	mes-sage	orig-i-nal
im-ag-i-na-tive	knock	mile-age	out-ra-geous
im-ag-ine	knowl-edge	min-i-a-ture	**P** pack-age
im-i-ta-tion	knuck-les	min-i-mum	paid
im-me-di-ate (-ly)	**L** la-bel	min-ute	pam-phlet
im-mense	lab-o-ra-to-ry	mir-ror	par-a-dise
im-mi-grant	la-dies	mis-cel-la-neous	para-graph
im-mor-tal	lan-guage	mis-chie-vous	par-al-lel
im-pa-tient	laugh	mis-er-a-ble	par-a-lyze
im-por-tance	laun-dry	mis-sile	pa-ren-the-ses
im-pos-si-ble	law-yer	mis-spell	par-tial
im-prove-ment	league	mois-ture	par-tic-i-pant
in-con-ve-nience	lec-ture	mol-e-cule	par-tic-i-pate
in-cred-i-ble	le-gal	mo-not-o-nous	par-tic-u-lar (-ly)
in-def-i-nite-ly	leg-i-ble	mon-u-ment	pas-time
in-de-pen-dence	leg-is-la-ture	mort-gage	pas-ture
in-de-pen-dent	lei-sure	moun-tain	pa-tience
in-di-vid-u-al	length	mus-cle	pe-cu-liar
in-dus-tri-al	li-a-ble	mu-si-cian	peo-ple
in-fe-ri-or	li-brar-y	mys-te-ri-ous	per-haps
in-fi-nite	li-cense	**N** na-ive	per-ma-nent
in-flam-ma-ble	lieu-ten-ant	nat-u-ral (-ly)	per-pen-dic-u-lar

Spelling

per-sis-tent
per-son-al (-ly)
per-son-nel
per-spi-ra-tion
per-suade
phase
phy-si-cian
piece
pitch-er
planned
pla-teau
play-wright
pleas-ant
plea-sure
pneu-mo-nia
pol-i-ti-cian
pos-sess
pos-si-ble
prac-ti-cal (-ly)
prai-rie
pre-cede
pre-cise (-ly)
pre-ci-sion
pre-cious
pref-er-a-ble
pre-ferred
prej-u-dice
prep-a-ra-tion
pres-ence
pre-vi-ous
prim-i-tive
prin-ci-pal
prin-ci-ple
pris-on-er
priv-i-lege
prob-a-bly
pro-ce-dure
pro-ceed
pro-fes-sor
prom-i-nent
pro-nounce
pro-nun-ci-a-tion
pro-tein
psy-chol-o-gy
pump-kin
pure

Q quar-ter
ques-tion-naire
qui-et
quite
quo-tient

R raise
re-al-ize

re-al-ly
re-ceipt
re-ceive
re-ceived
rec-i-pe
rec-og-nize
rec-om-mend
reign
re-lieve
re-li-gious
re-mem-ber
rep-e-ti-tion
rep-re-sen-ta-tive
res-er-voir
re-sis-tance
re-spect-ful-ly
re-spon-si-bil-i-ty
res-tau-rant
re-view
rhyme
rhythm
ri-dic-u-lous
route

S safe-ty
sal-ad
sal-a-ry
sand-wich
sat-is-fac-to-ry
Sat-ur-day
scene
sce-ner-y
sched-ule
sci-ence
scis-sors
scream
screen
sea-son
sec-re-tary
seize
sen-si-ble
sen-tence
sep-a-rate
sev-er-al
sher-iff
shin-ing
sim-i-lar
since
sin-cere (-ly)
ski-ing
sleigh
sol-dier
sou-ve-nir
spa-ghet-ti

spe-cif-ic
sphere
sprin-kle
squeeze
squir-rel
stat-ue
stat-ure
stat-ute
stom-ach
stopped
straight
strength
stretched
study-ing
sub-tle
suc-ceed
suc-cess
suf-fi-cient
sum-ma-rize
sup-ple-ment
sup-pose
sure-ly
sur-prise
syl-la-ble
sym-pa-thy
symp-tom

T tar-iff
tech-nique
tem-per-a-ture
tem-po-rary
ter-ri-ble
ter-ri-to-ry
thank-ful
the-ater
their
there
there-fore
thief
thor-ough (-ly)
though
through-out
tired
to-bac-co
to-geth-er
to-mor-row
tongue
touch
tour-na-ment
to-ward
trag-e-dy
trea-sur-er
tried
tries

tru-ly
Tues-day
typ-i-cal
U un-con-scious
un-for-tu-nate (-ly)
unique
uni-ver-si-ty
un-nec-es-sary
un-til
us-able
use-ful
using
usu-al (-ly)
u-ten-sil
V va-ca-tion
vac-u-um
valu-able
va-ri-ety
var-i-ous
veg-e-ta-ble
ve-hi-cle
very
vi-cin-i-ty
view
vil-lain
vi-o-lence
vis-i-ble
vis-i-tor
voice
vol-ume
vol-un-tary
vol-un-teer
W wan-der
weath-er
Wednes-day
weigh
weird
wel-come
wel-fare
where
whale
wheth-er
which
whole
whol-ly
whose
width
wom-en
worth-while
wreck-age
writ-ing
writ-ten
Y yel-low

Punctuation

Period

143   A **period** is used to end a sentence which makes a statement, or which gives a command which is not used as an exclamation.

> "That guy is coming over here."
> "Don't forget to smile when you talk."
> "Hello, Joe."
> "Hi."

Note: It is not necessary to place a period after a statement which has parentheses around it and is part of another sentence.

> Euny gave Jim an earwich (an earwich is one piece of buttered bread slapped on each ear) and then ran away giggling.

144   A period should be placed after an initial.

> Jack T. Bergin; Frances M. Neubert

145   A period is placed after each part of an **abbreviation**—unless the abbreviation is an acronym. An **acronym** is a word formed from the first (or first few) letters of words in a set phrase.

> **Abbreviations:** Mr., Mrs., Ms., Dr., A.D., B.C.
>
> **Acronyms:** WAC (Women's Army Corps); Radar (Radio Detecting and Ranging)

146   When an abbreviation is the last word in a sentence, only one period should be used at the end of the sentence.

> When she's nervous, she bites her nails, wrings her hands, squirms in her chair, etc.

147   An **ellipsis** (three periods) may be used for a pause in dialogue.

33

148 An ellipsis is used to show that one or more words have been left out of a quotation. (Leave one space before and after each period when typing.)

"Give me your tired . . . yearning to breathe free."

149 If the final words have been left out of a sentence, the ellipsis is placed after the period which is used at the end of the sentence.

"Ernest Hemingway was fond of fishing. . . .
His understanding of that sport is demonstrated in many of his writings."

Note: If the quoted material is a complete sentence (even if it was not in the original), use a period, then an ellipsis.

150 Use a period as a decimal point and to separate dollars and cents.

6.1 percent   28.9 percent $3,120.21

Comma

151 **Commas** are used between words, phrases, or clauses in a *series*. (A series contains at least three items.)

I like pepperoni, pineapple, and black olives on my pizza.

152 Commas are used to separate a series of numbers in order to distinguish hundreds, thousands, millions, etc.

Our school raised $1,720 from a fund-raising project.
Over 1,200,000 attended the State Fair this summer.

153 Commas are used to distinguish items in an address and items in a date.

They live at 2341 Pine Street, Willmar, Minnesota 56342, during the summer. (*Note:* Do not use a comma to separate the state from the ZIP code.)

Thousands of people celebrated the restoration of the Statue of Liberty on July 4, 1986, in New York City. New York was a very busy place in July 1986 as the city prepared for the celebration. (*Note:* If only the month and year are given, it is not necessary to separate them with a comma.)

154 Commas are used to set off the exact words of the speaker from the rest of the sentence.

"Didn't you know," she exclaimed, "that dirty socks cause ingrown toenails?"

Note: Use no comma before an indirect quotation. The circled comma should not be used.

Hank said ⊙he would never again move my piano.

34

155 Commas are used to separate a noun of direct address from the rest of the sentence. (A noun of direct address is the noun which names the person/s spoken to in the sentence.)

> Don't you understand, Dad, that every kid except for me is going to the roller-skating party?
>
> I'm sure, Larry! How am I going to get the money to attend a computer camp?

156 Commas are used to enclose a title, name, or initials which follow a person's last name.

> D.L. Jaunty, Ph.D., and S.J. Stutz, M.D., sat in their pajamas playing Old Maid.
>
> Sodbuster, A., Tumbleweed, B.J., and Ramshackle, Tyrone P., are three unknown pioneers.

157 A comma may be used between two independent clauses which are joined by coordinate conjunctions such as these: *but, or, nor, for, yet, and, so.*

> My friend always studies in school, and he expects to get good grades in all of his classes.

158 A comma should separate an adverb clause or a long modifying phrase from the independent clause which follows it.

> After a few hours of cooking, the spaghetti sauce is ready to pour over the noodles. (Long phrase)
> When you learn to make an Italian sauce, you will be able to make many good dishes. (Adverb clause)

159 A comma is used to separate an interjection or weak exclamation from the rest of the sentence.

> *Hey,* will you do me a favor?
> *Yes,* I'd be happy to help.
> *Wow,* that was quite a test.

160 Commas are used to set off a word, phrase, or clause that interrupts the main thought of a sentence. Such expressions usually can be identified through the following tests: 1) They may be omitted without changing the substance or meaning of a sentence. 2) They may be placed nearly anywhere in the sentence without changing the meaning of the sentence.

> I'm positive, *however,* that all little brothers and sisters don't have any brains.
> My little brother, *for example,* doesn't even know that it can be 7:00 in the morning and 7:00 at night.

161 Commas are used to separate an explanatory phrase from the rest of the sentence.

> Anchovies, *or small fish,* are popular on pizza.

162   An **appositive,** a specific kind of explanatory word or phrase, identifies or renames a noun or pronoun. (Do not use commas with single-word *appositives.* See the second example below.)

> My mother, *an expert cook,* makes the best Italian sauce in town.
> The spice *oregano* and a secret ingredient makes her sauce extra spicy.

163   Commas are used to separate two or more adjectives which modify the same noun.

> Mother cooks her Italian sauce in an *old, heavy* kettle.

Notice in the example that no comma separates the last adjective *(heavy)* from the noun.

> Most Italian sauces become very thick after they are cooked.

Note: In the example above, *most* and *Italian* are not separated by a comma because the two adjectives do *not* equally modify *sauces.* To figure out if adjectives modify equally, use these two tests: 1) Switch the order of the adjectives; if the sentence is clear, the adjectives modify equally. (If *most* and *Italian* were switched in the example above, the sentence would be unclear.) 2) Insert *and* between the adjectives; if the sentence reads well, use a comma when *and* is omitted.

Also Note: If the first adjective modifies the second adjective *and* the noun, use a comma.

> He sat down on the soft, velvet couch.

164   Commas are used to punctuate **nonrestrictive** phrases and clauses. (Nonrestrictive phrases or clauses are those which are not essential or necessary to the basic meaning of the sentence.) **Restrictive** phrases or clauses—those which are needed in the sentence because they *restrict* or limit the meaning of the sentence—are not set off with commas. Compare the following examples with their nonrestrictive and restrictive clauses.

> Rozi, *who likes to play with black cats,* is my sister.

> *(Note:* The clause, *who likes to play with black cats,* is merely additional information; it is **nonrestrictive** [not required]. If the clause were left out of the sentence, the meaning of the sentence would remain clear since the name of the girl is given.)

The girl *who likes to play with black cats* is my sister.

(*Note:* This clause is **restrictive**. The clause, *who likes to play with black cats,* is needed to identify the girl.)

Compare the following examples:

The Beatles, *a British rock group,* recorded many hit songs. (**nonrestrictive**)

The British rock group *the Beatles* recorded many hit songs. (**restrictive**)

Semicolon

165   A **semicolon** is used to join two independent clauses which are not connected with a coordinate conjunction.   (This means that each of the two clauses could stand alone as a separate sentence.)

I once had to share a bedroom with my brother; that was the worst time of my life.

166   A semicolon is also used to join two independent clauses when the clauses are connected only by a conjunctive adverb (*also, as a result, for example, however, therefore*).

My science teacher said that dissecting a frog will be exciting; *however,* she also said that seeing Halley's Comet was going to be exciting.

167   A semicolon is used to separate groups of words or phrases which already contain commas.

We visited many interesting places on our vacation, including Bangor, Maine; Hartford, Connecticut; Providence, Rhode Island; and Montpelier, Vermont.

Colon

168   A **colon** may be used after the salutation of a business letter.

Dear Ms. Asche:

169   A colon is used between the parts of a number which indicate time.

8:32 p.m.   6:00 p.m.   11:03 a.m.

170   A colon may be used to formally introduce a sentence, a question, or a quotation.

It was President John F. Kennedy who said these words: "Ask not what your country can do for you, but what you can do for your country."

171   A colon is used to introduce a list.

Amy brought her things: oil, popcorn, and salt.

Note: When introducing a list, the colon usually comes after a "summary" word(s)—*the following, these, things*—or a word describing the subject of the list, such as *sports* in the list below.

> *Incorrect:* Hubert enjoys: baseball, football, and mud wrestling.
>
> *Correct:* Hubert enjoys several sports: baseball, football, and mud wrestling.

Dash

172 The **dash** is used to indicate a sudden break or change in the sentence.

> There is one course that I always liked—social studies.
>
> I always felt that—But maybe I'd better not tell you that now.

173 A dash may be used to emphasize a word, series of words, phrase, or clause.

> He ran downstage, glared at the audience, screamed at the top of his lungs—and his pants fell down.
>
> She wanted a friend that matched her personality—crazy, fun-loving, and adventurous.
>
> Health, friends, and family—we are not thankful enough for these.

174 A dash is used to show that someone's speech is being interrupted by another person. (*Note:* A dash is indicated by two hyphens--without spacing before or after--in all handwritten and typed material.)

> Why, hello, Dear--yes, I understand--no, I remember--oh, I want to--of course, I won't--why, no, I--why, yes, I--it was so nice to talk with you again.

Hyphen

175 The **hyphen** is used to make a compound word.

> great-great-grandfather, run-of-the-mill, mother-in-law, three-year-old, twenty-six-year-old songwriter

176 The hyphen is used to join the words in compound numbers from *twenty-one* to *ninety-nine.* The hyphen is also used to join numbers which indicate the life span of an individual, the scores of a game, and so on.

> The score, *78-27,* told the whole story.

177 A hyphen is used between the numbers in a fraction, but not between the numerator and denominator when one or both are already hyphenated.

> four-tenths   five-sixteenths   (7/32) seven thirty-seconds

178 The hyphen is used to divide a word when you run out of room at the end of a line. A word may be divided only between syllables.

179

Additional Guidelines for Using the Hyphen

1. Always leave enough of the word at the end of the sentence so that the word can be identified.
2. Never divide a one-syllable word: *rained, skills, through.*
3. Avoid dividing a word of five letters or less: *paper, study, July.*
4. Never divide a one-letter syllable from the rest of the word: *omit-ted,* not *o-mitted.*
5. Always divide a compound word between its basic units: *sister-in-law,* not *sis-ter-in-law.*
6. Never divide abbreviations or contractions: *shouldn't,* not *should-n't.*
7. Avoid dividing the last word in a paragraph.
8. Never divide the last word in more than two lines in a row.
9. When a vowel is a syllable by itself, divide the word after the vowel: *epi-sode,* not *ep-isode.*
10. Avoid dividing a number written as a figure: *1,000,000* not *1,000,-000.* (If a figure must be broken, divide it after one of the commas.)
11. Always check a dictionary if you are uncertain where a word should be divided.

---

180 A hyphen is used to join a capital letter to a noun or participle.

> U-turn   B-teams   V-shaped

181 A hyphen is used to form new words beginning with the prefixes *self, ex, all,* and *great.* It is also used to join any prefix to a proper noun, a proper adjective, or the official name of an office. A hyphen is used with the suffix *elect.*

> ex-mayor, self-starting, all-knowing, pro-American, post-Depression, mid-May, president-elect, great-grandson

182 Use a hyphen with other prefixes or suffixes to avoid confusion or awkward spelling.

> re-cover (not recover) the sofa   shell-like (not shelllike)

183 Use the hyphen to join two or more words which work together to form a single adjective (a *single-thought* adjective) before a noun.

> well-designed bike   blueberry-filled donut
> flower-covered porch

Note: When words forming the adjective come after the noun, do not hyphenate them.

> My new bike is well designed.
> The donuts are blueberry filled.

Another note: When the first of the words ends in *ly,* do not use a hyphen; also, do not use a hyphen when a number or letter is the final part of a one-thought adjective.

> fresh*ly* painted barn   Grade A milk   number *360* sandpaper

Question Mark

184   A **question mark** is used at the end of a direct question (an interrogative sentence).

> Are your relatives mushy when you visit them?
> Are your grandparents heavy on the kissy-huggy stuff?

185   No question mark is used after an indirect quotation.

> My aunt always asks how I am doing in school.
> I always wonder what "doing in school" means.

186   Only one question mark should punctuate a question.   The following punctuation is both silly and incorrect.

> Do you mean that kid with the tall head???
> Really!   Why did you ever date him???

187   The question mark is placed within parentheses to show that the writer isn't sure a fact or figure is correct.

> Although my cousin is only 18 (?), he doesn't like to "waste his time" with his younger cousins.

Exclamation Point

188   The **exclamation point** is used to express strong feeling.   It may be placed after a word, a phrase, or an exclamatory sentence.   (The exclamation point should not be overused.)

> Help!   Mom!   Help!
> Wow, that was really awesome!
> The principal actually likes me!

189   Never write more than one exclamation point; such punctuation is incorrect and looks foolish.

> Isn't the Demon a great roller coaster!!!
> Who even thinks about going upside down!!!

Quotation Marks

190 **Quotation marks** are placed before and after direct quotations. Only the exact words quoted are placed within quotation marks.

> "I really don't know," he said, "whether roses are her favorite flowers or not."

Note: The words *he said* are not in quotation marks because the person did not say them. Also, the word *whether* is not capitalized because it does not begin a new sentence. (See the "Short Story" section for more information on using quotation marks.)

191 If more than one paragraph is quoted (as in a report or research paper), quotation marks are placed before each paragraph and at the end of the last paragraph (Example A). Quotations which are more than four lines on a page are usually set off from the rest of the paper with triple-spacing and indented ten spaces from the left. No quotation marks are placed either before or after the quoted material unless they appear in the original copy (Example B).

Example A   **Example B**

"_____   _____
_____   _____
____ .   _____
"_____   _____
_____   _____
____ ."   ____ .

192 Quotation marks are used to punctuate titles of songs, poems, short stories, lectures, courses, episodes of radio or television programs, chapters of books, and articles found in magazines, newspapers, or encyclopedias.

> "Uncle Wiggly Loses His Pants" (short story)
> "The Raven" (poem)
> "Beginning Photography and Printing" (course title)

Note: When you punctuate a title, capitalize the first word, last word, and every word in between *except* for articles, short prepositions, and short conjunctions.

193 Quotation marks also may be used (1) to set apart a word which is being discussed, (2) to indicate that a word is slang, or (3) to point out that a word is being used in a special way.

> My teacher replaced "disruptive" with "uncontrollable."
> He really thinks he's "with it."
> In order to be popular, she works very hard at being "cute."

194 Single quotation marks are used to punctuate a quotation within a quotation. Double and single quotation marks are alternated in order to distinguish a quotation within a quotation within a quotation.

"I never read 'The Raven'!"
"Did you hear him say, 'I never read "The Raven" '?"

195 Periods and commas are always placed inside quotation marks.

"I don't know," said Albert.   Albert said, "I don't know."

196 An exclamation point or a question mark is placed inside the quotation marks when it punctuates the quotation; it is placed outside when it punctuates the main sentence.

I almost died when he asked, "That won't be a problem for you, will it?"
Did the teacher really say, "Finish this by tomorrow"?

197 Semicolons or colons are placed outside quotation marks.

I read the poem "The Pasture"; "Chicago" is in another book.

Underlining (Italics)

198 **Italics** is a printer's term for a style of type which is slightly slanted.   In this sentence the word *happiness* is typed in italics.   In handwritten or typed material, each word or letter which should be in italics is underlined.

The novel Black Beauty tells a memorable story. (typed)
The novel *Black Beauty* tells a memorable story. (printed)

199 Underline the titles of magazines, newspapers, pamphlets, books, plays, films, radio and television programs, book-length poems, record albums, and the names of ships and aircraft.

When the Legends Die (novel)
The Cross and the Switchblade (film)
MASH (television program)
Motorists Handbook (pamphlet)
U.S.S. Arizona (ship)
New York Times or New York Times (newspaper)
Note: When the name of a city is used as part of the name of a newspaper, the name of the city need not be underlined.

200 **Exceptions:** Do not underline or put in quotation marks your own title at the top of your page.

Underline foreign words which are not commonly used in everyday English. Also underline scientific names.

E Pluribus Unum appears on most U.S. currency.
Mankind is also known as Homo Sapiens.

201 Underline any word, number, or letter which is being discussed or being used in a special way.

I got an <u>A</u> on my test because I understood the word <u>classify</u>.

Parentheses

202 **Parentheses** are used around words which are included in a sentence to add information or to help make an idea clearer.

> Abraham Lincoln began his political career in Springfield (Ill.) where he served four terms as a state legislator. Following his fourth term, Lincoln tried unsuccessfully to capture the Whig Party's nomination. (Lincoln later joined the Republican Party.) After failing a second time to secure the nomination, Lincoln decided to make one last effort; if he failed, he would retire from politics. His third attempt was a major triumph, for Lincoln won not only the nomination but the election as well (1846). "He was soon off to Washington, D.C., where he was to become one of the most controversial of all U.S. Presidents" (Sandburg, 42).

Note: Punctuation is placed within parentheses when it is needed to mark the material within the parentheses. Punctuation is placed outside the parentheses when it is needed for the entire sentence. Also note that words enclosed by parentheses do not have to begin with a capital letter or end with a period—even if the words make a complete sentence.

Brackets

203 **Brackets** are used before and after material which a writer adds when quoting another writer.

> His conclusion was that "they [the students] should be able to speak and read in at least one foreign language."

Apostrophe

204 An **apostrophe** is used to show that one or more letters have been left out of a word to form a contraction.

> don't—*o* is left out; she'd—*woul* is left out; it's—*i* is left out

205 An apostrophe is also used to show that one or more letters or numbers have been left out of numerals or words which are spelled as if they were actually spoken.

> class of '90—*19* is left out; good *mornin'*—*g* is left out

Note: When two apostrophes are called for in the same word, simply omit the second one.

> Be sure you follow closely the *do's* and *don'ts* (not *don't's*) on the checklist.

206 An apostrophe and *s* are used to form the plural of a letter, a number, a sign, or a word discussed as a word.

$$A - A's; \quad 8 - 8's; \quad + - +'s$$

207 The possessive form of singular nouns is usually made by adding an apostrophe and *s*.

Carter's daughter; John Denver's song

208 *Note:* When a singular noun ends with an *s* or *z* sound, the possessive may be formed by adding just an apostrophe. When the singular noun is a one-syllable word, however, the possessive is usually formed by adding both an apostrophe and *s*.

Thomas' cabin (or) Thomas's cabin
boss's; lass's (one-syllable nouns ending in *s*)

209 The possessive form of plural nouns ending in *s* is usually made by adding just an apostrophe. For plural nouns not ending in *s*, an apostrophe and *s* must be added.

Joneses' great-grandfather; bosses' office; children's book

Remember! The word immediately before the apostrophe is the owner.

kid's guitar	*kid* is the owner
kids' guitar	*kids* are the owners
boss's office	*boss* is the owner
bosses' office	*bosses* are the owners

210 When possession is shared by more than one noun, add an apostrophe and *s* to the last noun in the series.

VanClumpin, VanDiken, and VanTulip's fish. (All three own the same fish.)
VanClumpin's, VanDiken's, and VanTulip's fish. (Each guy owns his own fish.)

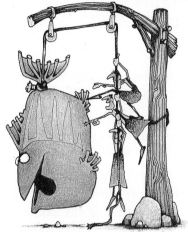

VanClumpin, Van Diken, and Van Tulip's fish

VanClumpin's, VanDiken's, and Van Tulip's fish

211 The possessive of a compound noun is formed by placing the possessive ending after the last word.

> his mother-in-law's (singular) husband;
> the Secretary of State's (singular) wife
> their mothers-in-law's (plural) husbands;
> the Secretaries of State's (plural) wives

212 The possessive of an indefinite pronoun is formed by placing an apostrophe and *s* on the last word.

> everyone's; anyone's; somebody else's

213 An apostrophe is used with an adjective which is part of an expression indicating time or amount.

> yesterday's news; a day's wage; a month's pay

Asterisk

214 An **asterisk** may be used in a short paper to indicate to the reader that additional information is included in a footnote at the bottom of the page.

> His first year* was very difficult.
> *1968

Diagonal

215 When quoting more than one line of poetry, use a **diagonal** at the end of each line.

> The following three lines from Frost's "The Road Not Taken" express clearly his thoughts on individuality: "Two roads diverged in a wood, and I—/I took the one less traveled by/ and that has made all the difference."

216	Punctuation Marks		
´	Accent, acute	·· (ö)	Dieresis
`	Accent, grave	. . .	Ellipsis
'	Apostrophe	!	Exclamation point
*	Asterisk	-	Hyphen
{ or }	Brace	. . .	Leaders
[ ]	Brackets	¶	Paragraph
∧	Caret	( )	Parentheses
و (ç)	Cedilla	.	Period
^	Circumflex	?	Question mark
:	Colon	" "	Quotation marks
,	Comma	§	Section
†	Dagger	;	Semicolon
—	Dash	~	Tilde
/	Diagonal/Slash	_____	Underscore

45

Usage and Commonly Mixed Pairs

217   **a, an:**   *A* is used before words which begin with a consonant sound; *an* is used before words which begin with a vowel sound.

> **Examples:**   *a* heap; *a* cat; *an* idol; *an* elephant; *an* honor; *a* historian

218   **accept, except:**   The verb *accept* means "to receive"; the preposition *except* means "other than."

> **Examples:**   Melissa graciously *accepted* defeat (verb).   All the boys *except* Zach were here (preposition).

219   **affect, effect:**   *Affect* is always a verb; it means "to influence."   *Effect* can be a verb, but it is most often used as a noun.   As a verb, *effect* means "to produce or make happen."

> **Examples:**   Mark's giggle *affected* the preacher.   Mark's giggle *effected* a pinch from his mother.

The noun *effect* means "the result."

> **Example:**   The *effect* of the pinch was a sore leg.

220   **allowed, aloud:**   The verb *allowed* means "permitted" or "let happen"; *aloud* is an adverb which means "in a normal voice."

> **Example:**   We weren't *allowed* to read *aloud* in the library.

221   **allusion, illusion:**   An *allusion* is a brief reference or mention of a famous person, place, thing, or idea.   An *illusion* is a false impression or idea.

> **Example:**   As he made an *allusion* to the great magicians of the past, Houdini created the *illusion* of having sawed his assistant in half.

222   **a lot:**   *Alot* is not one word; *a lot* (two words) is a very general descriptive phrase which should not be used in formal writing.

A *lot* should be written as two words, not one.   Luckily, Buzz *saw* through the problem.

223 **already, all ready:** *Already* is an adverb which tells when. *All ready* is a phrase meaning "completely ready."

> **Examples:** My little girl reads *already*. The class was *all ready* "to try out" the substitute.

224 **alright, all right:** *Alright* is the incorrect spelling of *all right*. *All right* is a phrase meaning "correct." (Please note, the following are spelled correctly: *always, altogether, already, almost.*)

225 **altogether, all together:** *Altogether* is always an adverb meaning "completely." *All together* is used to describe people or things which are gathered in one place at one time.

> **Examples:** This is *altogether* too much noise. My cousins were *all together* in the hay barn.

226 **among, between:** *Among* is used when speaking of more than two persons or things. *Between* is used when speaking of only two.

> **Examples:** Putrid socks were scattered *among* the sweaty uniforms. A single streamer dangled *between* the goalposts.

227 **amount, number:** *Number* is used when you can actually count the persons or things. *Amount* is used to describe things which can be weighed or measured, but not counted.

> **Examples:** The liquid produced a large *number* of burps. The burps were the result of a large *amount* of gas.

228 **annual, biannual, semiannual, biennial, perennial:** An *annual* event happens once every year. A *biannual* event happens twice a year (*semiannual* means the same as *biannual*). A *biennial* event happens every two years. A *perennial* event is active throughout the year and continues to happen year after year.

229 **ant, aunt:** *Aunt* is a relative. *Ant* is an insect.

230 **ascent, assent:** *Ascent* is "the act of rising"; *assent* is "agreement."

> **Example:** The pilot *assented* that the plane's *ascent* was unusually bumpy.

231 **bare, bear:** The adjective *bare* means "to be naked." A *bear* is a large, furry animal.

> **Example:** He chased the polar *bear* across the snow though his feet were *bare*.

The verb *bear* means "to put up with" or "to carry."

> **Example:** Dwayne could not *bear* another of his older brother's lectures.

232 **base, bass:** *Base* is the foundation or the lower part of something. *Bass* is a deep sound or tone. *Bass* (*a* pronounced as in *fast*) is a fish.

233 **be, bee:** *Be* is the verb. *Bee* is the insect.

234 **beat, beet:** The verb *beat* means "to strike, to defeat"; a *beet* is a carrot-like vegetable (often red).

Example: After our team *beat* Tom's team, four games to one, I was as red as a *beet*.

235 **berth, birth:** *Berth* is a space or compartment. *Birth* is the process of being born.

Example: We give up our most comfortable *berths* through *birth*.

236 **beside, besides:** *Beside* means "by the side of." *Besides* means "in addition to."

Examples: Jeff laid his gum *beside* his plate. *Besides* some burned toast, Bernice fed him some warm lemonade.

237 **billed, build:** *Billed* means either "to be given a bill" or "to have a beak." The verb *build* means "to construct."

Example: The horn-*billed* owl was able to *build* his nest without being *billed* for any material or labor.

238 **blew, blue:** *Blew* is the past tense of *blow*. *Blue* is a color; *blue* is also used to mean "feeling low in spirits."

239 **boar, bore:** A *boar* is a wild pig. *Bore* is a verb that means "to tire with dullness" or "to make a hole by drilling."

240 **board, bored:** A *board* is a piece of wood. *Board* also means "a group or council which helps run an organization."

Example: The School *Board* approved the purchase of fifty 1″ x 6″ pine *boards*.

Bored may mean "to make a hole by drilling" or "to become weary or tired of something."

Example: Dissecting fish *bored* Joe, so he took his tweezers and *bored* a hole in the tail of the perch.

241 **brake, break:** A *brake* is a device used to stop a vehicle. *Break* means "to split, crack, or destroy."

Example: I hope the *brakes* on my car never *break*.

242 **bring, take:** Use *bring* when the action is moving toward the speaker; use *take* when the action is moving away from the speaker.

Examples: *Bring* me another empty box. *Take* that full one out of here.

243 **by, buy:** *By* is a preposition meaning "near or through." *Buy* is a verb meaning "to purchase."

Example: Laurie stopped *by* the gate to ask if I would *buy* a painted toad.

244 **can, may:** *Can* means "able to" while *may* means "permitted to."

Example: "*Can* I eat this apple?" means the same as "Am I able to eat this apple?" "*May* I eat this apple?" means the same as "Am I permitted to eat this apple?"

245 **cannon, canon:** A *cannon* is a big gun; a *canon* is a rule or law made by an authority in a church or organization.

246 **canvas, canvass:** *Canvas* is a heavy cloth; *canvass* means "to go among the people asking them for votes or opinions."

247 **capital, capitol:** *Capital* can be either a noun or an adjective. The noun *capital* refers to a city or to money. The adjective *capital* means "major or important." *Capitol* is used only when talking about a building.

> **Examples:** The *capitol* building is in the *capital* city for a *capital* reason. The city government contributed the *capital* for the building project.

248 **cell, sell:** *Cell* means "a small room" or "a small unit of life which makes up all plants and animals." *Sell* is a verb meaning "to give up for a price."

249 **cent, sent, scent:** *Cent* is a coin; *sent* is the past tense of the verb "to send"; *scent* is an odor or smell.

> **Examples:** For twenty-two *cents*, I *sent* my girlfriend a mushy love poem in a perfumed envelope. She loved the *scent* but hated the poem.

250 **chord, cord:** *Chord* may be used to mean "an emotion or feeling," but it is more often used to mean "the sound when three or more musical tones are played at the same time," as with a piano *chord*. A *cord* is a string or rope.

251 **chose, choose:** *Chose* (choz) is the past tense of the verb *choose* (chooz).

> **Example:** This afternoon Mom *chose* tacos and hot sauce; this evening she will *choose* Alka-Seltzer.

252 **coarse, course:** *Coarse* means "rough or crude." *Course* means "a path or direction taken"; *course* also means "a class or series of studies."

> **Example:** Heidi took a *course* up the mountain which was very *coarse*.

253 **complement, compliment:** *Complement* means "completes or goes with." *Compliment* is an expression of admiration or praise.

> **Example:** I *complimented* Aunt Betty by saying that her hat *complemented* her coat and dress.

254 **continual, continuous:** *Continual* refers to something which happens again and again; *continuous* refers to something which doesn't stop happening.

> **Example:** Sunlight hits Peoria, Iowa, on a *continual* basis; but sunlight hits the world *continuously*.

255 **counsel, council:** When used as a noun, *counsel* means "advice"; when used as a verb, *counsel* means "to advise." *Council* refers to a group which advises.

> **Examples:** The jackrabbit *council counseled* all bunnies to keep their tails out of the old man's garden. That's good *counsel*.

256 **creak, creek:** A *creak* is a squeaking sound; a *creek* is a stream.

> **Example:** The old willow which leans over the *creek* is *creaking* in the wind.

257 **cymbal, symbol:** A *cymbal* is a metal instrument shaped like a plate. A *symbol* is something (usually visible) that stands for or represents another thing or idea (usually invisible).

> **Example:** The cracked *cymbal* left laying on the stage was a *symbol* of the band's final concert.

258 **dear, deer:** *Dear* means "loved or valued"; *deer* are animals. (*Note:* People will think you're strange if you write that you kissed your *deer* in the moonlight.)

259 **desert, dessert:** A *desert* is a barren wilderness. *Dessert* is food served at the end of a meal.

> **Example:** The scorpion tiptoed through the moonlit *desert*, searching for *dessert*.

The verb *desert* means "to abandon"; the noun *desert* also may mean "deserving reward or punishment."

> **Example:** The frightened rabbit *deserted* the boy; the loss of his pet was the cruel boy's just *desert*.

260 **die, dye:** *Die (dying)* means "to stop living." *Dye (dyeing)* is used to change the color of something.

261 **faint, feign, feint:** *Faint* means "to be feeble, without strength." *Feign* is a verb which means "to pretend or make up." *Feint* is a noun which means "a move or activity which is pretended or false."

> **Examples:** The little boy *feigned* a bruised, blood-spattered face and fell to the floor in a *feint*. His teacher, who didn't notice that the blood smelled like catsup, *fainted* beside him.

262 **farther, further:** *Farther* is used when you are writing about a physical distance. *Further* is used when you are not referring to distances; it can also mean "additional."

> **Examples:** Alaska is *farther* north than Iceland. *Further* information can be obtained at your local library.

263 **fewer, less:** *Fewer* refers to the number of separate units; *less* refers to bulk quantity.

> **Example:** There is *less* sand to play with, so we have *fewer* sandboxes to make.

264 **fir, fur:** *Fir* refers to a type of evergreen tree; *fur* is animal hair.

265 **flair, flare:** *Flair* means "a natural talent"; *flare* means "to light up quickly or burst out."

> **Example:** Hotheads have a *flair* for tempers which *flare*.

266 **for, fore, four:** *For* is a preposition meaning "because" or "directed to"; *fore* means "earlier" or "the front." *Four* is the number 4.

> **Example:** The dog had stolen one of the *four* steaks Mary had grilled *for* the party and was holding the bone in his *fore*paws when she found him.

267 **good, well:** *Good* is an adjective; *well* is nearly always an adverb.

Examples: The strange flying machines flew *well*. (The adverb *well* modifies *flew*.) They looked *good* as they flew overhead. (The adjective *good* modifies *they*.)

Exception: When used in writing about health, *well* is an adjective.

Examples: The pilots looked *good* at the start of the race. Not all of them felt so *well* at the finish.

The race made a *good* story for the young reporter. He wrote *well* and made the event come alive for his readers.

268 **hare, hair:** *Hair* refers to the growth covering the head and body of animals and human beings; *hare* refers to an animal similar to a rabbit.

Example: The *hair* on my head stood up as the *hare* darted out in front of our car.

269 **heal, heel:** *Heal* means "to mend or restore to health." *Heel* is the back part of a human foot.

Example: Bruce's badly bruised *heel healed.*

270 **hear, here:** You *hear* with your *ears.* *Here* is the opposite of *there* and means "nearby."

271 **heard, herd:** *Heard* is the past tense of the verb *hear*; *herd* is a large group of animals.

Example: The *herd* of grazing cows raised their heads when they *heard* the collie barking in the distance.

272 **heir, air:** *Heir* is a person who inherits something; *air* is the stuff we breathe.

273 **hole, whole:** A *hole* is a cavity or hollow place. *Whole* means "entire or complete."

274 **immigrate, emigrate:** *Immigrate* means "to *come into* a new country or area." *Emigrate* means "to *go out* of one country to live in another."

Example: Martin Ulferts *immigrated* to this country in 1882. He was only three years old when he *emigrated* from Germany.

275 **it's, its:** *It's* is the contraction of *it is.* *Its* is the possessive form of *it.*

Example: *It's* obviously a watchdog; it prefers to watch thieves rather than bark for *its* master.

276 **kernel, colonel:** A *kernel* is a seed or core; a *colonel* is a military officer.

277 **knew, new:** *Knew* is the past tense of the verb *know*. *New* means "recent or modern."

> **Example:** She *knew* that a *new* life began with graduation from kindergarten.

278 **know, no:** *Know* means "to understand or to realize." *No* means "the opposite of *yes*."

279 **later, latter:** *Later* means "after a period of time." *Latter* refers to the second of two things mentioned.

> **Example:** *Later* in the year 1965, Galen married Sam; the *latter*, Sam, is a lady.

280 **lay, lie:** *Lay* means "to place." (*Lay* is a transitive verb; that means it needs a word to complete the meaning.)

> **Examples:** I *lay* the cigar down today. I *laid* it down yesterday. I had *laid* it down before. (*Cigar* and *it* complete the meaning by answering the question *what*.)

> *Lie* means "to recline." (*Lie* is an intransitive verb.)

> **Examples:** The mutt *lies* down. It *lay* down yesterday. It has *lain* down before.

281 **lead, led:** *Lead* is a present tense verb meaning "to guide." The past tense of the verb is *led*. When the words are pronounced the same, then *lead* is the metal.

> **Example:** "Hey, Nat, get the *lead* out!"
> "Hey, cool it, man! Who gave you a ticket to *lead* me around?"

282 **learn, teach:** *Learn* means "to get information"; *teach* means "to give information."

> **Example:** If you want to test yourself on something you've just *learned*, try *teaching* it to others.

283 **leave, let:** *Leave* means "to allow something to remain behind." *Let* means "to permit."

> **Example:** Rozi wanted to *leave* her boots at home, but George wouldn't *let* her.

284 **like, as:** *Like* is a preposition meaning "similar to"; *as* is a conjunction meaning "such as." *Like* usually introduces a phrase; *as* usually introduces a clause.

> **Examples:** The glider floated *like* a bird. The glider floated *as* he had hoped.

285 **loose, lose, loss:** *Loose* (loos) means "free or untied"; *lose* (looz) means "to misplace or fail to win"; *loss* means "something lost."

> **Example:** Even though he didn't want to *lose* the *loose* tooth, it was no big *loss*.

286 **made, maid:** *Made* is the past tense of *make* which means "to cre-

ate." A *maid* is a female servant; *maid* is also used to describe an unmarried girl or young woman.

> **Example:** The *maid* asked if our beds needed to be *made*.

287 **mail, male:** *Mail* refers to letters or packages handled by the postal service. *Male* refers to the masculine sex.

288 **main, mane:** *Main* refers to the principal or most important part or point. *Mane* is the long hair growing from the top or sides of the neck of certain animals such as the horse, lion, etc.

289 **meat, meet:** *Meat* is food or flesh; *meet* means "to come upon or encounter."

290 **metal, meddle, medal, mettle:** *Metal* is an element like iron or gold. *Meddle* means "to interfere." *Medal* is an award. *Mettle*, a noun, refers to quality of character.

> **Examples:** The golden snoop cup is a *metal medal* which is awarded to the greatest *meddler*. Snooping is a habit of people of low *mettle*.

291 **miner, minor:** A *miner* digs in the ground for valuable ore. A *minor* is a person who is not legally an adult. A *minor* problem is one of no great importance.

The use of *minors* as *miners* is no *minor* problem.

292 **moral, morale:** *Moral* relates to what is right or wrong. *Morale* refers to a person's attitude or mental condition.

> **Example:** "I don't care whether hunting deer is *moral*," she said. "I care about my *morale*."

293 **morning, mourning:** *Morning* refers to the first part of the day before noon; *mourning* means "showing sorrow."

> **Example:** Abby was *mourning* her test grades all *morning*.

294 **oar, or, ore:** An *oar* is a paddle used in rowing or steering a boat. *Or* is a conjunction indicating choice. *Ore* refers to a mineral made up of several different kinds of material, as in iron ore.

295 **pain, pane:** *Pain* is the feeling of being hurt. *Pane* is a section or part of something, as in a framed section of glass in a window or door.

296 **pair, pare, pear:** A *pair* is a couple (two); *pare* is a verb meaning "to peel"; *pear* is the fruit.

297 **past, passed:** *Passed* is always a verb. *Past* can be used as a noun, as an adjective, or as a preposition.

> **Examples:** That Gremlin *passed* my 'Vette (verb). The old man won't forget the *past* (noun). I'm sorry, but I'd rather not talk about my *past* life (adjective). Old Blue walked *past* us and never smelled it (preposition).

298 **peace, piece:** *Peace* means "harmony or freedom from war." *Piece* is a part or fragment.

> **Example:** Someone once observed that *peace* is not a condition, but a process—a process of building goodwill one *piece* or one person at a time.

299 **personal, personnel:** *Personal* means "private." *Personnel* are people working at a particular job.

300 **plain, plane:** *Plain* means "an area of land which is flat or level"; it also means "clearly seen or clearly understood."

> **Example:** My teacher told me to "check the map" after I said that it was *plain* to me why the early settlers had troubles crossing the Rockies on their way to the Great *Plains*.

Plane means "flat, level, and even"; it is also a tool used to smooth the surface of wood.

> **Example:** I used a *plane* to make the board *plane* and smooth.

301 **pore, pour, poor:** A *pore* is an opening in the skin. *Pour* means "a constant flow or stream." *Poor* means "needy."

> **Example:** Long math tests on warm spring days make my *poor pores pour*.

302 **principal, principle:** As an adjective, *principal* means "primary." As a noun, it can mean "a school administrator" or "a sum of money." *Principle* means "idea or doctrine."

> **Examples:** His *principal* gripe is lack of freedom. "Hey, Charlie, I hear the *principal* chewed you out!" After twenty years, the amount of interest was higher than the *principal*. The *principle* of freedom is based on the *principle* of self-discipline.

303 **quiet, quit, quite:** *Quiet* is the opposite of noisy. *Quit* means "to stop." *Quite* means "completely or entirely."

304 **raise, rays, raze:** *Raise* is a verb meaning "to lift or elevate." *Rays* are thin lines or beams, as in rays of sunlight. *Raze* is also a verb which means "to tear down completely."

> **Examples:** As I *raised* the shade, bright *rays* of sunlight shot across the room and bounced to the ceiling. Across the street I could see the old theater which they plan to *raze* soon to build a parking lot.

305 **real, very, really:** Do not use *real* in place of the adverbs *very* or *really*.

> **Examples:** Pimples are *very* (not *real*) embarrassing. Her nose is *really* (not *real*) long.

306   **red, read:** *Red* is a color; *read* is a verb meaning "to understand the meaning of written letters, words, and symbols."

307   **right, write, wright, rite:** *Right* means "correct or proper"; it also refers to anything which a person has a legal claim to, as in copyright. *Write* means "to record in print." *Wright* is a person who makes or builds something. *Rite* is a ritual or ceremonial act.

    Example: Did you *write* that it is the *right* of the ship*wright* to perform the *rite* of christening—breaking a bottle of champagne on the stern of the ship?

308   **scene, seen:** *Scene* refers to the setting or location where something happens; it also may mean "sight or spectacle." *Seen* is a part of the verb "see."

    Example: An actor likes to be *seen* by making a *scene*.

309   **seam, seem:** *Seam* is a line formed by connecting two pieces of material. *Seem* means "to appear to exist."

    Example: The ragged *seams* in the old man's coat *seem* to match the creases in his face.

310   **sew, so, sow:** *Sew* is a verb meaning "to stitch"; *so* is a conjunction meaning "in order that." The verb *sow* means "to plant."

311   **sight, cite, site:** *Sight* means "the act of seeing." *Cite* means "to quote or refer to." *Site* means "location or position."

    Examples: Mark's *sight* was destroyed when a guy's cigarette exploded a gas can on the building *site*. The judge *cited* the man for careless use of smoking materials.

312   **sit, set:** *Sit* means "to put the body in a seated position." *Set* means "to place."

"How can you just *sit* there and watch as I *set* all these chairs in place?"

313   **sole, soul:** *Sole* means "single, only one"; *sole* also refers to the bottom surface of a foot or shoe. *Soul* refers to the spiritual part of a person.

    Example: A person's *sole* develops blisters on a two-mile hike while his *soul* walks on eternally.

314 **some, sum:** *Some* means "a certain unknown number or part." *Sum* means "an amount."

    Example: The total *sum* was stolen by *some* thieves.

315 **sore, soar:** *Sore* means "painful"; to *soar* means "to rise or fly high into the air."

    Example: Craning to watch the eagle *soar* overhead, our necks soon grew *sore*.

316 **stationary, stationery:** *Stationary* means "not movable"; *stationery* is the paper and envelopes used to write letters.

317 **steal, steel:** *Steal* means "to take something without permission"; *steel* is a metal.

318 **than, then:** *Than* is used in a comparison; *then* tells when.

    Example: *Then* he cried and said that his big brother was bigger *than* my big brother. *Then* I cried.

319 **their, there, they're:** *Their* is a possessive pronoun, one which shows ownership. *There* is a pronoun used to point out a location. *They're* is the contraction for *they are*.

    Examples: *They're* upset because *their* neighbor dumped garbage over *there*.

320 **threw, through:** *Threw* is the past tense of "throw." *Through* means "passing from one side of something to the other."

    Example: She *threw* the pillow *through* the window.

321 **to, at:** *To* should not be used in place of *at* in a sentence.

    Example: He is *at* (not *to*) school.

322 **to, too, two:** *To* is the preposition which can mean "in the direction of." (*To* also is used to form an infinitive.) *Too* is an adverb meaning "very or many." *Two* is the number.

    Example: The *two* divers were careful not *to* swim *to* the sunken ship *too* quickly.

323 **vain, vane, vein:** *Vain* means "worthless." It may also mean "thinking too highly of one's self; stuck-up." *Vane* is a flat piece of material set up to show which way the wind blows. *Vein* refers to a blood vessel or a mineral deposit.

    Example: The weather *vane* indicates the direction of wind; the blood *vein* determines the direction of flowing blood; the *vain* mind moves in no particular direction and is satisfied to think only about itself.

324 **vary, very:** *Vary* is a verb that means "to change." (The weather can *vary* from snow to sleet to sunshine in a single day.) *Very* can be an adjective meaning "in the fullest sense" or "complete." (His story was the *very* opposite of the truth.) *Very* can also be an adverb meaning "extremely." (The story was *very* interesting.)

325 **waist, waste:** *Waist* is the part of the body just above the hips. The verb *waste* means "to wear away, decay"; the noun *waste* refers to material which is unused or useless.

326 **wait, weight:** *Wait* means "to stay somewhere expecting something." *Weight* is the measure of heaviness.

327 **ware, wear, where:** *Ware* means "a product which is sold"; *wear* means "to have on or to carry on one's body"; *where* asks the question, "in what place? or in what situation?"

> **Example:** The little boy who sold pet fleas boasted, "Anybody can *wear* my *ware* any*where*, and he'll always know right *where* it is."

328 **way, weigh:** *Way* means "path or route." *Weigh* means "to measure weight."

> **Example:** After being *weighed* at Weight Watchers club, the two sad friends walked the long *way* home . . . past the malt shop.

329 **weather, whether:** *Weather* refers to the condition of the atmosphere. *Whether* refers to a possibility.

> **Example:** The *weather* will determine *whether* I go fishing.

330 **week, weak:** A *week* is a period of 7 days; *weak* means "not strong."

331 **which, witch:** *Which* is a pronoun used to refer to or point out something. *Witch* is an evil female who is believed to cast spells and keep company with black cats.

> **Example:** The cool *witch* drives a broomstick *which* has a tachometer.

332 **who, which, that:** *Which* refers to nonliving objects or to animals; *which* should never refer to people. *Who* is used to refer to people. *That* may refer to animals, people, or nonliving objects.

333 **who, whom:** *Who* is used as the subject in a sentence; *whom* is used as the object of a preposition or as a direct object.

> **Examples:** *Who* ordered this pizza? The pizza was ordered by *whom*?

Note: To test for *who/whom*, arrange the parts of the clause in a subject-verb-object order. (*Who* works as the subject, *whom* as the object.)

334 **who's, whose:** *Who's* is the contraction for *who is*. *Whose* is a possessive pronoun, one which shows ownership.

> **Examples:** "*Who's* that kid with the red ears?"
> "*Whose* ears are you talking about, big mouth?"

335 **wood, would:** *Wood* is the stuff which trees are made of; *would* is a part of the verb "will."

> **Example:** The captain who had a *wooden* leg *would* always be shortening his trousers whenever termites were on board.

336 **your, you're:** *Your* is a possessive pronoun, one which shows ownership. *You're* is the contraction for *you are*.

The Writing Process

337 The Personal Narrative

The stories that you share with your friends are often personal stories or narratives. This means that you tell about experiences that have actually happened to you—and you know when you have a good story to tell. It includes something funny, new, surprising, or interesting that you want to tell your friends. They probably won't want to hear about your little sister's birthday party, but they will be all ears when you tell them about your visit to the principal's office. This personal story will certainly be of interest to them. When you have a good story and you tell it well, you and your friends share in a very enjoyable experience. Everyone enjoys a good story.

Writing about your own experiences is a natural first step in developing your writing skills. For your writing to be good, it has to be just as fresh, exciting, and interesting as the stories you tell your friends. However, writing a personal narrative that holds your reader's attention requires a little more effort than simply telling a story. You have to capture your story on paper and make it come alive for the reader with written words. To do this, you—the writer—have to select your words very carefully and develop your story very creatively.

338 Writing the Personal Narrative

There are four basic steps you should follow when you set out to write a personal narrative. (These steps should be followed in all other forms of writing as well.)

Step 1 —	**Prewriting:**	*Selecting a Subject*
Step 2 —	**Planning:**	*Preparing to Write*
Step 3 —	**Writing:**	*Writing the First Draft*
Step 4 —	**Revising:**	*Improving the Writing*

339 Prewriting: *Selecting a Subject*

The first step in the writing process is prewriting. In this step you must select a subject for your narrative. Begin by thinking of several specific experiences which you know will interest your reader—those experiences which at one time you couldn't wait to tell your friends about. We all have these experiences. However, you might not remember them all immediately. A *free writing* can help you find these lost experiences. In a free writing for a personal narrative, simply write down everything that comes to mind about a certain time in your past. Use your senses to help you remember as many sights, sounds, smells, tastes, and feelings as you can. Write nonstop and freely until your ideas dry up. (See "Guidelines for Free Writing," 350, for a complete explanation.)

You might also talk to friends and family members since they might recall some experiences which you have forgotten. Make sure that the subject you select for your narrative meets the requirements of your assignment. For example, if you are assigned to write a short narrative about your preschool years, make sure that the specific experience or experiences you select for your paper are from that time in your life. Also, limit yourself to one or possibly two or three related experiences for short narrative assignments. (See "Guidelines for Selecting a Topic," 351, and "Sample Writing Topics," 352, for additional help in selecting a subject.)

340 Planning: *Preparing to Write*

Once you have selected a subject for your narrative, the next step is to prepare for the actual writing. Start by gathering details that will give your subject life. That is, you need to find specific details that will allow your readers to visualize (see in their minds) the experience as they read your finished narrative. For example, in a narrative about your preschool years, it is not enough to remember that you never crawled in the usual way as a child. Go a bit further and tell about the specific way in which you did move around before you walked. If you can't remember all the specific details, talk to your parents or older brothers and sisters.

If you have trouble finding enough details, you can do another free writing to search for information stored in your mind. To help you remember more details, ask yourself the *who, what, when, where, why,* and *how* of the experience. Remember, you can never have too many details in the planning stage of your narrative.

341 Add feeling.

As you gather details for your narrative, think about your attitude or feeling toward the subject of your paper. The way you feel about the subject will help you find a focus or purpose for your narrative. For example, if the experience in your paper is meant to be taken seriously, you will want to focus in on those details that are serious and factual. If the experience is light and funny, you will want to focus in on those details that capture the humor of the experience. In most cases, the focus or purpose of a narrative will be to explain or entertain.

Your feeling toward the subject of your paper will also help you write an effective beginning for your personal narrative. Readers are attracted to a paper which begins with an honest, sincere expression of an attitude or feeling. Note below the difference between the two beginnings for a personal narrative about a memorable teacher.

1. Mr. Brown is my seventh-grade gym teacher. (No expression of feeling is included.)

2. Mr. Brown does not allow any fooling around in his gym class. (An expression of feeling is included.)

342   Arrange your details.

After you have chosen a specific subject and feeling, you must next decide on a method of organization or order for arranging your details into a general outline:

Methods of Arrangement

Chronological (time) **order:** You can arrange your details in the order in which they happened.

Order of location: You can arrange your details in the order in which they are located *(above, below, alongside, beneath, etc.).*

Order of importance: You can arrange your details from the most important to the least—or from the least to the most.

A cause and effect arrangement: You can begin with a general statement giving the *cause* of a problem and then add a number of specific *effects*.

Comparison: You can explain a subject by showing how it is similar to another, better-known subject.

Contrast: You can use details which show how your subject is different from another, better-known subject.

Illustration *(general to specific):* You can arrange your details so that the general idea is stated first in the paragraph *(topic sentence).* Specific reasons, examples, facts, and other details are then added which *illustrate* or support the general statement.

343   Writing: *The First Draft*

The third step in the writing process is to write the first draft. Write freely and creatively, connecting your ideas together as naturally as you can. Keep the specific topic and purpose of your writing in mind and use your outline as a guide. However, don't be afraid to make changes. You'll be surprised at what you discover as you go along.   There are two important things to remember about writing the first draft: Say everything you can about your experience—and say it as creatively as possible.

344   Revising: *Improving the Writing*

The fourth step in the writing process is the revising and improving stage. No writing is complete after the first draft. As you revise, make sure your narrative reads clearly and smoothly. Remember, too, that your readers can share in your story only if you make it come alive with enough detail.

Read the two sentences which follow. You will notice that the second sentence contains more details than the first—details which help make the subject come alive for the reader.

1. Mr. Brown sent us in and went after the two. *(Original:* Not enough detail.)

2. With fire in his eyes, Mr. Brown quickly sent us in and went after the two transgressors. *(Revision:* Details added.)

Note: All the details in a personal narrative must help move the story along. If the details are used just to fill up the page, take them out. Also, if your details wander off the topic, change them or cut them.

345 Check your sentences.

Make sure you have used complete sentences—and complete sentences of different sizes. If, for example, you write a paper that contains only short, simple sentences, it may become boring to read. Notice the difference between the two examples below:

1. They reached the 50-yard line duck-walking. We could tell duck-walking was not easy. They were really struggling. (Three short, simple sentences)

2. By the time they reached the 50-yard line, we could tell duck-walking was not easy since they were really struggling. (One smooth, long sentence)

Note: For help in writing smoother, longer sentences, see "Sentence Combining." Also remember that too many long sentences is no more enjoyable to read than too many short ones.

346 Check your wording.

Check the beginning and ending of your narrative. The beginning should attract your reader to your story and make him or her want to read more; the ending should wind up your story and bring it to a natural stopping point. Make sure your thoughts are clear and interesting throughout your story. If your story starts to drag, check your word choice. Sometimes a simple word change can make the rest of the sentence much stronger. A thesaurus, which is a book of synonyms, can help you find strong, descriptive words for your narrative. Also, a thesaurus can help you find a replacement word for any word that you have used too often in your story. Finally, check for spelling, punctuation, and capitalization. A dictionary and your English handbook will help as you check the mechanics of your paper.

When you have finished your revising, proofreading, and polishing, write or type your final copy as neatly as you can. This makes it easier for your reader to share in your story—and stories are meant to be shared.

347 Model Narrative

Note the plan for the model narrative that follows. Then read the narrative which was developed from this plan.

Plan for Model Narrative

Assignment: Write a narrative about your last school year.

Subject: Seventh-grade gym teacher, Mr. Brown

Focus: One experience early in the school year that revealed that he is a strict teacher

Writer's attitude: Lightly humorous

Organization: Organized by time (in the order in which things happened)

Beginning: Introduces the subject and the writer's attitude — "Mr. Brown does not allow any fooling around in his gym class."

Ending: Brings the narrative to a stopping point — "We didn't want Mr. Brown to make us walk like a duck or any other type of animal for that matter."

Model Narrative

Mr. Brown does not allow any fooling around in his gym class. Unfortunately, two guys learned this the hard way. At the end of the first day of flag football, Mr. Brown blew his whistle to signal the end of the period. Most of us knew enough to stop and fall in line. He had made it very clear to us on the first day of class that when he blew his whistle, we had to stop our activity. Immediately! Kerry Schmidt and Joel Johnson, being brave or stupid, decided to test Mr. Brown on this rule. They ignored the whistle and continued throwing a football. With fire in his eyes, Mr. Brown quickly sent us in and went after the two transgressors. We all watched from the locker room doorway while Mr. Brown made them duck-walk on the football field. By the time they reached the 50-yard line, we could tell duck-walking was not easy since they were really struggling. He sent them in after another 20 yards when their duck-walk had turned into more of a crawl. We couldn't help giving a few duck calls when Kerry and Joel got into the locker room, but we didn't "Quack" very loudly. We didn't want Mr. Brown to make us walk like a duck or any other type of animal for that matter.

Summary:
Writing the Personal Narrative

Prewriting: *Selecting a Subject*

- Select an interesting or entertaining experience (or experiences) which meets the requirements of the assignment.
- Gather details for the experience by thinking and writing freely about all the possibilities.

Planning: *Preparing to Write*

- Examine your details and decide what feeling or attitude you should bring to your topic.
- Plan a method of organization (time? order of importance?).
- Write an outline.

Writing: *The First Draft*

- Write freely, naturally, and creatively.
- Use your outline as a guide.
- Keep your specific topic and audience in mind.

Revising: *Improving the Writing*

- Make sure the experience is described in a clear, yet colorful way.
- Take out details that *pad* rather than *add* to your paper.
- Check the beginning and ending. The beginning should attract your reader to the narrative; the ending should bring the story to a natural stopping point.
- Check the mechanics carefully—sentences, spelling, capitalization, and punctuation.
- Check word choice—use strong, descriptive words. Don't use the same word over and over, especially at the beginning of your sentences.
- Write or type a neat and clear final copy.

1. Follow the "Guidelines for Selecting a Topic" and find a topic that interests you and fits your assignment.

2. Follow the "Guidelines for Free Writing" and write down all of your ideas on the topic you've chosen. Write as freely and naturally as you can, much the same as you would if you were simply telling someone about the topic.

3. Keep writing until you are fairly sure you have gathered enough good information. Remember, for writing to be good, it must offer something to the reader—a new idea, an interesting experience, an unexpected ending, etc. Also make sure you have specific examples and personal experiences to use in your writing.

4. If you have listed all your thoughts on the topic, but still need more details, go to other sources for additional information. You can visit the library to read books, magazines, pamphlets, etc. You can also talk to people (parents, teachers, workers) who might be able to provide information from their personal experience. Observe people, places, things, and events which are somehow related to your topic. To help figure out where you need more details, ask the questions *who, what, when, where, why,* and *how* about your topic.

5. Select the details you plan to use in your paper and arrange them into a logical order. (See Handbook 342.) Make a list or an outline to help keep you on the right track as you write. Remember, though, that your list or outline is simply a guide. You may find a better way to organize your details as you write.

6. Once you have gathered and organized your ideas, you must next turn them into complete sentences which are both clear and colorful.

7. Your writing must have life. If your ideas are good, but they do not "sound" quite right on paper, your reader may lose interest. To add life to your writing, use strong words—action verbs (hissed, bubbled) and specific nouns. Use colorful modifiers—adjectives and adverbs—where needed. Also, you may want to use a "stylistic device" (simile, metaphor, alliteration, parallel structure, etc.) once in a while. However, remember that the best writing sounds natural. Don't make any part of your writing so "colorful" that it doesn't sound natural.

8. Your writing must read smoothly. If too many of your ideas are written in short, simple sentences, your writing will sound choppy. You must combine some of these short sentences into better-sounding sentences. Also, take out phrases or expressions that are overused. Finally, don't begin too many sentences with *it, he, she, I,* or *they.*

9. Your writing must get to the point. If you find yourself saying the same thing over and over, go back and trim. As a writer, you should repeat words and ideas only if they add to or make clearer what you have already said. Also, do not go looking for a "big" word when a small one will do; and don't use adjectives or adverbs which add nothing new (*loud* blasts, jerked *quickly*).

10. Test your writing by reading it out loud. Remember, for writing to be good, it must be both interesting and understandable. Your ideas should be clever, yet well organized. Your words should be lively, yet clear. And your sentences should be creative, yet natural. Use a revising checklist to make sure your writing is as good as it can be.

11. Lastly, your writing must be free of errors. Proofread your writing for errors in spelling, capitalization, punctuation, usage, agreement, and the like. Use a dictionary or handbook when in doubt. Write or type your final copy neatly so that it looks as good as it sounds.

Good observers make good writers.

350   Guidelines for Free Writing

Reminders . . .

1. Thoughts are constantly passing through your mind; you *never* have *nothing* on your mind.
2. Writing is simply getting these thoughts down on paper.
3. Your senses are always searching out details.
4. Many things seem difficult when you first try them; free writing is probably no different.
5. Some days will be better than others; don't be discouraged.
6. To succeed at anything, you must give it an honest effort.

The Process . . .

1. Start with plenty of paper and an extra pen.
2. Write whatever comes into your mind.
3. Don't stop to think about or correct your writing; that will come later.
4. Keep writing even when you think you have dried up.
5. Use all your senses and observe more closely than usual.
6. Continue to think about all sides of your topic until ideas and details begin to flow.
7. When a particular idea seems to be working, stick with it and record as many details as possible.
8. Listen to and read the free writings of others; learn from them.
9. Practice writing notes and reminders to yourself.
10. Carry a journal with you and write freely in it whenever you have an idea you don't want to forget, or even when you simply have nothing else to do. These free writings will help you become a better writer.

The Result . . .

1. You will often use your free writings as the starting point for a more formal writing assignment.
2. Make sure your free writing fits the topic and is also one you feel good about sharing.
3. Decide exactly what you plan (or are required) to write about and add details as necessary. (This may require a second free writing.)
4. If the topic seems to be working, keep writing; if you dry up, look for a new subject and begin with a new free writing.

1. **Use brainstorming techniques.** Brainstorming is a method of gathering as many details as possible on a particular subject. If you need a topic to write about, for example, you should simply begin listing as many potential topics as possible without taking the time to decide whether each one is good for your writing assignment. You simply want to get a list of as many topics as you can in the time you have. (Brainstorming works best when it is done in groups.)

2. **Sentence completion** can work well with either groups or individuals. Complete any sentence beginning in as many ways as you can. Try to word your sentence beginnings so that they lead you to a topic you can use for your paper.

   I wonder how...   I hope our school...   Our grading system...
   Television is...   One place I enjoy...   Too many students...

3. **Be alert for "found" topics.** These are topics which you *find* unexpectedly as you are shopping, playing, or walking home from school. You might come across an unusual event, person, or conversation which is different in some way. Often the best topics are found when people are just being themselves.

**Some of life's low points
can become high points of writing.**

4. **Keep a journal.** Write in your journal on a regular basis the same way you would if you kept a diary. Enter your personal feelings, opinions, and observations of what happens each day. This is good writing practice and a source of future writing topics.

5. **Observe.** Watch and listen carefully to everything and everybody when you are looking for a topic. Think about possible topics as you read. Talking to people (parents, grandparents, neighbors, workers) can also help you decide which topic to write about.

6. **Use a checklist.** Oftentimes, you can find lists of titles and topics in the library. These may be lists of articles kept in the vertical file or nonfiction titles recently added to the library. An issue of the *Reader's Guide to Periodical Literature* can be useful as a checklist of current topics also. (Ask your librarian for help in finding those.) Even a magazine or newspaper can remind you of the many topics being written about today. Below you will find a checklist of the things most needed in our daily lives. The checklist provides a variety of general subjects. If you want to use one of these subjects for a writing assignment, you must narrow that subject into a specific topic.

Example: *clothing* . . . fashionable clothing . . . the changing fashion in school clothing . . . The type of clothing students wear today varies with each group of students.

Things Most Needed in our Daily Lives

clothing	natural resources	agriculture	plants/vegetation
housing	personality/identity	environment	freedom/rights
food	recreation/hobby	land/property	energy
communication	love	trade/money	rules/laws
exercise	measurement	literature/books	tools/utensils
education	senses	entertainment	heat/fuel
family	machines	work/occupation	health/medicine
friends	intelligence	community	art/music
purpose/goals	history/records	science	faith/religion

Writing Topics...

COME IN ALL SHAPES, SIZES, AND SEASONS

Thoughts and Quotations

"A lie can travel halfway around the world while the truth is putting on its shoes."—Mark Twain

"I'm a great believer in luck, and I find the harder I work the more I have of it." —Thomas Jefferson

Some people make the world more special just by being in it.

"The impossible is often the untried." —Jim Goodwin

"Too often we give children answers to remember rather than problems to solve." —Roger Lewin

If you want a friend, be a friend.

"The man who makes no mistakes does not usually make anything." —W.C. Magee

"You can always tell a true friend; when you've made a fool of yourself, he doesn't feel you've done a permanent job." —Laurence J. Peter

Sharing with a friend makes twice as much fun.

"We can't all be heroes because someone has to sit on the curb and clap as they go by." —Will Rogers

Descriptive

Person: friend, teacher, relative, classmate, minister (priest, rabbi), co-worker, teammate, coach, neighbor, entertainer, politician, sister, brother, bus driver, an older person, a younger person, a baby, someone who taught you well, someone who spends time with you, someone you wish you were more like, someone who always bugs you

Place: school, neighborhood, old neighborhood, the beach, the park, the hangout, home, your room, your garage, your basement, the attic, a rooftop, the alley, the bowling alley, a classroom, the theatre, the locker room, the store, a restaurant, the library, a church, a stadium, the office, the zoo, the study hall, the cafeteria, the hallway, the barn, the dump, the street

Thing: a billboard, a bulletin board, a poster, a photograph, a camera, a machine, a computer, a video game, a music video, a musical instrument, a tool, a monkey wrench, a monkey, a pet, a pet peeve, a bus, a boat, a book . . . a car, a cat, a camp . . . a dog, a drawing, a diary . . . a model, a miniature, a muppet . . .

Narrative

stage fright, just last week, on the bus, learning a lesson, the trip, a kind act, homesick, a holiday experience, mysteries, a big mistake, field trips, studying, a reunion, a special party, getting lost, being late, asking for help, after school, Friday night, getting hurt, success, flirting, an embarrassing moment, staying overnight, moving, building a _____, the first day of _____, the last day of _____, learning to _____, the big game, miserable time, all wet, running away, being alone, getting caught, a practical joke, cleaning it up, being punished, staying after, a special conference, the school program, being a friend

Expository

How to . . . wash a car, make a taco, improve your memory, prevent accidents, care for a pet, entertain a child, impress your teacher, earn extra money, get in shape, study for a test, conserve energy, operate a computer, take a good picture

How to operate . . . control . . . run . . .
How to choose . . . select . . . pick . . .
How to scrape . . . finish . . . paint . . .
How to store . . . stack . . . load . . .
How to build . . . grow . . . create . . .
How to fix . . . clean . . . wash . . .
How to protect . . . warn . . . wave . . .

The causes of . . . acid rain, acne, hiccups, snoring, tornados, northern lights, shinsplints, dropouts, rust, birth defects, cheating, child abuse

Kinds of . . . music, crowds, friends, teachers, love, rules, compliments, commercials, punishment, dreams, happiness, pain, neighbors, pollution, poetry, taxes, clouds, stereos, heroes, chores, homework, fads, adoption, vacations, calendars, clocks, communication, mothers

Definition of . . . rock 'n' roll, best friend, "class," poverty, generation gap, free agent, a good time, a disabled person, hassle, a radical, a conservative, SALT, Arab, metric system, dialect, bankruptcy, "soul," grandmother, school, brain, arthritis, antibiotic, loyalty, credit union, astrology, CPR, Kosher, algebra

Persuasive

safety in the home, dieting, girls in all sports, organ transplants, sex education, homework, study halls, capital punishment, the speed limit, smoking in public places, shoplifting, seat belts, air bags, gun control, courtroom television, required courses, final exams, students on school boards, public housing, teen centers, something that needs improving, something that deserves support, something that's unfair, something that everyone should have to see or do, something . . .

Writing with Style

354   Do your written stories—the stories you turn in for assignments—seem as interesting and exciting as the stories you share with friends? If they do, you probably already write in a natural style. Writing in a natural style simply means that you write in a style which actually sounds like you when you tell a good story. You might not think that writing this way would be a difficult thing to do, but, for many of us, it is. For some reason, many of us switch to another personality when we write—the personality of someone who uses short, choppy sentences with strange, uninteresting words. And the stories we end up with sound like they were written by someone else. Before any of us can write well—tell a good story in words—we must "speak in our own voice." We must speak (write) to our audience using an honest, direct, and natural· style.

355 Use a Natural Style

      A natural writing style will not only make writing enjoyable for you, but it will also make reading what you have written enjoyable for your teachers and classmates. Those students whose stories are often read out loud in your English class usually write creatively and naturally. Something in these stories moves us in some way; it makes us say to ourselves, "Hey, I like that." That "something" is the ability of the writer to make a story seem real and alive. Read the parts of three junior high and middle school stories which follow.

> After that, I was underwater in a silent world, all alone. It was great. But my air was running out and I had to surface. I gave out a kick with my left leg; then two or three more and I surfaced. I dog-paddled to the side of the pool, paused, then lifted myself to the side. I was exhausted.

While we were walking, I looked up and saw the moon was out. It made the fog seem to glow. Off in the distance, I heard a dog bark and then a chorus of barks. I felt a shiver crawl up my spine, probably just the cold.

"I've thought it over.   I'm not going on the Demon."
"But it'll be fun.   C'mon!"
"No!   I just ate lunch.   I'm not going on it."
"Oh, gees!   It's not that bad.   You're not going to throw up."
"I know it, but I don't like going upside down."
"Yes you do."
"No I don't."
"I'll give you a dollar."
"Okay."

We got into the last car of the roller coaster and locked ourselves in. We started to move and slowly submerged into the Demon's tunnel. I felt like I was the camera on one of those National Geographic specials going into some creature's mouth and down its throat.

The examples above make us pay attention to what is being said because each seems real or natural.   And you can tell that each student is interested in telling a good story.   In the first student example, it is easy to visualize—see in your mind—the writer kicking to the surface of the water.   In the second example, you can share the writer's feeling of uneasiness while walking late at night.   In the last humorous example, we can share the writer's fear and uncertainty of a roller coaster called the Demon.

356 Improving Your Style Through Practice

Writing is a skill which must be practiced often before you can feel comfortable doing it.   Once the act of writing becomes easier for you, your style will become more and more natural.   One way to practice writing is to keep a personal journal or diary.   Use this journal to write down your thoughts as they enter your mind.   Don't worry about the way your journal writings look or how they sound.   If you practice in this way and keep at it, you'll soon find that your writing is more lively, interesting, and natural.

Another way to practice writing in a natural style is by "talking" to friends and close relatives in friendly letters.   Write these letters as if your friend or relative were in the same room with you, and you were actually talking to him or her in person.   Also, when you are given a writing assignment, begin by doing a *free writing*.   In a free writing, write down your thoughts about the subject of the assignment.   Keep writing until you can't think of anything else to say.   Many of these thoughts will be as interesting and creative as the ideas you share with friends.   Use some of these ideas in the actual writing assignment to make it sound more natural.   In addition, you should read as much as you can to see how the professionals write. You'll find that most of your favorite authors write in a natural style.

357 Improving Your Style Through Revising

Writing naturally is a very important skill—some might say the most important skill—to practice if you want to become a good writer. However, writing in this way won't guarantee that you will become another Mark Twain, a famous American author who wrote in an enjoyable, natural style. There are other characteristics or qualities of a good writing style that you will also have to learn and practice as well. You will find these characteristics especially helpful when you are revising or improving the first draft of one of your stories or other types of writing assignments.

Note: No one writes a story or other type of writing assignment which can't be improved by revising. Even the most successful writers make many changes before they are satisfied with their writing.

Anytime you write a first draft of a story or any other type of writing assignment, there will be parts of it which already sound interesting, creative, and natural. No changes should be made in these parts. However, there will also be parts of each writing assignment which simply don't sound right—something seems to be missing. Changes should be made in these sections so that the entire writing assignment will be enjoyable for your readers. To help you make these changes, use the following guidelines which identify and explain many of the important characteristics of a good writing style.

358 Use Strong, Colorful Words

A writer's style is greatly improved if he or she chooses the best words to use in any type of writing. The best words are the ones that effectively add to the meaning, feeling, and sound of the writing. Pay special attention to the nouns, verbs, and modifiers (adjectives and adverbs) that you use. These are the important words which add so much to your writing. The guidelines given below will help you use the best nouns, verbs, and modifiers.

359 **Choose specific words.** Some words are **general** *(car, house, animal)* and give the reader only a fuzzy picture. Other words are **specific** *(Corvette, igloo, llama)* and give the reader a much clearer, more detailed picture. When you want to share a specific idea or word picture with your reader, use a specific noun. In the chart which follows, the words on the top blanks are very general nouns. The words written in each of the second blanks are nouns which are more specific. Finally, each of the words in the bottom blanks is a very specific noun. These are the

74

kind of specific nouns which can make your writing clear and colorful.

360
Choosing Specific Words

person	place	thing	idea
woman	city	fluid	pain
actress	California city	nutritious fluid	mental pain
Jane Fonda	Los Angeles	milk	heartache

361   **Choose vivid verbs.** Use vivid, action-packed verbs to make your writing lively and interesting. For example, the vivid verbs *stared, glared, glanced, peeked,* and *inspected* all say more than an overused, ordinary verb like *looked.* The statement "Mr. Brown *glared* at the two tardy boys" is much more interesting than "Mr. Brown *looked* at the two tardy boys."

Helpful Hint: Avoid using the "to be" verbs *(is, are, was, were)* too often. Many times a better verb can be made from another word in the same sentence.

> A "to be" verb: Jack *is* a quick runner.
> A stronger verb.   Jack *runs* quickly.

362   **Choose words that "feel" right.** The words you include in your writing must not only be specific and colorful, but they must also have the right feeling or **connotation.** This means each word you choose must express both the exact meaning and the right feeling you are trying to get across in your writing. Let's say that you are writing about a friend who tried very hard to complete a 26-mile race, but couldn't quite make it. It wouldn't be right to say he tried "unsuccessfully" to finish the race because that word makes it

sound like your friend is a failure, and that isn't true. A better word would be "bravely"—he tried "bravely" to finish the race.

363   You can use a thesaurus to help you find the best words for your writing. A thesaurus is, in a sense, the opposite of a dictionary: you use it when you already know the definition but need to find the right word. The thesaurus lists synonyms, words with the same meaning. You pick the word which best fits the meaning, feeling, and sound of your writing assignment.

364   **Choose colorful adjectives.**   Use vivid, colorful adjectives to describe the nouns in your writing.   Strong adjectives can help make the nouns you choose even more interesting and clear to the reader.   For example, when you describe Tom Sawyer as "the mischievous Tom Sawyer," you are making him a much more interesting character with the addition of the adjective *mischievous.*

Note: Avoid adjectives which are used so frequently that they carry little meaning.   Some of these adjectives are: *neat, big, pretty, small, cute, fun, bad, nice, good, dumb, great,* and *funny.*

365   **Choose adverbs carefully.**   Use adverbs when you think they can help describe the action (the verb) in a sentence.   For example, the statement "Rover ran *wildly* after the rabbit" is more action-packed than "Rover ran after the rabbit."

Helpful Hint: Don't use a verb and an adverb when a single, vivid verb would be better.

> **Verb and adverb:**   Joan sat quickly on the sofa.
> **A single vivid verb:**   Joan plopped on the sofa.

366   **Use figurative language.**   You can also use figurative language from time to time to make your writing interesting, clear, and creative.   Three common types of figurative language are the *simile, metaphor,* and *personification*—each compares two different things.

367   ● A **simile** compares two different things using *like* or *as.*

> The car handled like a tank.
> The tank-like car handled poorly.

368   ● A **metaphor** compares two different things without using a word of comparison such as *like* or *as.*

> The car was a tank when it came to handling.
> The tank of a car handled poorly.

369   ● **Personification** is a form of figurative language in which an idea, object, or animal is given the characteristics of a person.

> The car fought you at every turn and corner.
> The car turned the corner reluctantly.

Helpful Hint: See "The Special Language of Poetry," 482, for an additional example of a simile, metaphor, and personification, as well as other types of figurative language.

A Final Reminder: Don't overdo it.   If your writing is already clear, natural, and interesting, remember to leave it alone.   Add vivid, colorful words only when you feel they can improve your writing.   If you add too many "vivid" words, your writing may sound "flowery" or artificial.

370 Use Strong, Clear Sentences

In addition to using a good balance of colorful and ordinary words, you can also improve your style by improving the smoothness and clearness of your sentences. Each of the sentences in your writing assignments should express or state a complete idea, and each should fit in with the rest of the writing. The guidelines which follow will help you use clear, correct sentences in your writing.

371 Use Complete Sentences

Use only complete sentences in your writing. A complete sentence contains a subject and verb and expresses a complete thought. Sentence fragments, comma splices, and run-on sentences are errors which should be avoided. Also, avoid using rambling sentences.

372 **A sentence fragment** may look and sound like a sentence, but it isn't. Instead, it is a group of words which is missing either a subject or a verb, or which doesn't express a complete thought.

> Sentence fragment: Can be quite a clown. (The subject is missing.)
> Complete sentence: My little brother can be quite a clown. (A subject has been added.)
>
> Sentence fragment: The rain on our garden. (The verb is missing.)
> Complete sentence: The rain poured on our garden. (A verb has been added.)
>
> Sentence fragment: That won the tournament. (The thought is incomplete.)
> Complete sentence: The team that won the tournament is our fiercest rival. (The sentence is now a complete thought.)

373 **A comma splice** is an error made when you connect two simple sentences with a comma instead of a period, question mark, or exclamation point.

> Comma splice: I never really enjoyed science, math is my favorite class. (A comma is used incorrectly.)
> Corrected sentences: I never really enjoyed science. Math is my favorite class. (A period has been added.)

374 **A run-on sentence** occurs when two simple sentences are joined without punctuation or a connecting word.

> Run-on sentence: Some run-on sentences are easy to recognize others are much more difficult. (Punctuation is needed.)

Corrected sentences: Some run-on sentences are easy to recognize.   Others are much more difficult. (Punctuation has been added.)

Corrected sentence: Some run-on sentences are easy to recognize, but others are much more difficult. (A connecting word has been added.)

375 A **rambling sentence** can appear in your writing when you connect several simple ideas with the word *and.*

Rambling sentence: I went to the dentist yesterday and when I got there, I had to wait forever to see him and when he finally examined my teeth, he found four cavities and now I have to go back next week to get fillings and I don't want to go.   (Too many *and*'s are used.)

Corrected sentences: I went to the dentist yesterday. When I got there, I had to wait forever to see him. When he finally examined my teeth, he found four cavities. Now I have to go back next week to get fillings, and I don't want to go. (The unnecessary *and*'s are omitted.)

376 ## Make Your Sentences Meaningful and Interesting

Use meaningful sentences in your writing. Meaningful sentences include more than the simple subject and the simple verb or predicate. They also include interesting and colorful modifiers—adjectives and adverbs—and descriptive phrases (groups of related words).

377 Add **adjectives** and **adverbs** to make your sentences more meaningful and interesting.

Sentence with no modifiers: The dog barked.

Revised sentence: The *huge, wooly* dog barked *fiercely.* (Adjectives—*huge* and *wooly*—and the adverb—*fiercely*—have been added.)

78

Phrases are groups of related words which make the main idea in a sentence clearer and more interesting. You should try to use three types of phrases in your writing: **prepositional phrases, participial phrases,** and **appositive phrases**.

378 Use **prepositional phrases** to add information to your sentences. (See "Prepositions," 74, in your handbook for a list of common prepositions.)

> The huge, wooly dog barked fiercely *at the mailman.*

379 **Participial phrases** can add both action and color to your sentences. (A participle is a "verb form" which ends in *ed* or *ing*.) A participial phrase describes a noun by telling what that person, place, or thing has done or is doing.

> *Rushing to the front door,* the huge dog barked fiercely at the mailman.

Note: A participial phrase is usually added to the beginning or the end of the sentence. Wherever you put it, make sure it is next to (or near) the word it modifies. Participial phrases are usually set off from the rest of a sentence with a comma or commas.

380 **Appositive phrases** can be used to help identify nouns more clearly. (An appositive phrase identifies or renames the noun that came before it.)

> The huge dog, a mixture of a collie and an Irish setter, barked fiercely at the mailman.

Note: An appositive phrase comes after the noun it modifies, and it is usually separated from the rest of the sentence with a comma or commas.

381 Use Sentences Which Read Smoothly

Use smooth-reading sentences in your writing, sentences which flow easily and sound natural. Young writers often use too many short sentences which make their writing sound choppy and unnatural. In real life, people use sentences of all lengths, not just short ones. The different ways to combine short, choppy sentences are given in the following section.

382 Ideas from shorter sentences can be combined into one sentence using *a series* of words or phrases.

> **Shorter sentences:**
> The cat is soft.   The cat is cuddly.   The cat is warm.
> **Combined sentence:**
> The cat is soft, cuddly, and warm. (A series of three words was used to combine the three sentences into one.)

383 *Helpful Hint:* All of the words or phrases you use in a series should be parallel—stated in the same way. (All should be nouns or *ing* words or the same in some other way.) Otherwise, your sen-

tences will sound awkward and unbalanced.

> Awkward series: The dog was friendly, reliable, and he showed exceptional intelligence.
> Corrected sentence: The dog was friendly, reliable, and intelligent. (The three items in the series are now parallel. That is, all of the items are single-word adjectives.)

384 Ideas from shorter sentences can be combined using **compound subjects** and **compound verbs** (predicates). A compound subject includes two or more subjects in one sentence. A compound verb includes two or more verbs in one sentence.

> Two shorter sentences: John ran into the glass door. Sarah ran into the glass door.
> Combined sentence with compound subject: John and Sarah ran into the glass door.
>
> Two shorter sentences: Mr. Fingers fumbled with the stack of papers. He dropped them down the stairs.
> Combined sentence with compound verb: Mr. Fingers fumbled with the stack of papers and dropped them down the stairs.

385 Ideas from shorter sentences can be combined into a **compound sentence.** A compound sentence is made up of two simple sentences which are *equal* in importance. The coordinating conjunctions *and, but, or, nor, for, yet,* and *so* are used to connect the two simple sentences. Place a comma before the conjunction in a compound sentence.

> Two simple sentences: A small brook trout looks like a minnow. It fights like a whale.
> One compound sentence: A small brook trout looks like a minnow, but it fights like a whale.

386 Ideas from shorter sentences can be combined into a **complex sentence.** A complex sentence is a type of sentence made up of two ideas which are *not equal* in importance. By combining two simple sentences into one complex sentence, you can make your ideas clearer and send a stronger message to the reader.

The more important of the two ideas should be included in an independent clause, a clause which could stand alone as a simple sentence. The other idea in a complex sentence cannot stand alone and is called a dependent or subordinate clause.

387 The two clauses in a complex sentence can be connected with **subordinate conjunctions.** *After, although, as, because, before, if, since, when, where, while, until,* and *unless* are common subordinate conjunctions. The two clauses can also be connected with the relative pronouns *who, whose, which,* and *that.*

Two shorter sentences: Janet returned to the team. We have won every game.

One complex sentence: *Since* Janet returned to the team, we have won every game. (The complex sentence was formed by using the subordinate conjunction *since* in the dependent clause.)

Two shorter sentences: Our coach works us very hard at practice. He is new this year.

One complex sentence: Our coach, *who* is new this year, works us very hard at practice. (The complex sentence was formed using the relative pronoun *who* in the dependent clause.)

Note: In most complex sentences, you should separate the dependent clause from the independent clause with a comma. (See the punctuation rules in your handbook for more information.)

388 Use Sentences Which Are Clear and Concise

Use sentences which are correct, clear, and to the point (concise). Any sentences which are incorrect, confusing, or wordy will make your writing assignments difficult to read. Use the following guidelines to check your sentences.

| John *likes* pizza. | His friends *like* pizza, too. |

389 **Agreement of subject and verb:** Make sure the subject and verb agree in *number* in your sentences. That is, if you use a singular subject, make sure you use a singular verb. (John likes pizza.) If you use a plural subject, make sure you use a plural verb. (His friends like pizza, too.) Be especially careful that you don't make agreement mistakes in the following types of sentences.

390 Sentences with compound subjects connected by *and* need a plural verb.

> *Mike and Marty spend* most of their spare time at the pizza parlor.

391   In sentences with compound subjects connected by *or* or *nor,* the verb must agree with the subject which is nearer the verb.

> Neither Mike nor *Marty likes* anchovies on his pizza.
> (Use a singular verb because the subject nearer the verb—*Marty*—is singular.)

> Neither Sarah nor her *sisters like* olives on their pizza.
> (Use a plural verb because the subject nearer the verb—*sisters*—is plural.)

392   In sentences with a singular indefinite pronoun as the subject, use a singular verb. (Use a singular verb with these indefinite pronouns: *each, either, neither, one, everyone, everybody, everything, someone, somebody, anybody, anything, nobody,* and *another.*)

> *Everyone* in John's family *likes* pizza.

393   Some indefinite pronouns (*all, any, half, most, none, some*) can be either singular or plural.

> *Some* of the pizzas *were* missing.
> (Use a plural verb when the noun in the prepositional phrase which follows the indefinite pronoun is plural. In the example sentence, the noun *pizzas* is plural.)

> *Some* of the pizza *was* missing.

> (Use a singular verb if the noun in the prepositional phrase is singular.)

394   When the subject is separated from the verb by words or phrases, you must check carefully to see that the subject agrees with the verb.

> John as well as his two friends works at the pizza parlor.
> (*John,* not *friends,* is the subject, so the singular verb *works* is used to agree with the subject.)

395   When the subject comes after the verb in a sentence, you must check carefully to see that the "true" subject agrees with the verb.

> There in the distance were the remains of the ghost town.
> (The plural subject *remains* agrees with the plural verb *were.*)

> Around the corner is my dad's store.
> (The singular subject *store* agrees with the singular verb *is.*)

> Has your sister read this book?
> (The singular subject *sister* agrees with the auxiliary or helping verb *has.*)

396   When a collective noun is the subject of a sentence, it can be either singular or plural. (A collective noun names a group or unit: *faculty, committee, team, congress, species, crowd, army, pair.*)

The crew of the sailboat is the best in the world.

(The collective noun *crew* is singular because it refers to the crew as one group. As a result, the verb *is* must also be singular.)

The faculty are required to turn in their room keys before leaving for the summer.

(The collective noun *faculty* is plural because it refers to the faculty as individuals within a group. As a result, the auxiliary verb *are* must also be plural.)

Note: Mumps, measles, news, mathematics, and *economics* require singular verbs.

397 *Helpful Hint:* Use the following chart of common verbs and contractions to help you remember their singular and plural forms.

singular		plural	
is	isn't	are	aren't
was	wasn't	were	weren't
has	hasn't	have	haven't
does	doesn't	do	don't

398 **Misplaced modifiers:** Make sure that your modifiers, especially the descriptive phrases you use, are located as close as possible to the words they modify. Otherwise, the sentence can become very confusing.

399 ● Do not put participial phrases in the wrong place.

Misplaced phrase: After seeing the movie, the space creatures seemed more believable than ever to all of us.

Corrected sentence: After seeing the movie, all of us felt space creatures were more believable than ever.

400 ● Do not put your prepositional phrases in the wrong place.

> **Misplaced phrase:** John walked into a room full of teachers who were talking about grading by mistake.
> **Corrected sentence:** By mistake, John walked into a room full of teachers who were talking about grading. (The prepositional phrase *by mistake* is moved to correctly modify the verb *walked.*)

401 **Wordy sentences:** Make sure your sentences contain no unnecessary words.

> Wordy sentence: The mountain climber was unable to descend *down* the mountain *by himself* and needed the help of another climber *to assist him.*
> Corrected sentence: The mountain climber was unable to descend the mountain and needed the help of another climber. (The words in italics add nothing new to the sentence, so they are omitted.)

402 **Problems with pronouns:** Sentences with unclear pronouns can be very confusing. Avoid sentences in which a pronoun does not agree with its *antecedent* (the word which the pronoun refers to).

> Agreement problem: Everyone going on the trip must bring their lunch.
> Corrected sentence: Everyone going on the trip must bring his lunch. (A pronoun must agree in number—singular or plural—with its antecedent. *Everyone* is singular so *his* not *their* is the correct pronoun to use to refer to *everyone.*)

403 ● Avoid sentences with a confusing pronoun reference.

> Confusing pronoun reference: As he pulled his car up to the service window, it made a strange rattling sound.
> Corrected sentence: His car made a strange rattling sound as he pulled up to the service window. (It is unclear in the sample sentence which noun the pronoun *it* refers to—the window or the car. To clarify this, the sentence has been reworded.)

404 ● Avoid sentences which include a pronoun shift.

> Pronoun shift: If *students* do not understand the assignment, *you* should ask for help.
> Corrected sentence: If *students* do not understand the assignment, *they* should ask for help. (Since *students* is a third-person subject, the pronoun which refers to it should also be in the third-person. That is why *you*—a second-person pronoun—has been changed to the third-person pronoun *they*.) See "Pronoun," 15, for an explanation of second- and third-person pronouns.)

405 ● Avoid sentences which include a double negative.

> **Double negative:**   Never give no one the wrong time as a joke.
> **Corrected sentence:**   Never give anyone the wrong time as a joke.   (*No* was changed to *any* because the word *never* is a negative word.   Do not include two negative words in the same sentence unless you are sure you understand how these words change the meaning of the sentence.)

Note: Do not use *hardly, barely,* or *scarcely* with a negative; the result is a double negative.

The centipede could *not hardly* keep his toenails clean.

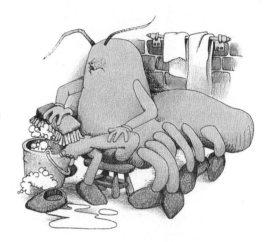

406 ● Avoid sentences which use *of* for *have.*

> **Incorrect usage:**   It would *of* worked out better if we could all have gone.
> **Corrected sentence:**   It would *have* worked out better if we could all have gone.   (*Of* was changed to *have* because an auxiliary verb and not a preposition was needed in the sentence.   *Of* is a preposition, and *have* is a verb.)

Very Important Note: If some of the sentences in a writing assignment don't sound right and you can't decide how to correct them yourself, make sure to ask your teacher for help.

407 # Write Clear, Natural Paragraphs

The paragraph is a unit of writing in which a writer develops an important or interesting idea.   Each paragraph must contain enough information—facts and details—so that your reader can understand and appreciate the main idea which is being developed.   Each sentence in a paragraph must be about the main idea.   Each paragraph must also read smoothly and naturally from start to finish.   Use the guidelines which follow to help you write paragraphs which read smoothly and naturally.

408 Use Linking Words

409 **Use transitions:** Make sure that the sentences in your paragraph move smoothly from one point to the next. Transitional words are especially helpful when you move from one point to the next in a paragraph. Note the use of transitions in the following section of a story. They make this part of the story easy to read.

> Yesterday was the worst day of my life. First, I overslept and missed my bus. As soon as my mom dropped me off at school, I realized that I had left my math assignment at home. Then, on the way to my locker, I saw Jill waiting for me, and I knew that I had forgotten something else—the $2.00 I had borrowed from her last week. After I apologized to her, I ran to my first-hour class....

Note: See "Useful Transitions and Linking Expressions," 442, for a list of transitions.

410 **Use repetition:** Another way to keep a paragraph smooth reading is to repeat a key word or a synonym for it. Note the repetition of the word *cold* (and synonyms) in the first part of a paragraph about January in Wisconsin.

> January in Wisconsin can be bitter *cold*. The temperature often drops to 20 or 30 degrees below zero. It is so *cold* at times that you can't go outside. On these *arctic-like* days, people are warned against traveling except for an emergency.

411 Use a Variety of Sentences

Make sure that you use a variety of sentences in your paragraph. Too many of the same type of sentence—especially short, choppy sentences—will make your paragraph difficult to read.

412 **Vary your sentence beginnings:** One way to add variety to your sentences is to vary (change) the way your sentences begin. That is, don't begin all of your sentences with the subject. Sentences which all begin with a personal pronoun as the subject as in *I did this... Then I did that... Also I did...* can be especially boring.

Look for modifiers—adverbs, prepositional phrases, participial phrases—and subordinate clauses which you can move to the beginning of some of your sentences for variety.

413 **Usual word order:** I silently studied the painting.
Beginning with a modifier: Silently, I studied the painting. (The adverb *silently* is moved to the beginning of the sentence.)

414 **Usual word order:** My mom and dad jog daily in the city park.

Beginning with a prepositional phrase: In the city park, my mom and dad jog daily. (A prepositional phrase is moved to the beginning of the sentence.)

415   Usual word order: Tammy, riding her bicycle, accidentally ran into her brother.
Beginning with a participial phrase: Riding her bicycle, Tammy accidentally ran into her brother. (A participial phrase is moved to the beginning of the sentence.)

416   Usual word order: I forgot to put the milk away when I ran outside to meet my friend.
Beginning with a subordinate clause: When I ran outside to meet my friend, I forgot to put the milk away. (A subordinate clause is moved to the beginning of this complex sentence.)

417   **Use different types of sentences:** Another way to add variety is to use different types of sentences. Use a mixture of simple, compound, and complex sentences in your writing.

418   ## Avoid Wordy Paragraphs

Make sure that your paragraphs do not sound too wordy. Trim any unnecessary words or phrases in the sentences so that a paragraph is clear and to the point. Note the changes made in the following sentences. All unnecessary words and phrases have been trimmed.

419   Wordy sentence: He had a way of keeping my attention by the way he raised and lowered his voice for every single word when he spoke.
Corrected sentence: He kept my attention by raising and lowering his voice when he spoke. (All of the unnecessary or repetitious words have been omitted.)

420   Wordy sentence: Some people they don't use their voices as well as they could.
Corrected sentence: Some people don't use their voices well. (The double subject *Some people they* has been changed to *Some people*.)

The Paragraph

421   Each personal story you tell your friends has a beginning, a middle, and an end. You naturally include these three parts in each of your stories because you want your friends to share in the entire experience. The beginning identifies the subject of your story and gets your friends interested in it. The middle part of your story tells your friends what actually happened. It gives the specific details of your story or experience. Your story ends with an idea that brings everything together and finishes the thought or point you were trying to make.

A paragraph is a group of related sentences that makes a specific subject or idea clear to the reader. The specific subject of a paragraph can be a story or narration, a description, an explanation, or an opinion. (See "Types of Paragraphs," 430, for examples.) Each paragraph is made up of a beginning, a middle, and an end, and these three parts are as important to a good paragraph as they are to any of the interesting stories you tell your friends. The beginning of a paragraph is called the topic sentence. The middle of a paragraph is called the body, and the end is called the concluding or clincher sentence.

The Basic Parts of a Paragraph

422   **Beginning:** The **topic sentence** tells the reader what the paragraph is going to be about. Note below a sample topic sentence and a simple formula for all good topic sentences:

> Mr. Brown must have been a drill sergeant before he became our gym teacher.
> *Formula:* A specific subject (*Mr. Brown, our gym teacher*) + a specific feeling or attitude (*must have been a drill sergeant before*) = a good topic sentence.

Note: A sentence like "Mr. Brown is a teacher" would not make a good topic sentence for a paragraph because it does not follow the formula. This sentence does not tell us what is special or different about Mr. Brown, so it does not have a specific subject. Also, there is no feeling or attitude given in the sentence.

423 **Middle:** The **body** is the largest part of the paragraph. All of the sentences in the body make the specific topic of the paragraph come alive for the reader. That is, all of the sentences in the body add details that make the topic clear. These sentences must be well written and organized in the best possible order. (See "Model Paragraph," 429, for an example of a well-written body of a paragraph.)

424 **End:** The **concluding** or **clincher sentence** comes after all the details have been included in the body of the paragraph. The clincher sentence reminds the reader of the topic of the paragraph. For example, let's say the topic sentence of a paragraph is "Mr. Brown must have been a drill sergeant before he became our gym teacher." A clincher sentence for this paragraph could be "I'm surprised that Mr. Brown doesn't make us march into the shower room after each class." This clincher sentence reminds the reader that the specific subject of the paragraph is Mr. Brown, the gym teacher, and that he is like a drill sergeant (the specific feeling or attitude).

A Closer Look

425 **Details:** A paragraph can be made up of three different types of details. Each type requires a different type of thinking.

1. The first type of detail comes from the writer's senses *(smell, touch, taste, hearing,* and *sight).* This type of detail is known as a **sensory detail.**

> Mr. Brown not only looks like a drill sergeant, he talks like one.

2. The second type of detail comes from the writer's memory. This type of detail is known as a **memory detail.**

> When we shot free throws during basketball, Mr. Brown gave us five seconds before he gave the ball to the other team.

3. The third type of detail comes as a writer wonders, wishes, or hopes about the topic of the paragraph. This type of detail is known as a **reflective detail.**

> I wonder how many pull-ups Mr. Brown can do?

426 **Well-written sentences:** A paragraph is made up of a series of well-written sentences.

1. The sentences in a good paragraph are smooth reading. Short, simple sentences (or ideas) are often joined to produce this smoothness. Special linking words are used to connect short sentences. These special linking words are often called transitions. (See "Useful Transitions and Linking Expressions," 442, and "Sentence Combining," 381, for a list of linking words and examples of connected sentences.) Note below the sets of simple sentences which are combined into one longer sentence that reads more smoothly. The linking words in each combined sentence are underlined.

> **Original sentences:** We shot free throws during basketball. Mr. Brown gave us five seconds. Then he gave the ball to the other team.
>
> **Combined:** <u>When</u> we shot free throws during basketball, Mr. Brown gave us five seconds <u>before</u> he gave the ball to the other team.
>
> **Original sentences:** Mr. Brown must have been a drill sergeant. He became our gym teacher.
>
> **Combined:** Mr. Brown must have been a drill sergeant <u>before</u> he became our gym teacher.

2. A good paragraph contains a variety of sentence types because a paragraph that contains mainly one type of sentence is boring to read. (See "Sentence Types," 98, for explanations and examples of the four types of sentences.) Note the different types of sentences used in the following example:

> At the start of each class, we have to stand at attention in straight lines while he takes attendance. (complex) Then we have to suffer through his warm-up exercises. (simple) His favorite is push-ups. (simple) We do them just as if we were in the army, and that means we have to keep our heads up, backs straight, and push up and down 25 times. (compound-complex) We also run in place until Mr. Brown can see that we are all "warmed up." (complex)

3. Sentences begin in different ways in a well-written paragraph. Sentences that all begin with the subject become monotonous and boring. Modifiers (individual words), phrases, and clauses are used to begin sentences in different ways. Note below the different ways to begin the same sentence:

> We stand at attention in straight lines. *(sentence with no beginning modifier)*
>
> Motionless, we stand at attention in straight lines. *(modifying word)*
>
> At the start of each class, we stand at attention in straight lines. *(phrases)*

> When each class starts, we stand at attention in straight lines. *(clause)*

Note: Also, avoid beginning too many sentences with the same word, especially *I, You, We, It, There,* or *The.*

427 **Sentence levels:** A well-written paragraph is made up of at least three levels of sentences. *Controlling sentences* are Level One sentences. They are the topic and clincher sentences which name the specific topic of the paragraph. *Clarifying sentences* are Level Two sentences. They add details to make the topic clearer to the reader. *Completing sentences* are Level Three sentences. Level Three sentences add details and examples that are more specific than Level Two sentences.

428 Note below that the three levels of sentences help organize the details about Mr. Brown. Each new level adds detail that is more specific, and each new level increases the reader's understanding and enjoyment of the topic of the paragraph. (The illustrations should help you understand the different levels of sentences.)

Level One   Level Two   Level Three

Level One — *Controlling Sentence:* Mr. Brown must have been a drill sergeant before he became our gym teacher.

Level Two — *Clarifying Sentences:* At the start of each class, we have to stand at attention in straight lines while he takes attendance. Then we have to suffer through his warm-up exercises.

Level Three — *Completing Sentences:* His favorite is push-ups. We do them just as if we were in the army, and that means we have to keep our heads up, backs straight, and push up and down 25 times. We also run in place until Mr. Brown can see that we are all "warmed up."

Note: A good paragraph will have at least two or three Level Two sentences. After most Level Two sentences, two or three Level Three sentences will follow.

429 Model Paragraph and Outline

Mr. Brown must have been a drill sergeant before he became our gym teacher. At the start of each class, we have to stand at attention in straight lines while he takes attendance. Then we have to suffer through his warm-up exercises. His favorite is push-ups. We do them just as if we were in the army, and that means we have to keep our heads up, backs straight, and push up and down 25 times. We also run in place until Mr. Brown can see that we are all "warmed up." All of the activities have to be done the right way, Mr. Brown's way. During physical fitness tests, he makes us climb ropes without using our legs. When we practice our dives during swimming, he gives us exactly seven seconds to complete each one. I'm surprised that Mr. Brown doesn't make us march into the shower room after each class.

Topic Sentence: Mr. Brown must have been a drill sergeant before he became our gym teacher.

I. At the start of each class, we have to stand at attention in straight lines while he takes attendance.
II. Then we have to suffer through his warm-up exercises.
    A. His favorite is push-ups.
        1. We do them just as if we were in the army.
        2. That means we have to keep our heads up, backs straight, and push up and down 25 times.
    B. We run in place until Mr. Brown can see that we are all "warmed up."
III. All of the activities have to be done the right way, Mr. Brown's way.
    A. During physical fitness tests, he makes us climb ropes without using our legs.
    B. When we practice our dives during swimming, he gives us exactly seven seconds to complete each one.

Clincher Sentence: I'm surprised that Mr. Brown doesn't make us march into the shower room after each class.

430 Types of Paragraphs

431 A **descriptive** paragraph gives a single, clear picture of a person, place, thing, or idea. (See "Guidelines for Describing a Person, ... Place, ... Object," 454.) The model paragraph above is an example of a descriptive paragraph.

432 A **narrative** paragraph gives the details of an event or experience. The details are given in the order that they happened. (See "Guidelines for Describing an Event," 458.) The "Model Narrative," 347, is an example of a narrative paragraph.

433 An **expository** paragraph gives facts or directions, explains ideas, or defines terms. (See "Guidelines for Writing a Definition," 457.)

> Complete one pull-up in Mr. Brown's gym class and you have really accomplished something. He makes us start by hanging from the bar with our arms straight. Our palms have to face forward on the bar. As we raise ourselves toward the bar, our bodies have to remain straight. Mr. Brown doesn't allow any kicking, wriggling, or squirming. He stands next to the bar and taps us on the stomach with a yardstick if we start to bend or wiggle. Our chins have to rest on the bar, if we are lucky enough to make it that far. We then have to lower ourselves until we are again hanging with our arms straight. This is one pull-up, unless Mr. Brown decides that something was done the wrong way.

434 A **persuasive** paragraph expresses an opinion and tries to convince the reader that the opinion is correct. (See "Guidelines for Persuasive Writing," 459.)

> Mr. Brown might not be a popular teacher, but he has three qualities that make him a good teacher. First, he is well organized for every class period. He always starts us off with exercises. Then we either learn or practice some skill or divide up into teams and play some sport. We always know ahead of time what we will be doing because Mr. Brown posts the day's activities on a blackboard in the locker room. Second, he is always concerned that we do our best, no matter what the activity. He expects us to work as hard in a game of dodgeball as we do during physical fitness tests. Mr. Brown's third and most important quality is that he treats everyone fairly. It doesn't matter if you're a jock or not. You know exactly where you stand with him. If you don't work up to your ability, he lets you know about it. If you work hard, he's satisfied. Some guys think Mr. Brown expects too much, but they all work hard for him.

435 Writing the Paragraph

436 **Prewriting:** *Selecting a Subject*

Selecting a specific subject for a paragraph should not be difficult. Your teacher will assign you the general subject for most of your paragraphs. You will have to pick a specific topic from the general subject. Pick a topic that interests you and will inter-

est your reader. *Remember:* It is important to have an interesting or exciting "story to tell." If you have trouble finding a specific topic, do a free writing or talk to friends and family members for help. (See "Guidelines for Free Writing," 350, and "Guidelines for Selecting a Topic," 351, for help.)

437 **Planning:** *Preparing to Write*

The planning stage is very important in writing a paragraph. First, you must write a topic sentence. Your topic sentence must identify the specific subject and state a feeling or attitude about the subject. Below is a sample topic sentence and a simple formula to follow when writing topic sentences:

> Uncle John is a real pest with his camera.
>
> A specific topic *(Uncle John)* + a specific feeling
> *(is a real pest with his camera)* = a good topic sentence.

After you have written a topic sentence, collect details to write about the topic. Again, you might want to do a free writing, talk to friends or family members, or do some reading on the topic to find details. Collect as many specific details as you can. Next, you should choose the best possible method of organization for your paragraph. Then, put the details into an outline according to the method of organization you have chosen.

438 **Writing:** *The First Draft*

As you write the first draft of your paragraph, start with the topic sentence, which is indented. Follow your topic sentence with the Level Two and Level Three sentences that you have organized in your outline. Write as naturally as you can. Don't be afraid to add or take out details as you go along. End your paragraph with a clincher sentence. This sentence will remind the reader of the topic and feeling stated in the topic sentence.

439 **Revising:** *Improving the Writing*

If you have planned your paragraph well, you won't need to do a lot of revising. As you do revise, make sure you have enough clear and creative details in your paragraph to make it understandable and entertaining. *Remember:* Level Three sentences contain the specific details and examples needed for good paragraphs. (See "Sentence levels," 427 , for examples of Level Three sentences.) Any details that don't help make the topic of your paragraph clear should be taken out. Make sure that the details are organized according to your plan or outline.

440   Also, make sure you have used complete sentences and that your sentences begin in different ways. (See "Sentence Beginnings," 412, for examples.) Add connecting words to any short, simple sentences that would read more smoothly if they were combined. Check the word choice of your paragraph. Strong, active words should be used. Find synonyms or replacements for any words that you have used too often. Also check the "Usage and Commonly Mixed Pairs," 217, for any usage questions. For example, if you're not sure if you should use "there, their, or they're" in a sentence, check the usage section in your handbook. Lastly, check the mechanics—spelling, punctuation, and capitalization—of your writing.

441 Summary: Writing the Paragraph

Prewriting: *Selecting a Subject*
- Select a specific topic that interests you and will interest your reader.

Planning: *Preparing the Subject*
- Write a specific topic sentence.
- Gather details.
- Select a method of organization.
- Write an outline or plan.

Writing: *Writing the First Draft*
- Start with the topic sentence.
- Follow with sentences that add interesting details.
- Write freely, and use your outline as a general guide.
- Write a clincher sentence.

Revising: *Improving the Writing*
- Make sure the topic is made clear with plenty of good details.
- Take out details that don't really add anything to the topic.
- Make sure all your sentences are complete thoughts.
- Make sure your sentences read smoothly.
- Check the word choice. Use strong, active words.
- Check the mechanics—spelling, punctuation, and capitalization—of your writing.
- Write or type a neat final copy. Indent the first line.

442 Useful Transitions and Linking Expressions

Transitions which can be used to **show location:**

above	behind	by	into	outside
across	below	down	near	over
against	beneath	in back of	off	throughout
along	beside	in front of	onto	to the right
among	between	inside	on top of	under
around	beyond			

Transitions which can be used to **show time:**

about	first	meanwhile	soon	then
after	second	today	later	next
at	third	tomorrow	afterward	as soon as
before	till	next week	immediately	when
during	until	yesterday	finally	

Transitions which can be used to **compare two things:**

in the same way	likewise	as
similarly	like	also

Transitions which can be used to **contrast things** (show differences):

but	even so	on the other hand	although	otherwise
however	yet	still	even though	

Transitions which can be used to **emphasize a point:**

again	for this reason	truly
to repeat	in fact	to emphasize

Transitions which can be used to **conclude or summarize:**

as a result	therefore	in short
finally	in summary	to sum up
in conclusion	lastly	all in all

Transitions which can be used to **add information:**

again	another	for instance	finally
also	and	moreover	as well
additionally	besides	next	along with
in addition	for example		

Transitions which can be used to **clarify:**

in other words	for instance	that is

The Composition

443   Once you are able to write good paragraphs, you are well on your way to being able to write good essays or longer compositions. The essay has the same basic characteristics as a paragraph: It has a single main idea or theme, it uses a variety of details to develop that idea, and all of the individual details are linked together into an effective, unified composition.

However, the essay is not the same as a paragraph. It is longer and it covers a larger portion of the subject than does a paragraph. Because an essay is longer than a paragraph, transitions and other methods of linking details are very important. They keep the composition unified. And since the essay is more complicated than the paragraph, it is usually a good idea to organize your thoughts into an outline. In other words, the essay must be planned and written carefully. Below are some guidelines which will be helpful when you are planning and writing your own essay.

444   ## Planning and Writing the Composition

1. Select a general subject area which interests you.

2. List all of your thoughts or ideas about the subject.

3. Use your list to help you focus on a specific topic within the subject area.

4. Decide what it is you would like to say about the topic and write a sentence which states this purpose. (This statement is sometimes called a *thesis statement.*)

5. Write a list of details which can be used to support your thesis statement.

6. Arrange this list of details into a well-ordered outline.

7. Do some reading, researching, or thinking if you need more detail for your outline.

8. Write the first draft of your paper, including an introductory and concluding paragraph.

9. Revise the first draft, paying special attention to the introductory and concluding paragraphs. The introductory paragraph should get your reader interested in your essay, and it should state the main idea of the essay. The concluding sentences should review the important points made in the essay.

10. Proofread your revised paper *twice:* once for spelling, punctuation, usage, and other mechanical errors and a second time for meaning and overall style. (Use your handbook when you have questions about errors.)

11. Neatly write (in ink) or type your final copy.

445   The Outline

An **outline** is an organized list of what you plan to write about. It is a *sketch* of what your final composition will look like. It is also a *guide* which keeps the writer on the right path when he or she is writing the first draft of an assignment. In the planning stages, your outline should be a changing, **working outline;** in its final form, your outline should be a "table of contents" of what is in your composition.

The details in an outline should be listed from general to specific. (The following details are listed from general to more specific: transportation, motor vehicle, car, Ford, Mustang.) If, for instance, you were assigned to write a paper about the subject of "Trees," you might choose to write about "Trees used in landscaping" (*topic*). In the planning of your paper, you might decide to divide your topic into "Trees used for landscaping in cold climates" and "Trees used for landscaping in warm climates" (*subtopics*). You might then further divide your subtopics into the different kinds of trees suitable in each climate (*supporting details*). To complete your outline, you could list examples of each kind of tree (*specific examples*). It is important to remember that each additional division in an outline must contain information which is more specific than the division before it. (See the sample outline below.)

446   Outlining Details—General to Specific

Subject: Trees

Topic

Many trees can be used for landscaping.

I. Subtopic

I. Some trees are best suited for cold climates.

  A. Supporting detail

  A. Evergreens are hardy and provide year-round color.

    1. Specific example
    2. Specific example

    1. Norway pine...
    2. Scotch pine...

  B. Supporting detail

  B. Maples hold up well and provide brilliant seasonal color.

    1. Specific example
    2. Specific example

    1. Red maple...
    2. Silver maple...

II. Subtopic

II. Some trees are better suited for warm climates.

447   A **topic outline** is a listing of the *topics* or ideas to be covered in your writing; it contains no specific details. Topics (ideas) are stated in words and phrases rather than complete sentences. This makes the topic outline useful for short compositions, especially those for which you have very little time as on an essay test. It is always a good idea to begin your outline by placing your *thesis statement* or controlling idea at the top of your paper. This will be a constant reminder of the specific topic you are going to be outlining and later writing about. Use the form shown below for starting the lines of your outline. Do not outline your introduction or conclusion unless your teacher tells you to do so.

Thesis statement: Africa will need all the help it can get to solve its hunger problem, yet it also can help itself.

| Outline Format | I.
  A.
  B.
    1.
    2.
      a.
      b.
        (1)
        (2)
          (a)
          (b)
II. | **Topic Outline**

Introduction
I. Natural resources in Africa
  A. Great areas of unused resources
  B. Capable of feeding Africa
  C. Planning will take time
II. India
  A. A similar hunger problem
  B. Planned for self-sufficiency
  C. Solved a serious problem
III. "Harare Declaration"
  A. A promise of self-sufficiency
  B. United African countries
  C. Already working in Somalia
Conclusion |

Note: No new subdivision should be started unless there are at least two points to be listed in that new division. This means that each *1* must have a *2;* each *a* must be followed by a *b.*

448   The **sentence outline** contains not only the major points to be covered in a paper, but it also lists many of the important supporting details as well. It is used for longer, more formal writing assignments; each point must, therefore, be written in a complete sentence. The sentence outline is useful when you find yourself asking others for help with your composition. It is much easier to understand an outline written in complete sentences than one written using single words and phrases. Given below is a sentence outline for the model essay.

Introduction
I. Africa is a land of many valuable resources.
  A. It contains great areas of unused land, water, and minerals.
  B. There are enough resources to feed all of Africa.
  C. Developing these resources will take time because many African countries are not very strong.
II. India should give the African countries hope.
  A. They experienced a similar hunger problem.
  B. The government planned for self-sufficiency and began producing enough food for its people.
  C. India is in much better shape than it was 25 years ago.
III. A group of agricultural officials produced the "Harare Declaration."
  A. This declaration promises self-sufficiency in Africa.
  B. This declaration also unified many African countries.
  C. Somalia is helping starving refugees from Ethiopia.
Conclusion

449 Writing: *Writing the First Draft*

Once your essay topic is well organized (outlined), you can begin writing your **introductory paragraph.** This opening paragraph must state the topic of the essay (*thesis statement*), gain the attention of the reader, and provide a smooth transition into the main part of the essay. There are several ways to develop the introductory paragraph:

- Use a series of questions about the topic.
- Use an interesting story about the subject.
- Use an unusual fact or figure.
- Use a reference to a famous person or place.
- Use a quotation from a well-known person or book.
- Use a definition of an important, topic-related term.

The **developmental paragraphs** make up the body (main part) of the essay. They must be developed and organized in a logical, yet interesting way. If, for instance, you are going to explain how to carve a figure from a bar of soap, you will most likely use a step-by-step explanation. Your paragraphs will naturally follow one another from the beginning of the explanation through the last step in the carving process. At the same time, you cannot let the explanation become so factual that the reader loses interest in it. Make sure that your paragraphs are vivid and colorful as well as accurate. (*Note:* The same methods of organization which are used for the single paragraph can also be used to arrange details in developmental paragraphs.)

A new paragraph is started whenever there is a shift or change to a new topic or subtopic from your outline. Each new paragraph should begin with a sentence which either serves as a transition or states a new or additional step in the essay. If a paragraph becomes too long, separate it into two paragraphs.

The **concluding** or summary paragraph should tie all of the important points in the essay together. It should leave the reader with a clear understanding of the meaning and the importance of the essay.

450 Revising: *Improving the Writing*

Proofread and revise your paper carefully. Check all of your paragraphs for effective links or transitions. Each paragraph should be linked or tied to the paragraph before and after it. You can use many of the same devices to link the paragraphs in an essay as you did to link the sentences in a paragraph. Write your final copy with black or blue ink. Use only one side of your paper; leave a margin of one inch on all sides. Place your name, subject, date, teacher's name, and other required information in the correct location. (See the checklist which follows the sample essay.)

Sample Student Essay

It is hard to ignore the hunger problem occurring in parts of Africa. Our television and newspapers have been bringing the hunger crisis to our attention for the past two or three years. Television has shown us relief camps packed with homeless and hungry Africans. Headlines in our newspapers warn us of what could happen in the drought-stricken areas of Africa: "Millions in Africa Face Starvation" or "Starving Countries Must Be Helped." The problem is so serious that Africa is going to need all the help it can get to save its hungry people. Yet Africa can also help itself.

Africa is a land of many valuable and unused resources—farmable land, water, and minerals. Because of these resources, this continent has the ability to feed all of its people. According to one study, if the farmlands were used properly, not only could all of Africa be fed, all of western Europe could be fed as well. Unfortunately, many of the countries in Africa are new, and a few of these countries are having problems forming strong, healthy governments. As a result, planning how to use the natural resources in the best possible way will take time in some parts of Africa.

However, none of the countries in Africa should lose hope. Twenty-five years ago, India, a large country in Asia, was experiencing a hunger crisis. Many people predicted that this country would be in worse shape than Africa is in today. Yet India now produces enough food for its entire country because its government spent so much time on farm and economic planning. India still has problems—many poorly nourished people and a high infant death rate—but overall India is in much better shape than it was 25 years ago.

Encouraged by the progress made in India, 30 African officials produced an official document in 1984 called the "Harare Declaration." This document states that the responsibility to feed the hungry people rests on the African government and the African people themselves. Its long-range goal is to make Africa a self-sufficient continent—a continent that produces all of its own food. A document like this can be a great help in uniting the Africans as they begin their work to solve their hunger problems. Already in Somalia, a country in eastern Africa, the government has accepted thousands of hungry refugees from Ethiopia. The government is presently thinking of ways to give the refugees land in Somalia so that they can produce their own food.

In order to meet the goals of the "Harare Declaration," Africa will need the help of the United States and other countries. The hunger problem is so serious that they can't presently fight it alone. They especially need the emergency supplies for those people suffering the most from hunger. Organizations from many countries have been sending tons of food and medical supplies to those areas in Africa where they are most needed. Also, some of these organizations have been helping with the long-term needs of Africa. They are training Africans in new farming techniques and teaching mothers how to help their undernourished and sick children. If the relief continues until the most serious problems of starvation are solved, the African people can work at becoming self-sufficient. They have the resources to do it.

Checklist for Revising and Proofreading

1. Set your writing aside for a day or two if possible before you begin revising it. Then read your paper out loud to see how it sounds. (Your writing should be clear and natural. If it isn't, simplify it—say exactly what you want to say as clearly as you can.)

2. Check your sentences. Is each sentence clear and colorful? Does each sentence express a complete thought (no fragments)? Is each punctuated as a complete sentence (no comma splices or run-ons)?

3. Have you used a combination of sentence lengths and types? Doing this will add variety and interest to your writing. (Look carefully at any sentence that is exceptionally long. Unless it is an especially strong sentence, consider breaking it into two or three single sentences.)

4. Check your sentence beginnings. Do not, for example, start sentence after sentence with the same word (*I . . .* , *There . . .* , *It . . .* , *The . . .*).

5. Make sure your writing is to the point. Take out any words, phrases, or ideas which are repeated or which *pad* rather than *add* to your explanation or description. (Don't overexplain the point you are trying to make.)

6. Replace any words or phrases that are too general or overused. Use nouns which are specific and adjectives and adverbs which are fresh and colorful. Use active verbs which are lively and vivid. (Avoid overusing the "to be" verbs: *is, are, was, were, as, been.*)

7. Replace any words or phrases which may confuse the reader. (Check for misplaced modifiers, double negatives, and agreement of subjects and verbs.)

8. Improve the style and clarity of your writing by using a simile, metaphor, or personification whenever you are describing something unusual to your reader. Also, define any terms which your reader may not understand.

9. Replace or take out any supporting facts and details which do not prove the point you are trying to make. Add supporting details (2nd- and 3rd-level details) wherever they are needed. (Ask *when, where, why, how, to what extent,* etc. about each of your ideas.) Use details from your personal experiences whenever possible.

10. Study each of your paragraphs. Does each paragraph have a clear purpose and focus (topic sentence)? Is each major idea developed and supported? Are the details arranged in a logical order? Have you used transitions within and between paragraphs so that your writing moves smoothly from start to finish?

11. Does your writing sound right for the audience who will be reading it? Does your writing accomplish what you set out to accomplish?

12. Follow all the rules and guidelines for spelling, capitalization, and usage. Use the correct paper, margins, and spacing. Always type or use ink for your final copy. Keep your paper neat and hand it in on time.

Writing Terms

Argumentation: Writing or speaking in which reasons or arguments are presented in a logical way.

Arrangement: The order in which details are placed or organized in a piece of writing.

Audience: Those people who read or hear what you have written.

Balance: The arranging of words or phrases so that two ideas are given equal emphasis in a sentence or paragraph; a pleasing rhythm created when a pattern is repeated in a sentence.

Body: The paragraphs between the introduction and conclusion which develop the main idea(s) of the writing.

Brainstorming: Collecting ideas by thinking freely and openly about all the possibilities; used most often with groups.

Central idea: The main point or purpose of a piece of writing, often stated in a thesis statement or topic sentence.

Clincher sentence: The sentence which summarizes the point being made in a paragraph, usually located last.

Coherence: The arrangement of ideas in such a way that the reader can easily follow from one point to the next.

Composition: A process in which a writer's ideas are combined into one, unified piece of writing.

Deductive reasoning: The act of reasoning from a general idea to a specific point or conclusion.

Description: Writing which paints a colorful picture of a person, place, thing, or idea using concrete, vivid details.

Details: The words used to describe a person, persuade an audience, explain a process, or in some way support the central idea; to be effective, details should be vivid, colorful, and appeal to the senses—seeing, hearing, etc.

Emphasis: Placing greater stress on the most important idea in a piece of writing by giving it special treatment; emphasis can be achieved by placing the important idea in a special position, by repeating a key word or phrase, or by simply writing more about this idea than the others.

Essay: A piece of factual writing in which ideas on a single topic are presented, explained, argued, or described in an interesting way.

Exposition: Writing which explains.

Extended definition: Writing which goes beyond a simple definition of a term in order to stress a point; it can cover several paragraphs and include personal definitions and experiences, similes and metaphors, and quotations.

Figurative language: Language which goes beyond the normal meaning of the words used; writing in which a figure of speech is used to heighten or color the meaning—simile, metaphor, etc.

Focus: Concentrating on a specific subject to give it emphasis or importance.

Form: The arrangement of the details into a pattern or style; the way in which the content of writing is organized.

Free writing: Writing openly and freely on any topic; *focused* free writing is writing openly on a specific topic.

Generalization: An idea or statement which emphasizes the general characteristics rather than the specific details of a subject.

Grammar: Grammar is the study of the structure and features of a language; it usually consists of rules and standards which are to be followed to produce acceptable writing and speaking.

Idiom: A phrase or expression which means something different from what the words actually say. An idiom is usually understandable to a particular group of people. (Example: *over his head* for *didn't understand.*)

Inductive reasoning: Reasoning which leads one to a conclusion or generalization after examining specific examples or facts; drawing generalizations from specific evidence.

Inverted sentence: A sentence in which the normal word order is inverted or switched; usually the verb comes before the subject.

Issue: A point or question to be decided.

Jargon: The technical language of a particular group (musicians, journalists) which is inappropriate in most formal writing.

Journal: A daily record of thoughts, impressions, and autobiographical information; a journal is often a source of ideas for writing.

Juxtaposition: Placing two ideas (words or pictures) side by side so that their closeness creates a new, often ironic, meaning.

Limiting the subject: Narrowing the subject to a specific topic which is suitable for the writing or speaking assignment.

Literal: The actual or dictionary meaning of a word; language which means exactly what it appears to mean.

Loaded words: Words which are slanted for or against the subject.

Logic: The science of correct reasoning; correctly using facts, examples, and reasons to support your point.

Modifier: A word, phrase, or clause which limits or describes another word or group of words. (See *adjective* and *adverb.*)

Narration: Writing which tells a story or recounts an event.

Objective: Relating information in an impersonal manner; without feelings or opinions.

Observation: Paying close attention to people, places, things, and events to collect details for later use.

Overview: A general idea of what is to be covered in a piece of writing.

Personal narrative: Personal writing which covers an event in the writer's life; it often contains personal comments and ideas as well as a description of the event.

Persuasion: Writing which is meant to change the way the reader thinks or acts.

Point of view: The position or angle from which a story is told.

Process: A method of doing something which involves several steps or stages; the writing process involves prewriting, planning, writing, and revising.

Prose: Prose is writing or speaking in the usual or ordinary form; prose becomes poetry when it takes on rhyme and rhythm.

Purpose: The specific reason a person has for writing; the goal of writing.

Revision: Changing a piece of writing to improve it in style or content.

Spontaneous: Doing, thinking, or writing without planning.

Subjective: Thinking or writing which includes personal feelings, attitudes, and opinions.

Theme: The central idea in a piece of writing (lengthy writings may have several themes); a term used to describe a short essay.

Thesis statement: A statement of the purpose, intent, or main idea of an essay.

Tone: The writer's attitude toward the subject; a writer's tone can be serious, sarcastic, tongue-in-cheek, solemn, objective, etc.

Topic: The specific subject of a piece of writing.

Topic sentence: The sentence which contains the main idea of a paragraph.

Transitions: Words or phrases which help tie ideas together.

Unity: A sense of oneness; writing in which each sentence helps to develop the main idea.

Universal: A topic or idea which applies to everyone.

Usage: The way in which people use language; language is generally considered to be standard (formal and informal) or nonstandard. You will use standard usage for most of your writing assignments.

Vivid details: Details which appeal to the senses and help the reader see, feel, smell, taste, and hear the subject.

Guidelines for Describing a Person

1. Whenever possible, write about someone you know well.

2. Begin gathering details about this person by observing him or her if possible. Notice in particular the details which make this person different from other people.

3. List the important physical characteristics, mannerisms, and personality traits, especially those which help to make your subject different from other people. Look for features like the way she smiles, laughs, or talks; the way she sits or moves her hands; and the way she dresses or wears her hair.

4. Next, notice the way other people seem to feel about your subject and the way your subject feels about other people.

5. Ask others about your subject. Often, they will be able to tell you things you would otherwise never have known.

6. Add details about what your subject has said or done in the past. Try to remember or find at least one specific incident which says something interesting about your subject.

7. Finally, interview the subject. Get his or her reactions to the details you have collected. Quote your subject directly whenever possible. (Read about your subject if he or she is well known and can't be interviewed.)

8. After you have collected as many details as you can, decide what overall impression your subject has made on you. Make this impression part of your topic sentence or *thesis statement* and list the points you plan to cover beneath it. This list can be used as a working outline for your description.

9. If you begin your description with your topic sentence, it must be well worded. It should create interest in your subject and help the reader to immediately "picture" the person you are describing. Instead of beginning with your topic sentence, you may choose to begin your description with a story or quotation.

10. Each of the sentences in your description must support the point you are trying to make about your subject. Your sentences should sound as natural as they would if you were simply talking to another person.

11. As you write, remember to use specific, vivid words. This is the only way you will be able to create a colorful, memorable picture of your subject. Use a simile or metaphor if you want to describe your subject by comparing him or her to someone else.

12. End your description in an interesting way. You might "come full circle" and end where you began. Or you might end with what you've learned, how you feel about the subject, or what makes your subject worth knowing.

455 Guidelines for Describing a Place

1. Whenever possible, write about a place you know well or one which left a big impression on you.

2. Begin gathering details by visiting the place you are going to describe. Jot down all the things which make your subject different from other places. (Remember that descriptive writing is only as good as the writer's observation of people, places, things, and events. The better the observing, the better the writing.)

3. List the important feelings, events, and people that contribute to making this place different. (Do not, however, try to describe every last detail about your place.)

4. Next, notice the way other people act in this place. This can tell you a great deal about their feelings about the place you are describing.

5. Ask others about your subject. Often you will be given information you would otherwise never know.

6. After you have collected as many details as you feel you will need, decide what overall impression your subject has made on you. Work this impression into a *topic sentence* or *thesis statement* and list the points you plan to describe beneath it. This list can be used as a working outline for your description.

7. If you begin your description with your topic sentence, it should be worded creatively enough to interest the reader. It should also help the reader to immediately "picture" the place you are describing. You may choose to begin your description with an incident, story, or historical background about your subject and place your topic sentence after it.

8. Each of the sentences in your description must add to the overall picture and help to build your description one piece at a time. Each sentence should sound as natural as it would if you were simply talking to another person about your subject.

9. As you write, remember to use specific, vivid words. This is the only way you will be able to convey a colorful, memorable picture to the reader. Use similes and metaphors if you need to compare your subject to something well known.

10. Avoid the use of **cliches** or **overused expressions:**

black as coal	black as pitch	covered like a blanket
cold as ice	blanket of snow	in all its glory
crack of dawn	blue as the sky	loomed on the horizon
dry as dust	mantle of snow	flat as a pancake
ocean's roar	green as grass	fresh as a daisy

456 Guidelines for Describing an Object

1. Select a topic you are familiar with or interested in knowing more about. (Look around your home, school, and neighborhood for objects which might make interesting subjects.)

2. Gather information by observing the object as closely as possible. Look for the details which make this object different from similar objects, objects in the same category or class.

3. Note the color, size, shape, and texture of the object. Look at each part and note its relationship to the other parts. Determine what the object is used for, what it can do, and how it works. Does it have a practical or everyday use? Or is it simply there to look at or listen to? Try to understand as much about the object as possible.

4. Observe how other people use or feel about this object.

5. Try to recall an interesting incident or story about this object.

6. After you have gathered plenty of details, decide what your main point is going to be and begin writing.

7. Remember, when you are describing something, you should *show* rather than *tell* what it is like. You can do this by using colorful details and interesting examples which make your object seem real to the reader. You can also compare your object to something your reader already knows about.

8. Avoid using **cliches** or worn-out expressions like *big as a house, flat as a pancake, old as the hills,* or *straight as an arrow.*

9. End your description with a final thought or feeling about this object, why this object is important, or a summary of what the reader should remember.

457 Guidelines for Writing a Definition

1. The first step in writing a **definition** is to place the term you are defining into the *class* or category of similar objects. Then add the special *characteristics* which make this object different from the rest of the objects in that class. See the example below.

   Term - *A computer . . .*
   Class - *is an electronic machine . . .*
   Characteristic - *which stores and arranges information.*

2. *Caution:* Do not use the term or a form of it in your definition. *Example:* "A computer is a machine that *computes.*"

3. Also avoid using either "is when" or "is where" in your definition. *Example:* "A computer *is where* you have a machine to do the thinking for people."

106

458   Guidelines for Describing an Event

1. Always write about an event you have actually been to or seen firsthand.

2. Observe closely (or recall) all the important details of the event you are describing. Notice things which happened even before the event began. These details can be especially useful in your introduction; they can help set the mood and prepare the reader to share the experience with you.

3. List the *who, what, when, where, why,* and *how* of the event—or at least as many of these six questions as you feel your reader needs to know to understand the event.

4. Now go back to the six questions and write freely about each. As you write, try to imagine yourself telling someone about this event—about what happened that made this event special.

5. After you have gathered all of your thoughts and recorded all of your details, decide what overall point or impression you would like to share with your readers.

6. Work this impression into a topic sentence and list the major points you plan to cover beneath it. This list can be the working outline for your description.

7. You can begin your description with your topic sentence, with a story or background about the event, or by setting the scene for the event. Begin with something interesting—something that will make the reader want to continue reading your description.

8. Each sentence in your description should somehow add to the "word picture" you are trying to draw. Most sentences will add details, some will explain details, and others will connect details. Try to make your description sound as if you were simply telling another person about the event. (See the list of "Useful Transitions and Linking Expressions" if you need help making your description fit together smoothly.)

9. Use specific, vivid details—details which will help your reader see, smell, taste, feel, and hear the event just as you did.

10. Avoid using **cliches** (overused expressions):

over a barrel	Mother Nature	slowly but surely
out of the blue	par for the course	few and far between
broad daylight	drop like flies	sell like hot cakes
cold sweat	eyes of the world	raining cats and dogs

11. End your description by emphasizing the importance of the event, how you feel about it, or if and when this event may take place again. This should leave your reader with a good feeling about having read your description.

1. Select a topic (issue) which is both current and controversial. This means the issue should be important to a group of people; also, the people in that group should have more than one opinion on the subject. This issue should also be one which you have strong, personal feelings about.

2. Begin collecting information by listing your personal feelings about the issue and the reasons you feel that way.

3. Ask other people how they feel about this issue. Listen closely, especially to those who have a different opinion. They will give you an idea of how your reader may feel about the topic. Ask them why they feel the way they do; test your opinion and reasons on them. You must understand how other people feel before you begin to write.

4. Next, gather any facts and figures which you now realize must be included in your writing to be convincing. Use the *Reader's Guide to Periodical Literature* in your library to help you find current magazine articles on the issue. Take careful notes on what you read and use these notes to build a strong case.

5. The writer of persuasion can use most of the same techniques of support and development used in expository writing.

6. Use a calm, reasoning tone throughout your writing; rely on logic, not emotion. Sometimes it's even a good idea to mention the reasonable arguments on the other side of the issue; then point out clearly why each argument is weak.

7. Use examples to illustrate your main points. Use very few statistics. Instead, make your point with strong word pictures. ("Every day we bury in our dumpsites enough garbage to completely cover the state of Rhode Island.") If you do use numbers, round them off. ("Each day we bury in our dumpsites nearly 50 million tons of garbage.")

8. Choose your words very carefully. Remember that words convey feelings (connotation) as well as meaning (denotation). Select words which your audience will react positively to. Avoid using "big" words just to impress your reader. If you must use a word your reader probably doesn't know, define it clearly.

9. Use your two strongest arguments first and last. People are much more likely to remember arguments placed in these positions than the others.

* Write freely and naturally. Do not try to "create" a writing style.

* Write with vivid action verbs and specific nouns. Don't overuse adjectives or adverbs.

* Use sentences of all shapes and sizes, and avoid beginning too many sentences in the same way.

* Include sensory details — details which describe how your subject looks, tastes, feels, sounds, and smells.

* Use familiar language. Don't look for a big or fancy word when a small one will do.

* Use an occasional figure of speech for color and emphasis.

* Look for a new twist or angle each time you write.

* Listen to the sound and rhythm of your writing. Use words which bounce and glide rather than plod along.

* Don't sacrifice clarity for style.

* Share what you've written with others.

The Classroom Report

460 Learning and Sharing

"What makes the clouds?"

"Why is grass green?"

If you have any little brothers or sisters, you know that they ask a lot of questions like the two given above. At times, you probably get tired of the many questions they ask. You must remember, though, that little children are just like the rest of us. They want to learn about things. Asking questions is simply the way they learn.

Once you get to junior high or middle school age, you still ask questions because you still want to learn. However, you don't ask as many questions as very young children do because you can read and learn a great deal on your own. The books, magazines, and newspapers you read contain interesting details, useful facts, and up-to-date information.

Just as we all like to learn, we also like to share what we have learned with others. Sharing the facts and details you have learned can be just as enjoyable as sharing a good story with your friends.

461 Writing the Classroom Report

When a teacher asks you to write a report, he or she is asking you to do two things. First, your teacher is asking you to learn facts and details about a specific report subject. You will find these facts and details in the same way that you have learned nearly everything: You will ask questions, and you will read. Second, your teacher is asking you to share this information in a clear, organized written report. Remember, sharing what you have learned is something you have enjoyed doing for a long time.

462 Prewriting: *Selecting a Subject*

Your teacher will identify the *general* subject for your report. It will be up to you to find a *specific* report subject that interests you. You should find it enjoyable to learn about a specific subject you are interested in.

Let's say you are assigned a report in your science class. The general subject is wildlife. Your teacher states that you must choose a specific wildlife mammal, bird, or fish which interests you as the specific subject or topic of your report. Check with your school library for books on wildlife. By paging through these books, you should be able to find a specific animal for your report. Keep in mind that when you select a topic, there must be enough information available to write a good report.

463 Planning: *Preparing to Write*

Suppose you pick a certain bird of prey—the peregrine falcon—for the topic of your report. The next step is to find a good number of interesting facts and details about the topic. Your library will have plenty of books on wildlife, books which will give you good background information on your topic.

You should, however, also look for other types of information. There are many organizations which offer free printed material with very valuable, up-to-date information. You simply have to write a letter to any of these organizations and ask for the material. For example, the National Wildlife Federation offers free wildlife notes on many animals, including the peregrine falcon.

464   Also, explore your own community or nearby communities for information for your report. A city museum or a city zoo would be a good source of information for a wildlife report since museums and zoos usually employ wildlife experts and often feature special wildlife displays. *Remember:* The books in your school library are not the only source of facts and details for your report.

465 Recording Your Information

Once you have found the books and materials for your report, the next step is to read through all of them and take notes on important facts and details. (See "Note-taking Skills," 722, for guidelines on good note-taking.)

To help you organize your reading and note-taking, it might be helpful to write some basic questions about the subject of your report which you would like to answer in your report. Put each of these questions at the top of a separate note card. Any time you find a fact that helps answer one of your questions, write this information on the note card with that question.

Example: In a report on the peregrine falcon, the following basic questions would be helpful in organizing the reading and note-taking:

1. What does the peregrine falcon look like?
2. Where does the peregrine falcon live and mate?
3. What does the peregrine falcon eat and how does it get its food?
4. What are its natural enemies?
5. How does it get along with man?
6. How many peregrine falcons are there?
7. What makes this bird interesting or different?

466

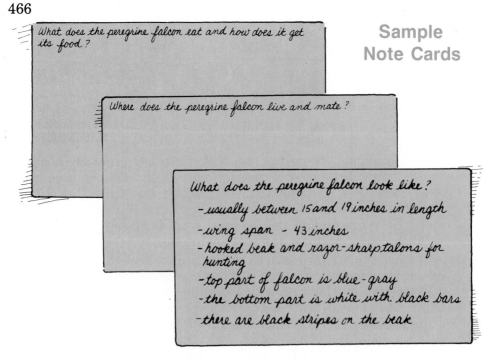

Sample
Note Cards

What does the peregrine falcon eat and how does it get its food?

Where does the peregrine falcon live and mate?

What does the peregrine falcon look like?
- usually between 15 and 19 inches in length
- wing span - 43 inches
- hooked beak and razor-sharp talons for hunting
- top part of falcon is blue-gray
- the bottom part is white with black bars
- there are black stripes on the beak

467 Organizing Your Information

Once you have finished your reading and note-taking, the next step is to begin arranging or organizing all the information you have found. Choose the information on one of your note cards to be the main point of your report. This information should be important and should come first as you organize your note cards.

If you had done research on the peregrine falcon, for example, you would have learned, among other things, that this bird is on the endangered species list. This means that the peregrine falcon is in danger of becoming extinct or dying out. This information could certainly be the main point for a report.

Next, you should arrange the rest of your note cards. Keep in mind the main point of your report and put the rest of your note cards in the best possible order.

468 Outlining Your Information

The final step in the planning stage of your report is to write an outline. An outline is a general plan of what the final report will look like. Begin your outline by listing on a clean sheet of paper the headings (questions) that are written on the top of your note cards. List them on this paper in the same order that you have already organized them. Leave enough space between each heading to list the important facts or details which are written on each note card. Think of this as the first draft of your outline. *Note:* You don't have to include all of the facts from your note cards. Only write those that are very important or interesting.

Then, rewrite the first draft of your outline into a clear sentence outline. The headings or questions are the main ideas of your outline and should follow Roman numerals (I., II., III., IV., etc.). The details under each heading or main idea should follow capital letters (A., B., C., etc.).

The beginning of a sentence outline for the model report on the peregrine falcon is given below. This section of the outline includes the first two main ideas and supporting detail for the report.

I. The use of pesticides is the main reason the peregrine falcon is an endangered species.

   A. The falcons are infected when they eat other birds already infected with pesticides like DDT.

   B. A peregrine's ability to reproduce may be upset by the pesticides.

   C. They can cause falcon eggs to have very thin and weak shells.

   D. The pesticides can kill full-grown falcons.

II. Man's movement into the peregrine's natural habitat or home has also caused it to be an endangered species.

   A. The use of wilderness land for farming and game preserves and parks has damaged the falcon's natural habitat.

   B. Sonic booms from modern aircraft may be hurting the peregrine population.

469   **Writing:**   *The First Draft*

If you have a complete and organized sentence outline, writing your report should be no problem. Each main idea will become the topic sentence for a paragraph in your report; the details under each main idea will become the sentences or supporting details for that paragraph.

However, before you write the main part of your report, you will need to write an introductory paragraph. This paragraph should say something interesting and catchy about the topic so that the reader will want to read your report. You might get the reader's interest with an unusual question, a surprising or fascinating fact, a direct quotation from an expert, or a definition which makes the reader think. The introductory paragraph should also state the main point of your report. (See the "Model Report" at the end of this unit for an example of an introductory paragraph.)

After you have written the main part or body of your report, you must add a concluding or summary paragraph. This paragraph should repeat the main point of your report so that the reader understands or remembers why you wrote it. In this paragraph you can also summarize other important points made in your report if you wish. Try to end your report with a good last sentence.

470   **Revising:**   *Improving the Writing*

Revising a report takes time since there are many things to think about. Use the following checklist as a guide to help you revise and improve your report:

_____   1.   Make sure your introductory paragraph gets the reader's attention and introduces the main idea of your report.

_____   2.   Make sure you have included enough detail in the main part of your report to make it interesting and educational.

114

_____ 3. Make sure your concluding paragraph repeats the main idea of your report and ends with a final, interesting sentence.

_____ 4. Make sure each paragraph begins with a clear topic sentence which contains an important point about your topic; also make sure that every sentence in each of your paragraphs relates to the topic sentence.

_____ 5. Make sure the paragraphs are arranged in the best possible order.

_____ 6. Make sure your sentences are clear, smooth, and easy to read. (See "Transitions," 442, for a list of words and phrases that can help tie your sentences together so that they form smooth-reading paragraphs.)

_____ 7. Make sure your report is written in your own words. (Use quotation marks when you use someone else's words.)

_____ 8. Make sure that your report is written in an interesting way and is enjoyable to read. Use strong verbs, colorful adjectives, and helpful similes, metaphors, and comparisons.

_____ 9. Make sure your writing is accurate. Check the spelling, usage, capitalization, and punctuation of your report. (Use your handbook if you have any doubts.)

_____ 10. Make sure to proofread your report carefully before you turn it in. You want the final copy of your report to be as error free and as neat as possible.

_____ 11. Make sure you have correctly given credit to an author's ideas or words if you are required to do so by your teacher. (Use "Giving Credit for Information Used in a Report" as a guide.)

_____ 12. Make sure you have correctly written the bibliography for your report if you are required to include one. (Use "Adding a Bibliography" as a guide.)

_____ 13. Make sure you have correctly written the title page and outline for your report if they are required as part of your assignment. (Use "Adding a Title Page and Outline" as a guide.)

_____ 14. Write your final copy in ink on unlined paper. Use only one side of the paper. Number your pages in the upper right-hand corner of each page starting with the second page. _Note:_ If you are typing your report, double-space the entire paper. Leave a 1 to 1½ inch margin on all sides of the paper.

If you are required to give credit to the authors whose ideas or words you have used in your report, follow the guidelines set by your teacher. Your teacher may ask you to identify the authors on each page of your report or in a list at the end of your report.

Traditionally, *footnotes* or *endnotes* have been used to identify the books and authors used in a report. Footnotes are listed at the bottom or *foot* of each page of a report; endnotes are listed at the *end* of a report on a separate page. More recently, it has become acceptable to list your sources of information right in the report. This can be done by placing the author's last name and the page number(s) on which you found the information in parentheses. Place this *note,* as it is called, at the end of the last sentence or idea taken from that author. The sample note below tells the reader that this information was originally written by the author Allen and was found on page 193. (For the author's full name and the title of the book, the reader can check the bibliography at the end of the report.)

> A peregrine's ability to reproduce may be upset by these pesticides. They can also cause falcon eggs to have very thin and weak shells (Allen 193).

If you use a book or material that doesn't have an author, use the title or a shortened form of the title in place of an author's last name. Also, page numbers are not required for one-page articles or articles in encyclopedias. The sample note given below tells the reader that the article about the peregrine falcon in Wildlife Notes was only one page long.

> Mated pairs of falcons may hunt as a team. One floats high in the air while the other falcon flies at a lower level. The falcon at the lower level scares up prey and the other falcon dives and attacks it (Wildlife Notes).

Important note: It is not necessary to list an author or book for every single bit of information you use in your report. If the information is common knowledge—already known by many people—you do not have to list an author even though you may have just read this information recently as you were preparing your report.

Very important note: You should, however, list an author and page number for the following kinds of information:

a. Information which is copied directly from another source. (You should not copy information directly unless the exact words of an expert, a poet, or some other person are very important to your report.)

b. Information which is written in your own words but contains important ideas, facts, or figures you didn't know before you read them.

472 Adding a Bibliography

If you are required to write a **bibliography,** make sure it follows the guidelines set by your teacher. A bibliography is a page at the end of a report which lists in alphabetical order the books and materials you have used in writing your report. *(Note:* If you use *notes* in your report, you must also use a bibliography.)

A bibliography listing for a book is usually written in the following way: *Author* (last name first). *Title. City where book is published: Publisher, Copyright date.* Double-space the information you include in your bibliography. The second line of each listing should be indented 1/2 inch (5 typed spaces).

(See the chart on the following page for bibliography listings for magazines, pamphlets, encyclopedias, etc. Also, see the model report on the peregrine falcon for a sample bibliography.)

473 Adding a Title Page and Outline

If you are required to write a **title page,** make sure you follow the guidelines set by your teacher. The title of your report, your name, your teacher's name, the name of the course, and the date are usually placed on the title page. This information should be centered on a separate sheet of paper. *Note:* Very often you will be told to simply place this information on the top of the first page of your report. (Check the first page of the "Model Report" for an example.)

If you are required to include an **outline** with the final copy of your report, make sure it includes enough detail to meet the requirements of the assignment. Also make sure to add, take out, or reorganize the points in your outline so that it follows the final report. *Note:* The outline which comes before the "Model Report" contains only the main ideas covered in the report.

Model Outline

Introductory Paragraph
I. The use of pesticides is the main reason the peregrine falcon is an endangered species.
II. Man's movement into the peregrine's natural habitat or home has also caused it to be an endangered species.
III. Man has not always treated the peregrine falcon so harmfully.
IV. The peregrine falcon is built for hunting.
V. The peregrine falcon feeds mainly on pigeons, songbirds, and ducks.
VI. This bird of prey usually lives and breeds on the sides of high cliffs.
VII. Today, not many peregrine falcons are found anywhere in the lower United States.
VIII. Steps are being taken to save this bird of prey.
Concluding Statement

Model Bibliographical Entries

One author	Allen, Thomas B. <u>Vanishing Wildlife of North America</u>. Washington, D.C.: National Geographic Society, 1974.
Two authors	Searles, Baird and Martin Last. <u>A Reader's Guide to Science Fiction</u>. New York: Facts on File, Inc., 1979.
More than three authors or editors	Brandes, Kathleen, et al., eds. <u>Vanishing Species</u>. New York: Time-Life Books, 1976. *Note:* For a book with more than three authors, simply drop *eds.* from the entry.
A single work from an anthology	Poe, Edgar Allen. "The Raven." <u>Selected Stories & Poems</u>. Ed. Joseph Wood Krutch. Danbury: Grolier Enterprises, 1978.
Encyclopedia article *(signed)*	Pettingill, Olin Sewall, Jr. "Falcon and Falconry." <u>World Book Encyclopedia</u>, 1980. *Note:* It is not necessary to give full publication information for encyclopedias. If the article is followed by the author's initials rather than his complete name, check in the index of authors (usually located in the front of each volume) for the author's full name.
Signed article in a weekly	Kanfer, Stefan. "Heard Any Good Books Lately?" <u>Time</u> 21 July 1986: 71.
Unsigned article in a weekly	"America on Drugs." <u>Newsweek</u> 28 July 1986: 48-50.
Signed article in a monthly	Heinrich, Bernd. "Why Is a Robin's Egg Blue?" <u>Audubon</u> July 1986: 64-71.
Signed newspaper article	Kalette, Denise. "California Town Counts Down to Big Quake." <u>USA Today</u> 21 July 1986, sec. A: 1.
Unsigned editorial or story	"A School Year Without a Strike." Editorial. <u>Chicago Tribune</u> 22 July 1986, sec. 1: 10. *Note:* For an unsigned story, simply omit *Editorial.*
Signed pamphlet	Laird, Jean E. <u>The Metrics Are Coming</u>. Burlington, Iowa: National Research Bureau, 1976.
Pamphlet with no author, publisher, or date	<u>Pedestrian Safety</u>. [United States]: n.p., n.d. *Note:* List the country of publication (in brackets) if known.
Recording	Frost, Robert. "The Road Not Taken." <u>Robert Frost Reads His Poetry</u>. Caedmon, TC 1060, 1956.
Radio or television program	"Latch-Key Kids." <u>Hour Magazine</u>. CBS, 15 Nov. 1983. *Note:* Other information (director, producer, narrator, writer) may be listed if appropriate.

Tim Larsen
Mrs. Frenz
Life Science
May 3, 1986

The American Peregrine Falcon: A Vanishing Bird

The peregrine falcon is one of the fastest birds in the air. In level flight it can reach a speed of 65 miles an hour. When this falcon dives and attacks its prey, it can reach speeds of over 200 miles per hour. No wonder the United States Air Force Academy has made the falcon its official mascot. This lightning-quick bird of prey, however, may not fly and attack much longer. The peregrine falcon is an endangered species.

The use of pesticides is the main reason the peregrine falcon is an endangered species. Pesticides are chemicals sprayed on plants to kill insects. The falcons are infected when they eat other birds already infected with pesticides like DDT. A peregrine's ability to reproduce may be upset by these pesticides. They can also cause falcon eggs to have very thin and weak shells (Allen 193). These eggs break before they should, and the hatched falcons die. Sometimes the pesticides can kill full-grown falcons.

Man's movement into the peregrine's natural habitat or home has also caused it to be an endangered species. The use of wilderness land for farming and game preserves and parks has damaged the falcon's natural habitat. Also, the sonic booms from modern aircraft may be hurting the peregrine population. The power and sound of a sonic boom possibly upsets nesting falcons and causes falcon eggs to crack too soon.

Man has not always treated the peregrine falcon so harmfully. The ancient Egyptians and Persians treated the falcon in a very special way. The Egyptians called the falcon "The Lofty One." During the Middle Ages, the very wealthy men of Europe used the falcon for hunting because of the bird's speed and intelligence. This type of hunting is called falconry. Falconry declined after the invention of guns ("Falcon" 37). However, some people still hunt with falcons in Holland, England, Japan, and the United States.

The peregrine falcon is built for hunting. It is a large bird, usually between 15 and 19 inches in length. The falcon's long, pointed wings spread to around 43 inches in full flight. Its hooked beak and razor-sharp talons or claws can slice its prey when it attacks. The top part of a peregrine falcon is blue-gray in color, and the bottom part is white with black bars or stripes. There are also black stripes on each side of the beak (Pettingill 14). The dull, natural colors of the falcon help keep it unnoticed when it is getting ready to attack.

PEREGRINE FALCON

The peregrine falcon feeds mainly on pigeons, songbirds, and ducks. Prey is often killed in the air after a quick dive by a peregrine. The prey is struck suddenly and viciously with the claws. Sometimes the prey is carried to the ground and plucked to death. Mated pairs of falcons may hunt as a team. One floats high in the air while the other falcon flies at a lower level. The falcon at the lower level scares up prey and the other falcon dives and attacks it. The main natural enemies of the falcon are predators like owls and raccoons which eat the young birds and the eggs.

This bird of prey usually lives and breeds on the sides of high cliffs. Peregrine falcons have the same mate for life and produce three or four eggs each season. The young are hatched after about 32 days of nesting. They stay in the nest for five or six weeks. It takes another month before the young can fly and hunt for food. Normally, a falcon will live for four or five years, although they may live up to 12 years or longer (Wilson 68).

Today, not many peregrine falcons are found anywhere in the lower United States. As of 1978, only 31 pairs were known to have been nesting in the wild (Wildlife Notes). These birds were found in the southwestern part of our country. The remaining falcons in North America live mainly in Alaska, western Canada, and Mexico. At one time, peregrine falcons were common in the central Rocky Mountain region of the United States. They used to breed east of the Rockies as well.

Steps are being taken to save this bird of prey. Environmentalists are trying to limit the use of pesticides. Also, the Peregrine Fund of the Cornell Laboratory of Ornithology in Ithaca, New York, has been created to breed peregrine falcons. A 10-year goal is in place by this organization to breed enough peregrines to populate its former habitats. Nearly 250 falcons have already been released (Brandes 82). Hopefully, these birds will be able to survive in the wild. It would be a tragedy to lose the peregrine falcon, one of the fastest and most spectacular birds in the air.

Bibliography

Allen, Thomas B.   Vanishing Wildlife of North America. Washington, D.C.: National Geographic Society, 1974.

Brandes, Kathleen, et al., eds.   Vanishing Species.   New York: Time-Life Books, 1976.

Caras, Roger, ed.   Vanishing Wildlife.   New York: Westover, 1970.

"Falcon."   The Audubon Nature Encyclopedia.   The Audubon Society.   12 vols.   Philadelphia: Cross, 1965.

Pettingill, Olin Sewall, Jr.   "Falcon and Falconry." World Book Encyclopedia, 1980.

Wildlife Notes: The American Peregrine Falcon. National Wildlife Federation, 1980.

Wilson, Ron.   Vanishing Species.   Secaucus, New Jersey: Chartwell Books Inc., 1979.

The Poem

477 What Is a Poem?

The poet Marianne Moore defines poetry as "imaginary gardens with real toads in them." This definition may seem unusual to you. When you think of a definition, you probably think of something like "a verb is a word which expresses action or a state of being." Poetry, however, is too creative and exciting to be effectively defined in such a factual way. That is why Ms. Moore chose such a different way to define poetry. She has given life to her definition and invites us to use our imaginations and share in her creation. A poem is an exciting and imaginative creation, an "imaginary garden." Poems come from our real world experiences—the "toads" which hop in and out of our lives every day.

"Imaginary gardens" might be new to you, but poetry is not. Your idea of poetry might be an old jump-roping jingle like "I like coffee/ I like tea/ I like the boys/ Do they like me?" Or, it might be the lyrics or words of your favorite song. Jingles and song lyrics may be considered poetry, but often they are not very creative or imaginative. More than anything, good poetry must present ideas in a new and different way, a way that makes poetry fun to listen to and interesting to read.

478 Some Imaginary Gardens

Read the three poems that follow. Each poem gives the reader an imaginative and interesting look at something or someone from our real world. The first poem looks at something we all take for granted—peanut butter. The second poem looks at something most of us dislike—spiders. The last poem looks at a somewhat mysterious junior high student. All of these poems are "imaginary gardens with real toads in them."

I Know Magic When I See (Er...Taste) It

The magic
that allows Peter Pan
to stay as young as he is
and do what is fun,
think magical thoughts
and live a charmed life,
fight for his rights
and soar into a room,
is found in his food.

He eats
his peanut butter,
the youth food,
that we all spread on our bread
(or eat by the spoonful).
All kids like it
much better than
broccoli and cauliflower,
liver and onions.

Only Peter Pan
eats nothing else.
Not only that...
The golden dust he sprinkles
on himself and his friends
for flying?
It's nothing more than
this magical food
specially freeze-dried.

Spiders

What of the spiders in the hall closet?
    They do not come to scare you.
    They bring no evil
    and do not wish to hurt you.
    No. They are the victims:
        tangled in cotton-polyester
        and old wool clothes
        doomed to be crunched
        between cold fingers
        masked by Kleenex
        and tumbled into plastic graves
        among soup cans and cracker boxes
            beneath the kitchen sink.

Manchild

When he did come,
Gordy always shuffled into
school
late and alone.
Small and rough-looking,
with grease-backed hair,
he worked on acting tough
and looking older than his
years
as we worked on math
problems
and understanding verbs.
After one month
he stopped coming altogether
and probably went on
with what was important to
him
while we continued on
with our junior high lives.

479 Poetry Is Not the Same as Prose

As you can see from the samples above, poetry is written in lines and stanzas (groups of lines). Poetry may or may not state ideas in complete sentences. Prose, on the other hand, is the ordinary way of writing using sentences and paragraphs as in reports and stories. Note the difference between the following prose paragraph and poem dealing with the same subject.

Prose Paragraph

A young boy who pretended he was Luke Skywalker rushed into the classroom. He was wearing saggy blue jeans and a flannel shirt. He slapped his paperback book on a desk top. The book was *Star Wars,* and Luke had read it many times. Immediately, he started talking about Chewbacca, Princess Lea, and Death Star. Luke didn't care whom he talked to. He just wanted to talk about the book because it really excited him.

Poem

Luke Skywalker,
saggy-jeaned and flanneled,
burst into the room,
slapped his well-read space book
on a desk top
and started talking of Chewbacca,
Princess Lea, and Death Star
to anyone who would listen.
He bubbled with the discoveries
he had made.

480 Poetry Can Add Life to an Idea

Even though poetry is usually briefer or shorter than prose, it can often give more life to an idea than prose. Suppose you are interested in dreams. A prose writing, such as you would find in an encyclopedia or textbook, would give you facts about dreams and dreaming. For example, the dictionary defines a dream as "a series of thoughts, images, or emotions occurring during sleep." This definition alone, however, might not be enough. It might not help the reader visualize—see in his or her mind—the strange and mysterious power of a dream. A poem that makes a dream come alive can do this.

Witches

*I wait
to feel happiness
familiar or brand new . . .
But I dream of witches.
Evil curls like smoke
from the corners of their eyes
and out between lips
parted in false smiles.
Spiny fingers reach for me.
My mind races,
but my feet are still.
I wake,
but still their cruel laughter
echoes through my head.
They'll return,
these wicked ladies,
to dance upon my bed.*

Writing Your Own Poem

Prewriting: *Selecting a Subject*

Before you begin writing your own poem, you must first select a good subject or idea. Poems have been written on just about any topic you can imagine. Choose as a subject something that you know about or often think about. This will naturally be something specific like your favorite food, a special person, an unforgettable experience, or an unusual dream.

Planning: *Preparing to Write*

Once you have selected a subject, think of an interesting way to write about it. For example, in the first model poem, the writer turns peanut butter into a magical food. In the second model poem about spiders, the spiders are treated as helpless victims. In the third model poem about the junior high student, the student is described as a mysterious loner. Remember, if you can't think of an interesting way to write about your subject, try a free writing. A free writing will help you unlock the interesting or creative ideas hidden in your mind. This writing will also help you gather details for your poem.

Writing: *The First Draft*

Once you have a specific subject and many interesting ideas or details about that subject, you are ready to write your poem. Don't worry about writing "the perfect poem" or a poem that looks or sounds like somebody else's. Write freely and naturally until you've said all that you need to say about the subject. Don't overlook the sounds, taste, or smells of your subject, and most importantly, remember how it looks or how you *feel* about it.

One of the nice things about writing poetry is that the form—the way it looks—is really up to you. You can arrange your details into any form you choose, as long as it looks good and makes sense to you. Very often the form of your poem will develop naturally as you write. Your poem might, for example, be a simple list of words and phrases, or it might be made up of complete sentences. As long as it makes sense to you and your reader, the poem can be anything you want it to be.

Most modern poetry is called **free verse,** which means it is not written in any special form. All of the model poems used earlier in this section are free verse poems. You can see that these poems are formed naturally. That is, they follow no special form.

Free verse poetry also doesn't require rhyme and meter. Meter is the pattern of accented and unaccented syllables which gives a poem a very regular rhythm or beat. Only the traditional or older forms of poetry have specific requirements for using rhyme and meter. (See "Traditional Forms and Terms of Poetry," for an explanation of rhyme and meter in traditional poetry.)

Note: Don't be afraid to use some rhyme in your free verse poem. Just remember that all the lines in your poem don't have to rhyme.

Revising: *Improving the Writing*

You will revise your poem many times before you are satisfied that it captures your subject. Your poem should contain strong, active words that *show* rather than tell something. Note below the difference in the words used to describe the eyes of the witches in the student poem.

> Their eyes were evil looking.
> "Evil curls like smoke
> from the corners of their eyes...."

The first sentence simply explains that the witches' eyes look evil. The second example creates an effective image (word picture)— smoke curling from the eyes of the witches.

482 The Special Language of Poetry

Poets also use language in a "figurative" way to help them produce interesting word pictures. **Simile, metaphor,** and **personification** are three popular forms of figurative language which can add a special, creative touch to poetry.

483 A **simile** compares two different things using either *like* or *as.*

> "Everywhere giant-finned cars nose forward like fish."

484 A **metaphor** compares two different things without using a word of comparison such as *like* or *as.*

> "The can of Pepsi was a lifesaver after the long, hot practice."

485 **Personification** is a form of figurative language in which an idea, object, or animal is given the characteristics of a person.

> "The moon suddenly stands up in the darkness."
> "Harsh winds frisk you to the bone."

Not only do you want your poem to say something imaginatively and clearly, you also want your poem to say it in a pleasing and effective way. In other words, you want your poem to sound good. **Alliteration, rhyme,** and **repetition** are three special forms of writing which can be used to give your poem a pleasing, musical sound.

486 **Alliteration** is the repeating of beginning consonant sounds as in "<u>cr</u>eamy and <u>cr</u>unchy."

487 **Rhyme** is the repeating of two or more words which sound alike as in "<u>fights</u> for his <u>rights</u>." Rhyme can occur at the ends of lines or within a line.

488 **Repetition** is the repeating of a word or phrase to add rhythm or to emphasize an idea, as in the following lines from "The Raven."

> While I nodded, nearly napping, suddenly there came a tapping,
> As of some one gently rapping, rapping at my chamber door—

489 **Additional Things to Check in Your Poem**

____ 1. Check the title of your poem. Make sure it adds something to your poem and catches the attention of the reader.

____ 2. Check your poem to make sure it is clear and complete.

____ 3. Check the form of your poem. The way your poem looks and sounds should help the reader enjoy it.

____ 4. Check the way your poem ends. A poem that fizzles and dies at the end won't leave a reader with much of an impression.

____ 5. Check the capitalization of your poem. The first word in each line of a traditional poem is capitalized. In free verse poetry, this is not the case. You may decide to capitalize the first word of each line, but you don't have to. You might decide to capitalize only a few words for emphasis.

____ 6. Check the spelling, punctuation, and usage in your poem.

____ 7. Finally, write your final copy neatly and clearly.

490 Reading and Appreciating a Poem

1.   Read the poem slowly and carefully.

2.   Read the poem aloud.   (If this isn't possible, "listen" to the poem as you read it silently.)

3.   Read the poem over several times.   Each reading will help you enjoy the poem more.

4.   Try to catch the general meaning of the poem during your first reading.   Knowing the general meaning will help you understand the more difficult parts of the poem.

5.   Share the poems you enjoy with your friends.

Note: To get a basic understanding and appreciation of most poems, you won't need to go beyond the five steps listed above.   If the poem is complicated, however, you should continue with the list below and study the poem more closely.

6.   Listen for voices.   A poet will sometimes use the voices or speech of other people to help carry the meaning of the poem.   Knowing who is "speaking" can help you understand what is being said.

7.   Read between the lines.   Sometimes a poem says more than it first appears to say.   Consider the full or "other" meaning of the poem before drawing any conclusions.

8.   When you find words or images (word pictures) that interest you, take the time to study and appreciate them.   Think how these words or images add to the overall picture or message of the poem.

9.   Think about your own feelings and experiences and compare them to the ideas presented in the poem; this will make the poem that much more meaningful to you.

Traditional Forms and Terms of Poetry
Introduction: Rhyme and Meter

Most traditional forms of poetry require rhyme. The rhyme is organized in patterns called rhyme schemes. Note below the rhyme scheme of the model poem, "Stopping by Woods on a Snowy Evening," by Robert Frost. The lines that rhyme are labeled with the same letter. (The rhyme scheme of this poem is *aaba bbcb ccdc dddd*.)

Stopping by Woods on a Snowy Evening

Whose woods these are I think I know. *(a)*
His house is in the village though; *(a)*
He will not see me stopping here *(b)*
To watch his woods fill up with snow. *(a)*

My little horse must think it queer *(b)*
To stop without a farmhouse near *(b)*
Between the woods and frozen lake *(c)*
The darkest evening of the year. *(b)*

He gives his harness bells a shake *(c)*
To ask if there is some mistake. *(c)*
The only other sound's the sweep *(d)*
Of easy wind and downy flake. *(c)*

The woods are lovely, dark and deep, *(d)*
But I have promises to keep, *(d)*
And miles to go before I sleep, *(d)*
And miles to go before I sleep. *(d)*

Also, traditional forms of poetry are written in meter. Meter is the pattern of accented and unaccented syllables in the lines of a poem. The regular beat or rhythm in a traditional poem comes from the meter. If you read a traditional poem carefully, you should be able to identify its meter.

The "Stopping by Woods . . . " poem is written so that every other syllable is accented. This pattern of an unaccented syllable followed by an accented syllable is the poem's meter. Note the first two lines of this poem given below. The accented (ʹ) and unaccented (ᵕ) syllables are labeled to show the meter.

> ᵕ　　ʹ　　ᵕ　　ʹ　ᵕ　ʹ　ᵕ　ʹ
> Whose woods these are I think I know.
>
> ᵕ　　ʹ　ᵕ　ʹ　ᵕ　　ʹ　ᵕ　　ʹ
> His house is in the village though;

There are six basic patterns of accented and unaccented syllables in traditional poetry. (See "Foot," 501, for the name and explanation of each pattern.)

492　**Assonance** is the repetition of vowel sounds, as in the following lines from "The Hayloft" by R.L. Stevenson.

> Till the shining scythes went far and wide
> And cut it down to dry.

493　**Ballad:** A ballad is a poem which tells a story. They are usually written in four-line stanzas called quatrains. Often, the first and third lines have four accented syllables; the second and fourth have three. (See "Quatrains," 512, for the possible rhyme schemes for the ballad.)

Ballad of Birmingham (first stanza)

> Mother dear, may I go downtown
> Instead of out to play,
> And march the streets of Birmingham
> In a Freedom March today?

494　**Blank Verse:** Blank verse is unrhymed poetry with meter. The lines in blank verse are 10 syllables in length. Every other syllable, beginning with the second syllable, is accented. (*Note:* Not every line will have exactly 10 syllables.)

Birches (first three lines)

> When I see birches bend to left and right
> Across the lines of straight and dark trees,
> I like to think some boy's been swinging them.

495　**Cinquain:** Cinquain poems are five lines in length. There are syllable and word cinquain poems.

Syllable Cinquain

Line 1:	Title	2 syllables
Line 2:	Description of title	4 syllables
Line 3:	Action about the title	6 syllables
Line 4:	Feeling about the title	8 syllables
Line 5:	Synonym for title	2 syllables

Word Cinquain

Line 1:	Title	1 word
Line 2:	Description of title	2 words
Line 3:	Action about the title	3 words
Line 4:	Feeling about the title	4 words
Line 5:	Synonym for title	1 word

496 **Consonance** is the repetition of consonant sounds. This is a lot like alliteration except it includes consonant sounds anywhere within the words, not just at the beginning. Listen to the "s" sounds in the following lines from "Singing" by R.L. Stevenson.

> The sailor sings of ropes and things
> In ships upon the seas.

497 **Couplet:** A couplet is two lines of verse that usually rhyme. Often, a couplet states one complete idea.

> Double, double, toil and trouble,
> Fire burn and cauldron bubble.

498 **Elegy:** An elegy is a poem which states a poet's sadness about the death of an important person. In the famous elegy "O Captain, My Captain," Walt Whitman writes about the death of Abraham Lincoln.

499 **End rhyme** is the rhyming of words at the ends of two or more lines of poetry, as in the following lines from "The Night Light" by Robert Frost.

> She always had to turn a light
> Beside her attic bed at night.

500 **Epic:** An epic is a long story poem which describes the adventures of a hero. *The Odyssey* by Homer is a famous epic which describes the adventures of the Greek hero Odysseus.

501 **Foot:** A foot is one unit of meter. (*Meter* is the pattern of accented and unaccented syllables in the lines of a traditional poem.) There are six basic feet:

Iambic — an unaccented syllable followed by an accented one (re peat')

Anapestic — two unaccented syllables followed by an accented one (in ter rupt')

Trochaic — an accented syllable followed by an unaccented one (old' er)

Dactylic — an accented syllable followed by two unaccented ones (o' pen ly)

Spondaic — two accented syllables (heart' break')

Pyrrhic — two unaccented syllables (Pyrrhic is very rare and seldom appears by itself.)

502 **Free Verse:** Free verse is poetry which does not require meter or a rhyme scheme.

503 **Haiku:** Haiku is a type of Japanese poetry which presents a clear perception or picture of nature. A haiku poem is three lines in length. The first line is five syllables; the second, seven; and the third, five.

> Water tumbles down
> In a gently flowing stream.
> Over rocks it trips.

504 **Internal rhyme** is the rhyming of words within one line of poetry, as in *Jack Sprat could eat no fat* or *Peter Peter pumpkin eater*.

505 **Limerick:** A limerick is a humorous verse of five lines. Lines one, two, and five rhyme, as do lines three and four. Lines one, two, and five have three stressed syllables; lines three and four have two.

> There once was a lady from Nantucket
> Who lived her whole life in a bucket.
> Her pleasures unknown,
> Were completely thrown,
> When in a mudhole her bucket got stuckit.

506 **Lyric:** A lyric is a short poem that expresses personal feeling.

My Heart Leaps Up When I Behold (first 5 lines)

> My heart leaps up when I behold
> A rainbow in the sky;
> So was it when my life began;
> So is it now I am a man;
> So be it when I shall grow old.
> William Wordsworth

507 **Meter:** Meter is the repetition of stressed and unstressed syllables in a line of poetry. (See "Foot," 501.)

508 **Ode:** An ode is a long lyric that is deep feeling and rich in poetic devices and imagery. "Ode to a Grecian Urn" is a famous ode by John Keats.

509 **Onomatopoeia** is the use of a word whose sound makes you think of its meaning, as in *buzz, gunk, gushy, swish, zigzag, zing,* or *zip*.

510 **Parody:** A parody is a poem which humorously copies or exaggerates the style of another poem or poet.

511 **Poetry:** Poetry is a concentrated or compact form of writing which shows imagination, emotion, and thought.

512 **Quatrain:** A quatrain is a four-line stanza. The lines in a traditional quatrain are written with meter and rhyme. Common rhyme schemes in quatrains are *aabb, abab,* and *abcb*.

> I wish I had no teachers.
> That's what I'd like to see.
> I'd do whatever I wanted to,
> And nobody'd yell at me.

513 Sonnet: A sonnet is a fourteen-line poem which states a poet's personal feelings.   One common sonnet is the Shakespearean sonnet which follows the *abab cdcd efef gg* rhyme scheme.   Each line in a sonnet is 10 syllables in length; every other syllable is stressed, beginning with the second syllable.

514 Stanza: A stanza is a division in a poem named for the number of lines it contains.   Given below are the names of the common stanzas.

Couplet . . . . . two-line stanza	*Sestet* . . . . six-line stanza
Triplet . . . . three-line stanza	*Septet*. . . . . seven-line stanza
Quatrain . . . four-line stanza	*Octave* . . . . eight-line stanza

515 Tanka: A tanka is a form of Japanese poetry which gives a clear picture of nature in five lines.   The first and third lines have five syllables; the other lines have seven.   (Compare this form to the "Haiku," 503.)

> A parched, brown meadow,
> Baking in the midday heat
> Of early autumn,
> Serves as the hunting domain
> Of a keen-eyed, floating hawk.

516 Verse: Verse is a name for a line of traditional poetry written in meter.   Verse is named according to the pattern of accented and unaccented syllables in the line (See "Foot," 501.) and the number of patterns repeated.   The names for the number of patterns or feet per line are given below.

Monometer . . . . one foot	*Pentameter* . . . . five feet
Dimeter. . . . . two feet	*Hexameter* . . . . six feet
Trimeter. . . . . three feet	*Heptameter* . . . . . . seven feet
Tetrameter . . . . four feet	*Octometer* . . . . eight feet

The verses or lines in "Stopping by Woods . . . ," 491, are written in iambic tetrameter.   This means that this poem is written in iambic feet, and there are four iambic feet per line.

Alternative and Experimental Poetry

517 Alphabet Poetry: A form of poetry which states a creative or humorous idea using part of the alphabet.   An alphabet poem is often written as a list.

> **H**ighly
> **I**gnorant
> **J**umping
> **K**angaroos
> **L**ove
> **M**aking
> **N**oise
> **O**bnoxiously

518 **Clerihew Poetry:** A form of humorous or light verse created by Edmund Clerihew. A clerihew poem consists of two rhyming couplets. (See "Couplet," **497,** for an explanation.) The name of some well-known person creates one of the rhymes.

> The only way to pitch Pete Rose
> Is to throw the ball near his nose.
> Throw a pitch which he can hit
> And he'll blast a drive no one will get.

519 **Concrete Poetry:** A form of poetry in which the shape or design helps express the meaning or feeling of the poem.

520 **Contrast Couplet:** A couplet in which the first line includes two words that are opposites. The second line makes some sort of comment about the first line.

> It really doesn't matter if you're young or old.
> There's always someone to say: "Do as you're told."

521 **Definition Poetry:** A form of poetry which defines a word or idea creatively.

> Stryofoam —
> a strange stuff
> which bends, dents, and rips
> when poked or pulled.

522 **Dream Poetry:** A form of poetry which describes a personal dream. (See "Witches," **480,** for an example.)

523 **Headline Poetry:** A form of poetry which is created from the words of newspaper or magazine headlines. The words in the headlines are organized in a creative way.

524 **List Poetry:** A form of poetry which lists words or phrases.

Rooms

> There are rooms to start up in
> Rooms to start out in
> Rooms to start over in
> Rooms to lie in
> Rooms to lie about in
> Rooms to lay away in
> Rooms to lay up in
> Rooms to lay over in
> Rooms to lie low in . . .
>
> Ray Griffith

525 **Name Poetry:** A form of poetry in which a name is used as the first letter of each line in the poem.

> **B**asically
> **A**ll kinds of activity and
> **R**eading a good book
> **B**ring out
> **A**ll that is
> **R**ight
> **A**bout me.

526 **Phrase Poetry:** A form of poetry which states an idea with a list of phrases.

> **Cross Country**
>
> Off with a bang
> around the bushes
> up the exhausting hill
> toward the finish
> without any breath

527 **Riddle Poetry:** A form of poetry which makes the reader guess the subject of the poem. "I Like to See It Lap the Miles," by Emily Dickinson is a good example of a riddle poem.

528 **Terse Verse:** A form of humorous verse made up of two words that rhyme and have the same number of syllables.

Old Flower	**Worms**	**Braces**
Lazy	Great	Tin
Daisy	Bait	Grin

529 **Title-down Poetry:** A form of poetry in which the subject of the poem is used as the first letter in each line.

> **B**eing down is
> **L**ousy,
> **U**gh, but
> **E**veryone is down sometimes.

The Short Story

Getting Started: Finding an Idea

The best ideas for a short story are found in your own mind—the same place ideas for a poem, a play, or any other form of creative writing are found. When you search your mind for ideas for a short story, look for ideas that you think can be made into an interesting and creative story. Think of people you know who might make interesting characters; think of any problems in your own life or in the lives of others that might work as starting points for the plot of a story; or think of attitudes or feelings held by you or other people that might make interesting or worthwhile themes for a short story.

The three illustrations above show the thoughts of three different students, thoughts which are all possible starting points for a short story. Surely, ideas such as these pass through your own mind. Let's examine each of the ideas presented in the illustrations to see how each might be used in starting a short story.

The first student is thinking about a boy named Rocky who wears "funny clothes." Maybe his clothes are funny because they are old and worn. Maybe the student sees Rocky's clothes as funny because they are wild and flashy, and Rocky is as wild as his clothes. Or possibly, Rocky wears a suit and tie to school every day, and he always has his nose stuck in a book. Whatever the case may be, if the person is interesting and different, he could very well serve as a main character and a starting point for a short story. *(Note: Don't create a character in your story that resembles a real person so closely that he or she might be offended or hurt if your story is going to be shared with others.)*

The second student is thinking about the recent change in his brother's personality. A main element or part of a short story—some might say the most important part—is the problem or conflict which creates the action in a story. (See "Conflict," 753, for an explanation of the different types of conflicts.) Certainly the change in the personality of a close family member could be a worthwhile conflict for a story, and thus, a good starting point for developing a short story.

The third student is thinking about a celebration her family had recently and the fun she had with her relatives. Being with her family might be the best part about celebrations for this girl. A feeling or attitude such as this one could be used as the theme for a story, or could at least be a good starting point for developing a theme. (See "Theme," 829, for an explanation.)

The main character, the conflict, and the theme are all important parts of a short story. All three of these elements have to be considered when you are planning a story, and any one of the three may serve as the starting point. If you have trouble finding a particular person, problem, or belief which can get you started on your own short story, try a free writing or two.

531 Characteristics of a Short Story

Before you begin planning your own short story, you will need to know more about short stories and what makes them different from other forms of writing.

A short story is a form of fiction which can be read in one sitting. A good short story will leave a reader with a particular feeling after the story has been read. Often, a short story is about the real world. It contains believable characters, realistic problems, and honest feelings. However, not all short stories are about the real world. Science fiction and fantasy are also subjects of short stories. (*Note:* Science fiction and fantasy stories are not easy to write. Beginning writers will find it much easier to write short stories about real life.)

532 Characters

A good short story unfolds or develops mainly through action, description, and dialogue or conversation. One of the characters of the short story often serves as the narrator or teller of the story. However, a writer may create a narrator who is outside of the story. (See "Point of View," 806, for an explanation of the different types of narrators.)

Only a few characters are introduced into a short story, and, generally, only one or two of the characters plays an important role. The reader gets to know the characters through their actions, conversations, and details given by the narrator. The main character will often change in some important way by the end of the story because of the conflict or problem he or she has had to deal with.

533 Plot

The plot or action of a short story is well organized and limited. That is, world wars are not fought in short stories. (See "Plot," 803, for a definition.) The time and place of the action in a story is limited to one or possibly two settings. Note below the plot line which identifies the basic parts and organization of the action of a short story.

534 **Exposition:** Usually, a short story begins right in the middle of the action. Once-upon-a-time beginnings are for fairy tales, not short stories. The main character, the conflict, and the setting are quickly worked into the action in the beginning or *exposition* of the story.

535 **Rising action:** Minor problems or complications (usually three or four) are then added in a short story to build suspense or interest. These minor problems get the main character deeply involved in the conflict and get the reader deeply interested in the story. The creation of suspense or interest in this part of a story is very important. If everything goes too smoothly, the short story will become too predictable — the readers will be able to figure out what is going to happen.

536 **Climax:** The rising action builds to the *climax,* which is the most important part of a short story. In the climax, the main character comes face-to-face with the major conflict or problem of the story. The main character will always be changed in some way as he or she faces up to the conflict, even if he or she doesn't succeed in overcoming or solving it.

537 **Falling Action and Resolution:** Any additional events leading to the end of the story are part of the *falling action.* Any loose ends in the plot caused by the climax are taken care of in this section. The *resolution* or conclusion in a well-planned plot brings the short story to a believable ending. Perfect, happy-ever-after endings are not usually found in good short stories, just as they are not frequently found in real life. This means that a short story may be better and more believable if the main character simply learns to live with his or her problem rather than completely solve it. Realistic short stories should leave the reader with a better understanding of the real world.

Model Short Story

The short story which follows was written by a junior high school student. It is the story of a girl and her family one particular Christmas. A number of "problems" come up just before the holiday and threaten to spoil the celebration. The story describes the problems and how things work out in the end.

538

The Faces of Christmas

As soon as I woke up, I knew I was late. When I glanced at my clock, I found I was right. I jumped out of bed, threw open my closet door, and searched for something to wear. I ran around the house trying to get ready and dashed out the door just in time to catch the bus.

On the bus my best friend Laura was saving a seat for me. I sank into the seat and was about to tell her how my morning had started out when I saw her face.

"What's wrong, Laura?"

"Oh, Vicki! Christmas is going to be so terrible this year," she moaned. "Mother and Dad have to be out of town on Christmas, and I'm being sent to my Aunt Jane's house. I hate my Aunt Jane. She treats me like a five-year-old. Worse than that, she's a terrible cook, yet she always wants to feed me."

"It can't be as bad as that. Can it?" I asked.

"You haven't met my Aunt Jane! I wish I had a big family like you, so I could go somewhere else. You're so lucky."

Actually, my family is not that big. It includes Mom, Dad, and four kids, including me. Sarah is the oldest child. Jim comes next. Then there's me and Mike, who is the baby of the family. I only have one living grandparent, my Grandma Potter. I do have tons of aunts and uncles, along with many cousins on both sides of the family.

Every Christmas since I can remember, the whole family has gathered at either Grandma's or at our house to exchange gifts and see everyone. This year's annual gathering was just two days away. Since this year it was going to be at our house, Mom had thrown herself completely into Christmas baking.

By this time the bus had reached the high school, and I was caught up in the noisy halls before I could say anything more to Laura.

During school I thought about what Laura had said to me. I guess I am pretty lucky, especially compared to Laura. Laura's mom is always traveling with her dad, and her family isn't big on holidays. Mom is almost always home for us when we get home from school, and we make a big deal about every holiday.

While I was sitting in the kitchen after school, I told Mom about Laura having to be away from her parents on Christmas.

"Oh, that's a shame. Why don't you ask Laura to spend Christmas at our house while her parents are away?" Mom asked.

"Oh, Mom, that would be great! I'm sure Laura would love to come."

"There will be an extra place at the table anyway," she said. "Sarah, along with a few of her friends, has a chance to go to France with one of her college professors."

"But, Mom, she can't go. She'll miss Christmas with the family. We've always spent it together."

"The rest of us will still be together, Vicki," Mom said.

I opened my mouth to say something more, but the telephone rang. It was Aunt Grace calling to say that she, Uncle Ted, and my cousin Mary wouldn't be able to make it for Christmas. I wasn't all that sorry Aunt Grace and Uncle Ted weren't coming, but Mary is the same age as I am, and we always have had fun together on the holidays.

During dinner that night the telephone rang again. This time it was my brother Jim calling. He was wondering if Mom and Dad wouldn't mind too much if he didn't come home for Christmas. Some of his college friends were going on a skiing trip, and he wanted to go along. Of course, Mom and Dad said Jim could go, but I had wanted them to say no.

After dinner I called Laura to ask her over. She got permission from her parents and planned to come over the next day.

All morning we cleaned. It was Christmas Eve, so my brother Mike, Mom, Dad, and I were trying to get everything ready for Christmas Day. The four of us had fun, but something seemed to be missing. Sarah and Jim were what were missing. The six of us would always laugh and talk while we worked. Without Sarah and Jim it just wasn't the same.

Later that afternoon Laura came over, which cheered everyone up a lot. Soon after Laura came, Dad drove up the driveway with Grandma in the car. Because Grandma is in her seventies, she has trouble walking, but her mind is as alert as ever. After Grandma got settled, I went over to talk to her.

"Where are Sarah and Jim?" she asked me.

"They've made other plans, so they aren't coming home. Uncle Ted, Aunt Grace, and Mary aren't coming either," I said. "Christmas just isn't going to be the same this year without them."

"Of course this Christmas won't be the same as last year," Grandma said. "No two Christmases are ever the same. People change, children grow older, new additions are added to the family, and sometimes people die. You have to learn that sometimes things have got to change. Do you understand that, Vicki?"

"Yes, Grandma," I said. "I think I do."

The next day I woke up and saw that it was snowing out. It was a perfect day for Christmas. Laura was already awake, and when we went into the living room, we found everyone else was awake too. We opened our presents; then we went to get dressed. As soon as breakfast was over, Mom started to make the ham and duck for dinner.

Everyone was so busy that we didn't realize how late it was until the doorbell rang, telling us that the first of our relatives had arrived. People arrived steadily from then on, and we were busy greeting everyone.

Finally they had all arrived, so we sat down to eat dinner. As I looked around the table, I really began to understand what Grandma had tried to tell me. I saw the new faces of babies, my aunt's fiance, and my best friend, and I saw the old familiar faces that would always be there. No, I thought. No two Christmases are ever the same.

539   The Plan for "The Faces of Christmas"

Look at the plan used by the student who wrote the sample short story. Notice that the plan covers such things as characters, plot, narrator, setting, and theme. By looking at this plan, you should be better able to understand how short stories are written. The sample plan should also help you to plan your own short story.

Plan: The Faces of Christmas

I. Main Character: Vicki
  A. Eighth grade student
  B. Very friendly
  C. Sensitive
II. Minor Characters
  A. Laura
    1. Vicki's best friend
    2. Spends Christmas with Vicki
  B. Vicki's mother
    1. Plans the family's Christmas gathering
    2. Patient and understanding
  C. Grandmother
    1. Gathers with the family for Christmas
    2. Offers Vicki advice in dealing with her problem

III. Plot
   A. Exposition: Vicki rushes to catch the bus the day before her Christmas vacation and then has a conversation with Laura, her best friend. (The story begins right in the middle of the action. The characters and setting are worked into the story naturally.)
   B. Conflict: Vicki has a hard time accepting the fact that her older brother and sister will not be home for Christmas. (The main character's conflict is with herself, not another person.)
   C. Rising Action (Complications)
      1. Laura has to spend Christmas away from her parents.
      2. Vicki's older sister will not be home for Christmas.
      3. Vicki's aunt and uncle and favorite cousin will not make the Christmas Day gathering.
      4. Vicki's older brother will not be home for Christmas.
   D. Climax: Vicki's talk with her grandmother
   E. Falling Action and Resolution
      1. Christmas Day starts enjoyably with the opening of presents.
      2. Later in the day when everyone is seated for the Christmas meal, Vicki understands what her grandmother had tried to tell her: Since time changes things, no two Christmases can ever be alike. (Vicki accepts the fact that members of her family are not home for Christmas.)
  IV. Narrator: The main character
   V. Setting
      A. Vicki's school (briefly at the beginning)
      B. Her home
  VI. Theme: Our lives continually change.

Writing Your Own Short Story

540 **Planning Your Story**

Once you have selected an idea for your story, the next step is to plan as much of the story as you can before you start writing the first draft. Use the questions included in the sample plan which follows to help you write a plan for your story. If this plan is too complicated or too brief for your story, create your own. (All of the terms in the plan are explained in the "Literary Terms" section of your handbook.)

Sample Plan

   I. Who is the main character(s)?
      A. What does this character look like?
      B. What is his or her personality like?
      C. What problem or conflict will he or she deal with in the story?

II. Who are the minor characters? What part will each minor character play in your story?
- A.
- B.
- C.

III. What will happen in your story?
- A. How will your story start? (Remember to start your story right in the middle of the action if possible.)
- B. What will the conflict or problem of your story be?
- C. What are two or three possible events that will get the main character deeply involved in the conflict?
  1.
  2.
  3.
- D. What will be the climax of your story—when will the main character come face-to-face with his or her conflict or problem?
- E. How will your story end? (Remember to make the ending believable as well as interesting.)

IV. Who will tell your story? Will it be someone in the story or someone outside of the story?

V. Where and when will the action take place? (Limit yourself to one or two settings.)

VI. What idea or belief will your story present, if in fact you have one in mind? (Remember to work this idea or belief into your story naturally. Don't tack it onto the end as a moral.)

Note: You might not be able to plan all parts of your short story, but do the best that you can. Your plan will help you control your story as you write.

541 Write Your First Draft

Write your first draft freely and naturally. However, don't go too far outside the boundaries of your plan, unless you see that you can improve your story by moving in a different direction. You probably won't finish writing your first draft in one try. Each time you continue working on your story, reread what you have already written. If you're not happy with some part of your story up to that point, you might want to make changes before you start writing again. Keep your story organized and believable. Include as much detail, action, and dialogue as you can.

542 A Short Story Checklist

Once you have completed your first draft, use the following checklist to help you judge the progress of your story.

____ 1. The main character is believable. The reader gets to know the main character through his or her actions and dialogue.

_____ 2. The main character is influenced in some way by the conflict.

_____ 3. Each of the minor characters is necessary to the story. (A short story does not need a long list of characters.)

_____ 4. The plot is not too predictable or easy to figure out. That is, the reader must read the entire story to learn the outcome.

_____ 5. The story begins creatively and moves quickly to the action. The main character, the conflict, and the setting are worked into the beginning or *exposition* of the story.

_____ 6. At least two or three minor problems or events are included to get the main character and the reader deeply involved in the story. These problems in the *rising action* are believable and move the main character toward the *climax*.

_____ 7. The *climax*—the main character's showdown with the conflict—is interesting and realistic.

_____ 8. The end or *resolution* brings the story to a believable finish.

_____ 9. The story develops naturally and contains a good deal of action, detail, and dialogue. (A short story should not sound like a report.)

_____ 10. Dialogue has been used correctly. The characters have enough dialogue to "tell" the story without a lot of help from the narrator.

_____ 11. The narrator tells the story from one point of view. Jumping from one point of view to another confuses the reader.

_____ 12. The time and place of the action is limited to one or possibly two settings. Since a short story, by its very nature, is a rather brief story, there is not enough time for other settings.

_____ 13. The theme or point of the story, if there is one, is worked into the story. It is not tacked onto the end of the story in the form of a moral or lesson.

In addition to using the above checklist when you revise, you should also check the sentences, word choice, usage, capitalization, and punctuation of your story. Write your final copy neatly and clearly. Use only one side of the paper.

543 Using Dialogue

Dialogue is the written conversation between two or more people. Dialogue makes a short story more realistic because it gives the exact words of the speakers. Note below that the dialogue in the second example makes the same idea seem much more realistic.

Larry asked Mr. Smith for help with a math problem.

"Ah . . . Mr. Smith? Do you think you could help me with this math problem?" asked Larry.

544 Guidelines for Punctuating Dialogue

1. Place quotation marks (" ") before and after the exact words of the speaker.

> Julie whispered, "Beth, do you understand this assignment?"

2. Capitalize the first word of the quotation.

> Sam burst into the room and yelled, "Someone ransacked my locker!"

3. Separate a quotation from the rest of the sentence with a comma, question mark, or exclamation point.

> Lori whispered, "He's cute."
>
> "Do you like that new song?" asked Mary.
>
> "Watch out!" screamed Jeff.

4. Start a new paragraph when a different speaker talks.

> Jim asked, "Hey, Bill, what are you doing after school?"
>
> "I'm going down to the new bike shop. I hear they have a lot of new models, and I need a new bike. Mine is really beat."
>
> Jim shook his head, "Don't bother. I went down there yesterday. They only have really cheap bikes."

5. Do not capitalize the second part of a broken quotation. It simply continues and completes the idea started in the first part of the quotation.

> "We will be very busy today," said Mr. Smith, "because we have to finish the chapter on percentages."

6. When a speaker's conversation is made up of two or more uninterrupted sentences, place a quotation mark before the first word of the first sentence and after the last word of the final sentence.

> "I couldn't believe it," Jane said. "I walked into the guidance office expecting to see boring old Mr. George. I flipped when I saw this young, really neat-looking woman in his office. I found out that Mr. George has retired, and this woman, Mrs. Peterson, is our new **counselor.**"

7. Avoid overusing the word "said." Check a thesaurus for different words. *Note:* It is not necessary to identify the speaker at all when it is obvious who is talking.

8. Do not use quotation marks for indirect quotations. A quotation is indirect in a story when the narrator simply tells us what

a character has said.   Note the difference between the indirect and direct quotations given below.

> Uncle Hank said, "I will never again move your player piano."   (Direct Quotation)
>
> Uncle Hank said he would never again move my player piano.   (Indirect Quotation)

Uncle Hank said, "I will never again move your piano." (Direct Quotation)

Uncle Hank said he would never again move my piano. (Indirect Quotation)

545 Appreciating and Evaluating a Short Story

To best appreciate a short story, read the entire story in one sitting, and, if at all possible, read it more than once.   During the first reading you should simply enjoy the story: Meet the characters, take note of the setting, and experience the action along with the characters.

During the second reading look a little more closely at the story.   Evaluate the characters, the plot, the setting, and the theme of the story.   Use the checklist, 542, to help you in your evaluation.   Also, consider if the story moves you in any way, and if you would have done anything differently.   Use this section and the checklist, 542, when you write about a short story.   One or two of the ideas in the checklist may serve as the focus of your writing assignment.

The Letter

546 The Friendly Letter

We all enjoy receiving cards and letters from friends and relatives, especially from those special people who have moved or live far away. Letters from friends may make a friendship stronger or may renew an old friendship. Letters from relatives draw you closer to the many people who are related to you.

However, don't rely on friends or relatives to decide suddenly to write you. Give them a reason to write—a letter from you. Sometimes friends and relatives need to be reminded that you are thinking about them and want to hear from them. Once you "reach out" to people with letters, you will receive mail yourself.

Note below the model friendly letter written by a junior high school student. This letter, which was written to a friend who had moved, continues the close friendship built between the two boys.

547 Model Friendly Letter

2525 First Street
Muskego, WI 53150
November 12, 1985

Dear Scott,

How have you been doing in the warm tropics? I know you are probably swimming in your pool and in the ocean. We're not so lucky back here. The last remaining leaves have just blown off the trees. On Monday we had the first trace of snow on the ground. It was so cold we nearly froze to death at the bus stop.

This month in school we're going to have a parent/kid exchange day. That means the parents are going to go to school instead of us. My mom said she would go while I stay home and watch all of the soaps. Are you doing something like that in your school?

School has been going pretty well since my violin was hit by the bus. It was "totalled." I've been kind of lucky in school, though, because I haven't had a whole lot of homework. My favorite class is math because I have a really nice teacher. Her name is Miss Johnson. Did Ray ever have her for math?

I haven't been doing too much since we've talked. In December I will be playing at the Domes with my school orchestra. We will be playing a whole mess of Christmas songs.

Have you seen the Brewers on TV? On the local stations they were interviewing the Brewer players and Harvey Kuenn with his cheek full of tobacco. The stations showed the people in the streets of Milwaukee after they won their first series game. Boy, were they going crazy. After the World Series there was a huge parade to honor the Brewers because they did so well.

The reason I'm writing is because we have to write a friendly letter in my English class. My teacher says that we have been writing our letters the wrong way, and this is the right way. I hope. That is the reason why my letter is so different from the last one. I hope I get a good grade. Please write back soon!

Your best friend,

Mike

548 Form of a Friendly Letter

There are five basic parts in a standard friendly letter: the **heading,** the **salutation,** the **body,** the **closing,** and the **signature.** Your letter does not have to include all of these parts, especially in a friendly letter to a very close friend or relative. For example, the heading, which includes your address, certainly isn't necessary if the person you're writing to already knows your address. Also, the standard form for the salutation doesn't have to be followed in a letter to someone close to you.

However, in a friendly letter to someone you don't know very well, it is best to follow the standard form for a friendly letter. Given below is an explanation of the five parts of a standard friendly letter.

• The **heading** includes your address and the date. The heading is located in the upper right-hand corner of the letter.

• The **salutation** or greeting begins with the word Dear and is followed by the name of the person who will receive the letter. A comma is placed after the name. Write the salutation at the left-hand margin, one or two lines below the heading. Examples of common salutations are given below:

Dear Janet, Dear Grandma, Dear Uncle Eric,
Dear Mr. Smith, Dear Miss Jones, Dear Dr. Long,

• The **body** is the main part of the friendly letter in which you present (write) your information and ideas. Usually, the paragraphs in the body are fairly short for easy reading. Skip one line after the salutation before you begin the body. Also, you should skip one line between paragraphs.

• The **closing** is written two lines below the body of your letter. It begins just to the right of the middle of the letter. Only the first word is capitalized. The closing is followed by a comma. Examples of common closings are given below:

Your friend, Sincerely, With love,

Note: Be creative and use an original closing if you wish.

• The final part of a friendly letter is your **signature.** It is written beneath the closing. Usually, you will just write your first name. Include your last name if you think there will be a question as to which *Bob, Sue, John,* or *Julie* you are.

549 Writing a Friendly Letter

550 Prewriting: *Selecting a Subject*

Write to someone who deserves a letter: a person you haven't written to in a long time, a person who has already written to you, or a special person you want to "talk to" personally in a letter.

551 **Planning:** *Preparing to Write*

Make a list of all of the main ideas you want to include in your letter. Gather all of the facts and details you will need to make each of these ideas clear and entertaining to your reader. You might also decide the order in which these ideas will appear in your letter.

If this is a return letter, reread the letter you received before you begin your own. Make sure to answer any questions asked in that letter. Also, think of one or two creative or "surprise" sections to make your letter more than just answers to the questions which were asked. Below are some ideas for creative sections:

1. Share a good joke or story.
2. Recreate a conversation.
3. Describe a memorable day (hour by hour, etc.).
4. Include a sketch or cartoon.
5. Include a photograph or newspaper article.
6. Write a poem.
7. Start a story which your friend will continue or complete.

552 **Writing:** *The First Draft*

Write your first draft freely and naturally. Write as if you were face-to-face with your friend or relative, sharing stories and information. Make sure you cover all of the main ideas which you listed as you planned your letter.

553 **Helpful Tips**

If you haven't done much letter writing, or if you're writing to someone you don't know that well, the guidelines which follow will help you write a good friendly letter:

- Start your letter in a way which gets your reader interested in your letter. Don't start by saying you don't really have anything exciting or important to report.

- Write in a style which will interest your reader. Don't say something like "School is okay this year," unless you add something to it such as "School is okay this year, but...."

- Your reader will want to know what is going on in your life, so don't ask too many questions of him or her.

- If this is a return letter, answer any questions clearly. Repeat part of a question so that your reader will know what you are writing about: "You asked how Carol is doing in school this year."

- What you say in your letter has a lot to say about you, so avoid gossiping or saying something you'll later regret.

- End your letter in a creative and positive way. Don't apologize by saying that your letter has been boring and not worth reading. Also, ask for a return letter.

554 **Revising:** *Improving the Writing*

Make sure that your letter is easy to read. This means your sentences should read smoothly; your paragraphs should be fairly short and should develop one main idea in each. Include enough facts and details so your ideas are clear and entertaining.

Check your letter for spelling, capitalization, punctuation, and usage errors. (Use your handbook to help you correct any errors.) Check the form of your friendly letter. It is especially important that your letter follow the standard form when you are writing to someone who is not a close friend or relative. A letter correctly written will make a good first impression.

Neatly write or type the final copy. Center your letter on the page, and keep your margins as equal as possible. Use at least one-inch margins on all sides. Address the envelope neatly and correctly, and make sure you fold your letter so that it fits into the envelope.

555 The Social Note

A special type of friendly letter is the social note. In a social note you don't share stories and information. Instead, you share a very short social message. This message may be an invitation or a reply to an invitation. A social note may also be a thank-you note for a gift or for someone's kindness.

Write social notes on the same paper or stationery you use for regular friendly letters. You might also use one of the special note cards made for social notes. These special note cards are often very colorful and attractive.

Social notes usually begin with a salutation. However, a heading is important if you expect an answer to an invitation. The body of a social note is usually one paragraph in length. This paragraph is short and to the point. If you are sending an invitation and need to know how many people will be able to come, ask for an answer in your letter. (Or you can add *RSVP* and your telephone number in the lower-left corner.) "Sincerely" or "Love" are common closings.

540 Elm Drive
Racine, WI 53405
June 15, 1986

Dear Mary,

    On Tuesday, June 25, I'm celebrating my birthday. I'm inviting all of my friends for a party. The party will begin at four o'clock and end around eight o'clock.

    Supper will be served. We will play softball after supper. Let me know if you can come.

Sincerely,
Hilda

556 The Business Letter

Sharing information with a friend or relative is not the only reason to write a letter. Writing a letter can also help you find information. In fact, writing a letter may be the best or the only way to get information about certain things. Often, the books, magazines, and newspapers which you read will contain addresses of people and places you can write to for free material on a variety of topics. The only way to get this information is by letter.

A business letter asking for information or answers to your questions should be written differently than the friendly letters you write to close friends and relatives. A business letter should be written more formally than a friendly letter, and it should follow an accepted form or style for a business letter as well.

Note below the model business letter requesting information on an endangered species. It is written very formally and follows the *full-block* style.

557 Model Business Letter

413 Chicago Street
Racine, WI 53405
March 1, 1986

Director—Wildlife Notes
National Wildlife Federation
1412 16th Street NW
Washington, DC 20036

Dear Director:

I am an eighth-grade student writing a science report on the American peregrine falcon.

I would appreciate any up-to-date information you have on this endangered bird. I am especially interested in the following types of information:

1. The history of the peregrine falcon.
2. The falcon's nesting areas in the United States.
3. Present efforts to save the falcon.
4. A bibliography of current information.

Thank you for your help.

Sincerely,

Jim Smith

Jim Smith

₅₅₈ Form of a Business Letter

The business letter is made up of six basic parts: the **heading, inside address, salutation, body, closing,** and **signature.** The placement of these parts is somewhat different in the two basic styles of business letters: the **full-block** style and the **semi-block** style. Note in the illustrations below the placement of the letter parts in the two basic styles of business letters:

559 **Styles of the Business Letter**

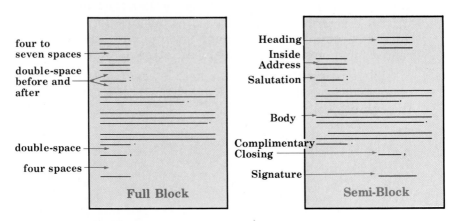

560   The **heading** for a business letter includes the sender's complete address and the full date. The heading is placed about an inch from the top of the page. In a business letter following the full-block style, the heading is placed at the left-hand margin. In a letter following the semi-block style, the heading is placed in the right-hand corner of the letter.

561   The **inside address** is placed at the left-hand margin, four to seven spaces below the heading. It should include the name and complete address of the person and/or company you are writing. (Place a person's title after his or her name. Separate the title from the name with a comma. If the title is two or more words, place the title separately on the next line.)

562   The **salutation** is placed two spaces below the inside address. For a specific person, use a salutation like *Dear Miss . . . , Dear Ms. . . . , Dear Mr. . . . .* For a letter addressed to a person by title, use *Dear Sir, Dear Madam,* or *Dear (Title).* For a company, group, or organization, use *Gentlemen, Dear Sirs,* or *Dear (Company name).* Place a colon at the end of the salutation. (Check the first line of the inside address to determine the right salutation to use.)

563   The **body** of the business letter is placed two lines below the salutation. The information in the body should be clearly and brief-

ly written. Double-space between each paragraph. In a letter following the full-block style, do not indent the first line of each paragraph. In a letter following the semi-block style, indent the first line of each paragraph. (Indent five spaces if typed.)

564   The **closing** is placed two spaces below the body. Use *Very truly, Yours truly,* or *Sincerely* for a business letter closing. Place a comma at the end of the closing. In a full-block letter, the closing is placed at the left-hand margin. The closing should line up with the heading in a letter following the semi-block style.

565   Your full **signature** should end a business letter. It is written beneath the closing. If you are typing your letter, skip four lines and type your full name. Then, write your signature between the closing and your typed name.

566 Types of Business Letters

You're not in business, and business letters, by their very nature, are written for business reasons. So why should a junior high or middle school student know how to write a business letter?

You may need special information for a school report, as in the model business letter. As a member of your school and community, you may feel the need to "sound off" or express an opinion. As a consumer you may need to order a product or complain about a product you've already bought. And as a teenager in need of money, you may need to apply for a part-time job. For these reasons it's important for you to know how to write a good business letter.

The four situations presented in the last paragraph all require a different type of business letter. When you ask for information in a letter, you are writing a letter of inquiry. When you express an opinion by letter, you will probably write a letter to an editor or official. You may write a letter of complaint when you are unhappy with something you've purchased. And, you should write a letter of application when you are applying for a job by letter.

567 Letter of Inquiry

A **letter of inquiry** in which you ask for information or answers to your questions should be short and to the point. Word your letter so that there can be no question as to what it is you need to know. (See 557 for an example of a letter of inquiry.)

There are many organizations which offer up-to-date information at no cost. (Others may charge a small fee.) When you are doing research for a school report, one of these organizations will very likely offer valuable facts about your report topic. Your teachers and school librarians may have some suggestions for places to send for up-to-date information.

568 Letter to an Editor or Official

A **letter to an editor or official** is written to complain about something or to compliment someone. As with all business letters, this type of letter should be clear and to the point. Don't be overly complimentary or overly critical. Also, back up your opinions with specific facts and examples. Opinions supported by facts have a better chance of being listened to (or published if you are writing to a newspaper). When you are complaining, end your letter by suggesting ways to change or improve what you see as a bad situation.

569 Model Letter to an Editor

511 State Street
San Antonio, TX   78212
January 21, 1986

Editor
Goode Times
Goode Junior High
San Antonio, TX   78217

Dear Editor:

As we all know, the lunch hours here at Goode are a real mess! We are rushed through our lunches and then herded outside to stand around or goof off. What a waste of time!

What we need in our school is a more organized, meaningful noon hour for those students who don't like to waste their time. I have four suggestions as to how this could be done:

1. Those students who don't like to gulp down their lunches should be given more time in the cafeteria to enjoy their meals.
2. The gym should be opened for organized activities like volleyball and basketball.
3. The computer lab should be opened for students interested in computer activities.
4. A silent reading and study area should be created for those students who want to read or do homework.

I don't think my suggestions are out of line. We already have teachers and aides assigned to noon-hour supervision. I'm sure a teacher or aide would rather supervise or participate in more meaningful activities. And the students, at least all of my friends, would gladly participate in the activities I've suggested.

If you feel the same way I do about the noon-hour situation, contact your student council representative. Talk to your teachers and Mr. Jones about the situation. Also, talk to your parents. Ask them to discuss this topic at the next Parent-Teacher Council meeting.

If we all work together, I'm sure we can make some much-needed improvements.

Thank you,

Dawn Smith

Dawn Smith

570 Letter of Complaint

Caveat emptor, a Latin term meaning "let the buyer beware," is a caution to everyone to be very careful when buying something. If you are a careful buyer, you reduce the amount of risk of ending up with something that doesn't do what you had hoped. However, even the careful buyer is going to have trouble with a product at some time.

When you do have a problem with something you buy, your first step naturally will be to contact the store where you bought the product. Sometimes the local store can take care of the problem. Other times, however, the store will not be able to help you. Or, maybe you purchased the product by mail. In both cases, you will need to write a letter of complaint.

In a **letter of complaint,** carefully and clearly *describe the product.* · Then, *describe the problem* and what may have caused the problem. (Don't waste a lot of time explaining how unhappy you are.) Explain any *action you have already taken* to solve the problem. End your letter with *the action you would like the reader* (company) *to take* to solve the problem.

571 Model Letter of Complaint

625 Oak Avenue
Fort Atkinson, WI   53538
October 5, 1986

Customer Service Manager
Rightway Fund Raisers
2525 Capital Drive
Springfield, IL   62701

Dear Sir:

At the beginning of the semester, I ordered a hooded sweatshirt from your company through a fund raiser sponsored by our school's music department. When I received my sweatshirt, I experienced quite a shock. The hood was sewn on the wrong way.

The hood is on the front of the sweatshirt—the same side with our school name printed on it. I showed the sweatshirt to our music director who was as surprised as I was when he inspected it. He suggested that I return the sweatshirt along with a letter explaining my problem and a copy of my receipt of payment.

I'm sure once you read this letter and inspect the sweatshirt, you'll want to send me a new sweatshirt with the hood sewn on the right way. I would appreciate receiving my new sweatshirt as soon as possible since I'm very anxious to wear it.

Sincerely,

Martin Miller

Martin Miller

572 Letter of Application

The jobs available to junior high or middle school students are limited, as you well know. Typically, students at your age do some babysitting, lawn work, or other jobs around the neighborhood. When a job opportunity does come along for something like summer work in a camp or city park, there will naturally be a lot of other students interested in that job. Your chances of being hired will be greatly improved if you make a good first impression. This can be done very nicely in a well-written letter of application.

573 Model Letter of Application

229 Main Street
Elk Grove, WI 53410
April 14, 1986

Director
Camp Watumen
2323 Lake Drive
Elk Grove, WI 53224

Dear Sir:

I am applying for the position of Day Camp counselor which was posted on the job board at our school, Elk Grove Middle School.

I am 13 and in the eighth grade. I'm 5'4", weigh 105 pounds, and am very athletic. There are five members in my family, and I am the oldest child.

While I was an elementary student, I attended Camp Watumen Day Camp for three summers. Because of my experience as a day camper, I know that it takes hard work, dependability, and athletic ability to be a good counselor. I feel I have these qualities.

I'm an honor student at my school, and I've missed only three days over the past two years. I've also been a member of the volleyball team and student council at Elk Grove. Last summer I earned my Junior Lifesaving Certificate as well.

Please feel free to contact Miss Jill Capewell, Elk Grove student council advisor, and Mrs. Eileen Jones, a neighbor for whom I babysit, for references. They have agreed to talk with you about my abilities.

May I call you after 3:00 p.m. on Wednesday, April 17, to set up a time for an interview? If this is not convenient, please call me any day after 2:30 p.m. at 256-5494. I look forward to meeting you.

Sincerely,

Julie Johnson

Julie Johnson

574 As in all business letters, a letter of application should be clear and to the point. In the first paragraph, you should identify the job you are applying for and explain how you heard about the job. In the second paragraph, you should give your age, year in school, and,

possibly, information about your size and health if that is important for the job. You might also add information about your family (family size, parents' occupations, etc.) in this paragraph.

In the third paragraph, describe your personal qualifications for the job. Since you probably have few job-related experiences, think of things you do around your house or neighborhood that are related to the job. Also, think of your classes and extracurricular activities in school. Make sure that you sound interested and qualified for the job when you write this paragraph. (*Note:* This section of your letter might be more than one paragraph in length.)

You might want to include a paragraph in which you give two or more people as references. References are people other than family members who know you well and would be willing to talk to an employer about you. Make sure you get permission from that person to use him or her as a reference.

End your letter by asking for an interview at the employer's convenience. Give your telephone number and when you can be reached.

Carefully proofread your letter of application before you send it. This letter is your first contact with an employer, so you want it to read smoothly and be free of careless errors.

575 Writing the Business Letter

Use the following summary checklist to help you write a good business letter.

576 Prewriting: Selecting a Subject

- Write a business letter
  - ...if you need to send for information.
  - ...if you want to express an opinion.
  - ...if you want to complain about something you've bought.
  - ...if you want to apply for a job.

577 Planning: Preparing to Write

- Check your handbook for the requirements for the different types of business letters.

  > Letter of Inquiry
  > Letter to an Editor or Official
  > Letter of Complaint
  > Letter of Application

- Gather all of the details and facts you need.
- Organize your ideas and facts in a general topic outline.

578 Writing: The First Draft

- Write honestly and naturally, but keep the style somewhat formal.
- Follow your topic outline.
- Write short paragraphs. (This does not mean that a paragraph should be only one or two sentences.)

579 Rewriting: Revising the First Draft

- Make sure you have included the necessary facts and details.
- Make sure you have written honestly and sincerely.
- Make sure your letter is easy to read.
- Make sure you have followed one of the business letter styles.
- Make sure you proofread for punctuation, capitalization, and usage errors. (Pay special attention to the capitalization and punctuation of the heading, inside address, and salutation.)
- Make sure your letter is neatly written or typed.
    - Center the letter and keep the margins even.
    - Use consistent and even spacing.
    - Use only one side of the paper.

(Note: If the body of your letter carries over to a second page, the name of the person you're writing should be placed at the top left-hand margin. Skip two lines after the name.)

580 Addressing the Envelope

- Place the full name and complete address of the person to whom the letter is being sent slightly to the left of the middle of the envelope.
- Place your return address in the upper left-hand corner of the envelope.
- Place the correct postage in the upper right-hand corner of the envelope.

MR JAMES EVANS
512 N ADAMS AVE
WINONA MN 55987

NORTHERN CORP
ATTN D J HENKHAUR
XYZ CORP RM 4A
MAJOR INDUSTRIAL PARK
CLEVELAND OH 44135

Note: There are two acceptable forms for writing the addresses on the envelope. In the traditional form, you use upper- and lower-case letters as well as punctuation and abbreviations. In the newer form preferred by the postal service, four important steps must be followed:

1. Capitalize everything in the addresses.
2. Use the list of common abbreviations found in the National ZIP Code Directory.
3. Don't use any punctuation.
4. Use the special two-letter abbreviations found in the ZIP Code Directory.

Note below the difference between the traditional form and the new form for addressing an envelope.

Old System

Mr. James Evans
512 North Adams Ave.
Winona, MN 55987

New System

MR JAMES EVANS
512 N ADAMS AVE
WINONA MN 55987

There are various combinations for addresses. Here are some examples:

MISS TRISH DATON
BOX 77
HOUSTON TX 77008

ACCOUNTING DEPT
STEVENSON LTD BLDG 18
2632 FOURTH ST
DULUTH MN 55803

MS JOAN JACKSON
261 MASON ST APT 44
TORONTO ONTARIO
CANADA

NORTHERN CORP
ATTN D J HENKHAUR
XYZ CORP RM 4A
MAJOR INDUSTRIAL PARK
CLEVELAND OH 44135

MR TEDDY BARE
PRESIDENT
ACME TOY COMPANY
4421 RANDOLPH ST
CHEYENNE WY 82001

581 Folding the Letter

The *preferred* method for folding a letter is used with a standard-sized (4 1/4" x 9 1/2") business envelope.

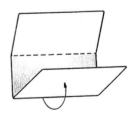

1. Begin by folding the bottom edge of the letter so that the paper is divided into thirds.
2. Next, fold the top third of the letter down and crease the edges firmly.
3. Finally, insert the letter into the envelope with the open end at the top.

A second method of folding is used when your envelope is smaller than the traditional business envelope.

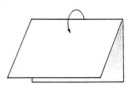

1. Begin by folding the letter in half.
2. Next, fold the letter into thirds.
3. Insert the letter into the envelope.

The Book Review

582   A book review is a special type of persuasive writing. In a book review, you state an opinion about a part (or parts) of a book you have read. You then support that opinion with specific facts and details taken from the book. The subject for a book review usually comes from one or more of the four main parts of a book—the plot, the characters, the setting, or the theme.

Note: A book review is different than a traditional book report in which you usually summarize the plot or state whether or not you liked the book.

583   ## Preparing to Write

To write a good book review, you need to read a book very carefully. And, you will need to reread those parts of the book you plan to use in your review. Also, you will need to know what kind of book you are reading—modern romance novel, historical novel, science fiction, biography, and so on. It would be wrong to criticize a biography because it lacks action and suspense. A biographer attempts to write about the life of an important person in a special way, a way that helps the reader understand that person better. A biographer isn't trying to write an action-packed story.

In addition, you need to have some understanding of the basic parts of a story when you write a review. The basic parts of a short story or novel are the plot, characters, setting, and theme. (See the "Literary Terms," 736, for an explanation of each basic part.) A book review, at times, will also include information about the style of the book. Style deals with the way in which a book is written—the word choice, the sentences, and the paragraphs. Junior high and middle school students often find it difficult to write about style since they are still learning the art of writing themselves. As a result, it would be best for you to concentrate on the four basic parts of a book when you write a review.

Use the "Summary: Thinking and Writing," 660, to help you write your book review. As you do, keep in mind that a review is a type of persuasive writing. (Persuasive writing includes a statement of opinion supported by facts and details.) Also, use the list of ideas which follows to help you choose a specific subject (statement of opinion) for your review. If you are asked to write a one-paragraph review, begin by choosing one of the basic parts of a story (plot, characters, theme, or setting) to write about. If you are assigned a longer book review, choose related ideas from more than one basic part of a story (theme and character, for example). Finally, always use the present tense when writing about a story.

584 Ideas for Book Reviews

585 Plot (The action of the story)

1. The story includes a number (2, 3, 4 . . .) of suspenseful and surprising events.
2. The story includes some or many predictable events.
3. Certain parts of the story are confusing.
4. The climax (the most important event) changes the story in an interesting way . . . in a believable way . . . in an unbelievable way.
5. There are a number (2, 3, 4 . . .) of important events which lead to the outcome or ending of the story.
6. The ending is surprising . . . predictable . . . unbelievable.

586 Characters

1. The main character changes from _____ to _____ by the end of the story.
2. Certain forces or circumstances—people, setting, events, or ideas—make the main character or characters act as they do.
3. A certain character acts believably or unbelievably when . . .
4. _____ is the main character's outstanding personality trait. (You may choose to point out more than one outstanding trait in some cases.)
5. The main character does the right thing when . . .
6. I can identify with the main character when . . .

Note: Concentrate on the main characters if you write about the characters in your review.

587 Setting (The time and place of the story)

1. The setting helps make the story exciting.
2. The setting has an important effect on the main character.
3. The setting (in a historical novel) increased my knowledge of a certain time in history.
4. The setting (in a science fiction novel) creates a new and exciting world.
5. The setting in this book offers nothing new and exciting.
6. The setting could have played a more important role in this story.

588   Theme   (The author's statement or lesson about life)

1. Ambition... courage... greed... happiness... jealousy... is clearly a theme in (title of book).
2. The moral, "Don't judge a book by its cover" . . . "Haste makes waste" . . . "Hard work pays off," is developed in (title of book).
3. This book showed me what it is like to be . . .

589   ## Model Book Review Paragraph

The following is a model plan and book review paragraph about *Tom Sawyer*, a novel by Mark Twain.   The writer decided that the novel's main character, Tom Sawyer, has a very adventurous spirit, and he used this important personality trait as the subject of his review.   Four specific events from the book were used to support the writer's opinion or belief.

590   ### Plan

Topic Sentence: Tom Sawyer's adventurous spirit makes his boyhood exciting and, at times, very dangerous.

List of events that show (display) this trait:

1. Tom sneaks out of his house at midnight to join Huck Finn in a graveyard.
2. Tom, along with Huck and another friend, runs away to be a pirate.
3. Tom looks for hidden treasure.
4. Tom reenters the same cave where he and Becky Thatcher almost lost their lives.

591   ### One-Paragraph Book Review

Tom Sawyer's adventurous spirit makes his boyhood exciting and, at times, very dangerous.   One thing Tom likes to do is prowl around the town at all hours of the night.   One night Tom sneaks out of his house at midnight and joins his friend Huckleberry Finn in the town's graveyard.   Here, the boys witness Injun Joe killing the town doctor and are very nearly caught by the killer.   Tom also likes to read adventure stories and imagine himself as a daring adventurer.   At one point in the story, he decides to run away and become an adventurous pirate.   He convinces Huckleberry and another friend to join him, and the newly formed band of pirates is off to Jackson Island.   Another one of Tom's favorite pastimes is looking for hidden treasure.   Once, while searching an old, abandoned shack, Tom and Huck find a hidden treasure belonging to Injun Joe, a dangerous criminal.   At the end of the story, Tom reenters the cave where he and Becky Thatcher almost lost their lives once.   Tom knows that Injun Joe has moved his treasure from the shack to the cave, and he can't resist going after it.   His need for adventure and excitement gets Tom Sawyer into plenty of tight spots.

The Essay Test

592   The key to writing a good essay test is being well prepared. You must begin by organizing and reviewing the material
you have studied. Review the important names, dates, places, and
ideas and be ready to work them into your essay test answer. Also,
read and study the guidelines which follow. They will help you
prepare for and take the essay test.

593   ## Guidelines for Taking the Essay Test

1. Make sure you are ready to take the test. (See the "Test-Taking Skills," 728.) Bring all the needed materials (paper, two
   pens, etc.).

2. Practice writing short sample essays as you study. Begin reviewing several days before the test. Review the most difficult
   materials right up to the time the test begins.

3. Listen carefully to your teacher's instructions. How much time
   do you have for the test? Do all the questions count equally? Can you use any notes, a dictionary, or other books? Are
   there any corrections, changes, or additions to the test?

4. Look over the entire test to get an idea of what it covers. Jot
   down any important points you want to make sure to include later when you answer that question. Remember to spread out
   your time. Don't spend so much time answering one question
   that you run out of time before you can answer the others.

5. Read each essay question carefully, paying special attention to
   the "key word." Ask your teacher to explain any question you
   do not understand.

6. Follow the steps for "Planning and Writing the Essay Answer"
   which are given later in this section.

594 Understanding the Essay Test Question

Understanding what the teacher is asking for in an essay test question is very important. Too many students make the error of thinking that the best way to answer an essay question is to write down everything they know about the topic as fast as they can. But this is not the best way. The best way is to think carefully and plan before you write.

The first step in planning your essay answer is to read the question several times or until you are sure you know what the question is asking. As you read, you must pay special attention to the "key words" that are found in every essay question. These key words will tell you the kind of thinking and writing needed to answer the question correctly. For example, if the question asks you to *evaluate* an event or idea, but you simply *explain* what it is, you have not answered the question correctly. You have not thought "deeply" enough about the question. Your grade will probably be disappointing.

595 Key Words

The list which follows includes the most common key words used on essay tests. It also includes a definition of each word. Study these words carefully: It is the first step to improving your essay test scores.

596 **Classify:** When you are asked to *classify*, you must place people and things (especially plants and animals) together in a group because they are alike in some ways. In science there is an order which all groups follow when they are classified: phylum (or division), class, order, family, genus, species, and variety.

597 **Compare:** To *compare*, you must use examples to show how two things are alike.

598 **Contrast:** To *contrast*, you must use examples to show how two things are different.

599 **Define:** To *define*, you must tell what the word or subject in the question means. (See "Writing a Definition," 457.)

600 **Describe:** To *describe*, you must tell in "story" form how something or someone looks, feels, sounds, etc. You should use enough vivid details to create a clear word picture of the subject.

601 **Discuss:** To *discuss*, you must look at the topic from all sides and try to come to some conclusion about the importance of the topic. A discussion answer can get quite long, so plan carefully.

602 **Evaluate:** To *evaluate*, you must give your opinion (or an expert's opinion) of the value or worth of the subject. You must write about both the good points (advantages) and bad points (disadvantages).

603 **Explain:** To *explain*, you must tell how something happens or show how something works. Use reasons, causes, or step-by-step details when you explain.

604 **Identify:** To *identify*, you must answer the *who, what, when, where, why,* and *how* questions in an organized paragraph or essay.

605 **List:** To *list*, you must include a specific number of examples, reasons, causes, or other details. You will number your answer in some way: *first, second, finally,* etc.

606 **Outline:** To *outline,* you must organize your answer (facts and details) into main points and sub-points. In some cases, you will use an actual outline to do this; other times, you will present your main points and sub-points in paragraph form.

607 **Prove:** To *prove*, you must present facts and details which show clearly that something is true.

608 **Relate:** To *relate*, you must show how two or more things are connected.

609 **Review:** To *review*, you must summarize the most important points about the subject.

610 **State:** To *state*, you must present your ideas about the subject using sentences which are brief and to the point.

611 **Summarize:** To *summarize*, you must present just the main points. Details, illustrations, and examples are seldom included in a summary.

612 **Trace:** To *trace*, you must present (one step at a time) those details or events which show the history or progress of the subject.

Planning and Writing the Essay Answer

In addition to a good understanding of the key words used in essay questions, you must also understand how to actually write the essay answer. The following steps should help:

1. **Read the question** several times or until you clearly understand what the question is asking you to write. (Pay special attention to the "key word.")

2. **Reword the question** into a topic sentence. *Note:* It often helps to drop the key word and add a word (or words) which states the overall point or topic you are going to cover in your answer. (Notice these changes in the following examples.)

> **Question:** *Describe* one important fund-raising event staged to help famine victims in Africa.
>
> **Topic Sentence:** One important fund-raising event staged to help famine victims in Africa was the Live Aid concert. (The key word, *describe,* has been dropped; the main topic, *the Live Aid concert,* has been added.)

3. **Outline the main points** you plan to cover in your answer and arrange them in the best possible order (time, order of importance, cause and effect). Don't try to include too many details in your outline—you may run short on time.

4. **Write your essay.** Your opening sentence will be your topic sentence (the reworded question). Then include any additional information needed to make the rest of your answer clear. Use connecting words (*first, second, third,* etc.) to keep you on track.

> **One-paragraph answer:** If you feel that only one paragraph is needed to answer the question, use all of your main points in this one paragraph. Arrange the information in the best possible way. Your arrangement will depend on the question being asked. It might be chronological (time order), order of importance, comparison, contrast, and so on.
>
> **Two- or Three-paragraph answer:** If the question is too complicated to be answered in a single paragraph, use your topic sentence in the first paragraph. Also include one of your main points in the first paragraph. Use facts, examples, reasons, or other details to back up your first point.
>
> Begin your second paragraph with another one of your main points and add details as you did in paragraph one. Do the same for a third paragraph if one is necessary. End your essay with a sentence (or two) which summarizes the overall point you are trying to make.

Note: For a sample essay test answer, see the "Model Understanding Paragraph," 625, on the Live Aid concert.

To write well, you must be able to __think__ well.

1. *Recalling*
2. *Understanding*
3. *Generalizing*
4. *Judging*

Thinking and Writing

614   When you are with friends, it is easy to talk about what you like and don't like about school or what you like and don't like about popular music and television shows. It is a little different when you're talking to someone you don't know very well because you're never sure how he or she will react to something you say. If this person questions something you say, you might have to support or back up one of your ideas or opinions. And, as you probably know, this is not an easy thing to do.

It is especially difficult to share your ideas and opinions in one of your classes. Your teachers expect you to support or back up what you say or write with clear facts and details. They know that supporting your ideas and opinions is a very special skill which requires careful thinking. This is why teachers give you so many assignments each year to practice this skill. Anytime you write a factual or persuasive paragraph or answer an essay test question, you are practicing the skill of supporting your ideas and opinions.

But learning how to support your ideas and opinions is not easy. There are no real shortcuts. You simply have to practice thinking and writing as much as you can. You must also practice and improve your reading, listening, and study skills. These skills help you form opinions which are based on facts. They also help you collect and organize facts and details to support your opinions.

Conclusion: Thinking and writing are very closely related. Your ability to write clearly and effectively is closely related to your ability to think clearly and effectively.

615 Levels of Thinking

Generally, in junior high or middle school, you will use four general levels of thinking when you work on factual or persuasive writing assignments. These levels of thinking are **recalling, understanding, generalizing**, and **judging**. *Recalling* is a very basic level of thinking; *judging* is a very advanced level. All of these levels of thinking are connected. That is, you never use just one level of thinking for an assignment, except if you are asked to simply recall or list information. For example, if you are asked in an assignment to use a very advanced level of thinking like *judging*, you must also be able to use the other types of thinking: *recalling, understanding*, and *generalizing*.

An explanation of each level of thinking follows. These explanations will help you understand and use the different levels of thinking in your writing assignments. Some common writing assignments which use each level of thinking will be given at the beginning of each explanation. Also, a list of key words related to the different levels of thinking will be given. These key words are often used by teachers when they give you writing assignments or essay tests. Knowing that these words are related to a certain level of thinking will help you work on your writing for assignments and tests. Each explanation will end with a sample thinking and writing assignment.

616 **Recalling Information**

Key Words: Each of the following words is often used in writing assignments and essay test questions which ask you to recall information.

Recall   Identify   List   Name   Remember   Repeat   Report

617 Listening, Reading, and Remembering

The most basic type of thinking you practice in school is recalling information. This type of thinking is needed when you are asked to remember and repeat information which you discussed in class or read about in a textbook. Since your teachers expect you to recall the most important information, make sure that you listen carefully in class and that you read carefully in your textbook. You don't want to miss any important facts and details needed for an assignment. Also, take good notes as you listen in class and as you read in your textbook. Always underline the important facts and details in your notes. Think of the five W's—the *who, what, when, where,* and *why*—of an event or idea when you underline information. In addition, think of the facts and details that your teacher emphasized in class and those that were emphasized in your textbook.

171

618 Reviewing

To help you remember important information, review your notes as often as you can. Pay special attention to the facts and details you have underlined. Also, review the chapters you've read in your textbook to make sure you haven't missed any important facts and details in your notes. In addition, try reading your notes out loud and reviewing them with a friend. If you follow these suggestions, recalling information will be no problem for you.

619 Recalling on Tests

Recalling is a level of thinking most often used when you answer multiple-choice, matching, and fill-in-the-blank questions on a test. Your teachers will give very few writing assignments in which they want you simply to recall information. Usually, this level of thinking is combined with other more advanced levels of thinking in writing assignments. However, some very basic essay test questions might ask you simply to recall information. Also, your teacher might give you a review writing assignment and ask you to write down what you remember from a class discussion or from a chapter in your textbook.

Let's say you are studying the world hunger problem in your social studies class. As one part of this unit, you read about Live Aid, a project which was organized to save the lives of starving people in Africa. As a basic essay question, your teacher might ask you to list in sentences five important facts you have learned about the concert organized by Live Aid officials. (When your teacher asks you to *list* information, he or she is really asking you to *recall* information.) Read carefully the sample answer which follows. Each point in the list includes important information which has been recalled about the concert.

620 Using Recall to Answer a Test Question

Essay Test Question: List in sentences five important facts you have learned about the Live Aid concert.

Answer:
1. In 1985, the Live Aid concert was organized to raise money for hunger relief in Africa.
2. Over 60 rock stars like Bob Dylan and Sting performed at the concert for no charge.
3. There were really two Live Aid concerts held at the same time, one in Philadelphia and one in London.
4. The two concerts were televised throughout the world.
5. Live Aid earned over $70 million for relief aid.

Understanding Information

Descriptive Paragraph
Summary Paragraph
Essay Test Questions
Review Writing
Paraphrasing

621 Understanding Information

Key Words: Each of the following words is often used in writing assignments and essay test questions which ask you to understand information.

Understand Describe Explain Paraphrase
Restate Review Summarize

Your teachers will often ask you to do more than simply recall information in list form. You will be asked to understand the information as well. Understanding means that you not only have to recall or remember information, but you also must know this information well enough to reword—put into your own words—what you've learned in a writing assignment like a paragraph. And, just as understanding is a more advanced level of thinking than recalling, a paragraph is a more advanced level of writing than a simple list of remembered information.

622 Rewording Your Notes

To help you understand important information, try rewording the facts and details in your notes which you've underlined or identified as important. If you are able to clearly reword this information, you probably have a good understanding of the facts and details in your notes. If you can't do this, make sure that you ask your teacher for help in understanding any information in your notes which confuses you.

173

623 Reading and Understanding

To understand information from a textbook, you must be a careful reader. Preview each chapter you read before you begin a complete (thorough) reading. This will give you a general understanding of the chapter. Read all of the titles and headings. They will also help you understand the information in a chapter. Then, read slowly and carefully so that you don't miss any important facts and details. Make sure to study all maps, charts, graphs, and illustrations as you read. And make sure to take good, clear notes which you can study later on.

To understand information, you must be a careful reader. You must read the headings, study the charts, examine the illustrations, and take good notes.

624 Understanding in Paragraphs and Essay Tests

Understanding is a very important level of thinking which you will use when you work on the basic paragraphs and essay test questions assigned to you by your teachers. Anytime one of your teachers asks you to **describe**, **explain**, or **summarize** ideas or events, he or she is asking you first to understand information, and, then, to retell what you've learned in a paragraph(s). This type of assignment lets your teacher know how well you understand the information covered in class or in a reading assignment. Always concentrate on being clear and complete when you retell what you've learned. However, you don't need to include everything you remember and understand. Stick to the very important ideas. (See "Paragraphs," 430, for an explanation and examples of this basic type of writing.)

Let's say as a writing assignment (or essay test question) your social studies teacher asks you to describe in a paragraph the Live Aid concert, a fund-raising event you talked about in class. In an assignment of this type, your teacher is really asking you to **understand** as well as **recall** the important facts and details—the *who*, *what*, *when*, *where*, and *why*—about this event. He or she then wants you to retell this information in your own words in a clear paragraph. The paragraph below is a sample of what you might have written in a description of the Live Aid concert.

625   **Model Understanding Paragraph**

    One important fund-raising event staged to help famine victims in Africa was the Live Aid concert. This concert was organized in London by a group of concerned people under the direction of Irish rock singer, Bob Geldof. Live Aid took place in Philadelphia and London on July 13, 1985, and featured over sixty of the world's most famous rock stars. Older stars like Bob Dylan and Mick Jagger joined new stars like Sting and Lionel Richie. All of the musicians performed at no charge. Live Aid attracted 162,000 rock fans in person, and twelve television satellites showed the concert to over a billion viewers in 150 countries. More than $70 million was raised from ticket sales, television rights, and donations. Most of the money came from the donations of large corporations and from the donations of people who pledged money by phone during the concert. Live Aid ended up being the biggest money-making event staged to help the hunger victims in Africa.

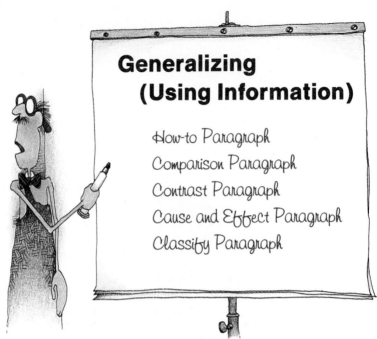

**Generalizing
(Using Information)**

How-to Paragraph

Comparison Paragraph

Contrast Paragraph

Cause and Effect Paragraph

Classify Paragraph

626 Generalizing (Using Information)

Key Words: Each of the following words is often used in writing assignments and essay test questions which ask you to generalize or use information.

Choose Compare Contrast Classify Demonstrate
Give Group Map Organize Show Select Use

Generalizing is an advanced level of thinking. Generalizing is using the specific facts and details you have learned about a topic to arrive at a general conclusion or a more meaningful understanding. You might, for example, use the specific facts you've learned in a geography class to show how two countries are very much alike or not alike at all. Or you might use the information you've gathered in a science class or lab to come to an understanding of why light travels faster than sound. Your teachers will ask you to use this level of thinking when they feel you have had enough practice using the first two levels of thinking—recalling and understanding. Generalizing is especially important when you are asked to think and write about more than one main idea or event.

627 Deciding the Purpose

Basically, you must answer three important questions when you are thinking and writing at this level. The first important question you have to ask is "What is the purpose of this writing assignment?" Is it to give directions, to show how things are alike (comparing), to show how things are different (contrasting), to put similar ideas into groups (grouping), or to give reasons? These are the most common purposes for assignments which require you to generalize.

628 Selecting Facts and Details

The second important question you have to answer is "Which facts and details are the right ones to use for this assignment?" Let's say the purpose of an assignment is to give the directions for making something. You will want to select the facts and details which will make your directions clear and complete.

629 Organizing the Facts and Details

The third question you have to answer is "How should the facts and details for this writing assignment be organized?" Will you organize the details in the order in which they happened (chronological or time order), in the order of importance, or in the order of location? For example, chronological order would be the best way to organize a paper giving directions since giving the facts and details in the right order is very important in how-to paragraphs.

To help you generalize for certain writing assignments, use the following chart. It explains five common writing assignments which ask you to use the third level of thinking.

Writing Generalizations

630 How-to Paragraphs

Sample assignment: Give the complete directions on how to make a book cover.

Purpose: To give the full directions on how to do or make something.

Selecting details: Choose facts and details which make your directions clear and complete.

Organizing: Usually, how-to paragraphs are organized chronologically (by time).

631 Comparison Paragraphs

Sample assignment: Make a comparison between a fund-raising effort(s) organized in England to fight world hunger with any effort(s) organized in the United States to fight world hunger.

Purpose: To show that two (or more) ideas are alike in several important ways.

Selecting details: Choose facts and details which show the important similarities. (You need to select at least two or three similarities for a comparison to be worthwhile.)

Organizing: Usually, comparison paragraphs are organized by order of importance. That is, the most important similarity is either given first or, more commonly, last.

632 Contrast Paragraph

Sample assignment: Contrast two fund-raising efforts staged to fight world hunger.

Purpose: To show the important differences between two (or more) similar ideas or events.

Selecting details: Choose facts and details which identify important differences. (Select at least two or three important differences for a paragraph.)

Organizing: Contrast paragraphs are usually organized by order of importance. That is, the most important difference is given first or, more commonly, last.

Note: At times, your teacher might ask you to compare and contrast in the same writing assignment. This means you must include both similarities and differences. Check with your teacher for the number of similarities and differences you should include in an assignment of this type.

633 Grouping (Classifying)

Sample assignment: In a paragraph, *identify* different groups of people within one of the following subject areas: friends, teachers, aunts, cousins, sports fans, concert goers, etc. Include at least three groups for a paragraph.

Purpose: To identify or point out the different groups within a general subject area. This subject area can be anything from pet cats to sports fans to bus drivers.

Selecting details: Choose facts and details which identify meaningful or interesting groups. These groups should be related to some general idea or theme. For example, in a paragraph which groups different types of concert goers, the "concert personality" of different people could be the general idea or theme. You might know or have seen on television people who yell or scream throughout an entire concert, those who pretend they are a part of the band by singing and playing an "air guitar," and those who very seriously study the musicians and their special effects and equipment.

Organizing: Paragraphs which identify the groups within a subject area can be organized by order of importance or in chronological order.

634 Giving Reasons (Cause and Effect)

Sample assignment: In a paragraph, *identify* the important reasons for the hunger problem in Africa. (See the "Model Generalizing Paragraph," 637, for the completion of this assignment.)

Purpose: To identify the reasons or steps which "caused" or led to an important condition, decision, or result. Or, at a more advanced level, to come to a better understanding of a condition, decision, or result after thinking and writing about the reasons behind it.

Selecting details: Choose good reasons and enough facts and details to make each reason clear to the reader.

Organizing: Paragraphs which give reasons for something are organized chronologically or by order of importance.

635 More About Generalizing

Also, look for paragraphs or articles in textbooks, newspapers, and magazines which have purposes like those discussed above and see how other writers use generalizing, the third level of thinking and writing. The ways in which they generalize when they compare, contrast, or group information might help you understand better how to think and write at this level. Look closely for the facts and details each writer selects and the method of organization he or she chooses. If you have trouble finding paragraphs or articles yourself, your teacher should be able to help you find examples of writing at this level.

636 Generalizing in Writing Assignments

Generalizing is a level of thinking which you will use in more advanced paragraphs and longer assignments. Let's say as part of a world hunger unit that your social studies teacher asks you to write a paragraph which gives the reasons for the hunger problem in Africa. After studying your class notes and reading carefully, you decide that there are four important reasons for the hunger problem in Africa. The model which follows is an example of what you might have written for this assignment.

637 **Assignment:** In a paragraph, identify the important reasons for the hunger problem in Africa.

Model Generalizing Paragraph

Most areas in the world, except for Africa, have made progress in ending hunger. In Africa, there is less food per person today than there was in 1960. The most important reason for the hunger problem is the serious drought which has been going on in many parts of Africa. Some areas have not had a decent amount of rain for three years. Another important reason for the hunger problem is the lack of planning by many African nations for times of drought. For example, there are few food storage or irrigation systems in the drought stricken areas. Without these systems, people have no chance to prepare for difficult times. The hunger problem has also been caused by the poorly-run governments within certain African countries—especially Ethiopia and Chad. Governments in these countries are so concerned about staying in power that they spend very little time helping hunger victims. A final reason for the hunger problem is the lack of a good transportation system in most of the areas. Without good roads or railroads, transporting supplies to hunger victims who live in remote areas is almost impossible. Unless these conditions improve soon, it is estimated that over 35 million people will face starvation in Africa.

638 Judging Information

Key Words: Each of the following words is often used in writing assignments and essay test questions which ask you to judge information.

Judge Evaluate Criticize Decide Rate
Value Persuade Argue Convince Prove

639   Judging is the most advanced level of thinking and writing you will use in junior high or middle school.   Generally, when your teachers ask you to use this level of thinking for an assignment, they are asking you to do one of two things.   They are asking you to *evaluate* (rate the value of) the information you've learned.   Or, your teachers are asking you to *persuade* the reader (make the reader believe) that one of your opinions is a good one.

640 Evaluating

When you are asked to evaluate information for a thinking and writing assignment, you are, in effect, being asked to think like an "expert" on the topic.   You must understand a subject well enough to decide how important or valuable it is.   To become an expert, you must carefully study all the facts and details you've learned about a subject.

641 Studying a Subject

As you study, you must ask yourself whether these details reveal strengths or weaknesses about your subject. When you "know" your subject well enough to judge its value, you are ready to begin an evaluation. Start with a sentence—the topic sentence—which identifies your overall evaluation or rating of the subject's value. Then, follow with facts and details which prove your evaluation is a good one.

Note: Most of the important ideas and events you study in school will have both strengths and weaknesses, good points and bad points. Because of this, it is often difficult to evaluate a subject as completely successful and valuable or completely worthless. For example, the writer of the "Model Evaluating Paragraph" was unable to call Live Aid a complete success because getting supplies to famine victims in Africa was going to be so difficult.

642 Practicing Evaluating

To become a good evaluator of ideas and events, it might be helpful to study or review your class notes and your reading assignments in a new way. Normally, you study simply to remember and understand information. Try studying in a more advanced way, evaluating important ideas and events as you go along. Sometimes, you will find that you really don't have enough facts and details to make a good evaluation. When this is true, you will need to do a little extra research so that you can better evaluate the ideas you've been studying.

Thinking about your notes in this new way will help make *evaluating* a routine part of your studying or reviewing. Then, when your teacher asks you to *evaluate* in a writing assignment, you should be better prepared to think and write at this level.

You might also want to practice evaluating with a friend (or family member). Select an important topic you've studied in class and talk about it. Each person should bring up as many good points and bad points about the topic as possible. You might find that your friend has different facts and details about the topic than you do. A conversation of this kind should make it easier for you to evaluate the worth or importance of your topic. *Note:* Don't be surprised if you and your friend disagree about a topic's value. We don't all "see" things the same way.

643 Evaluating in Writing Assignments

Your teachers will probably not give you too many thinking and writing assignments at the evaluating level. (You will be expected to do much more evaluating in high school than in junior or middle school.) But your English teacher might ask you to evaluate the importance of a personal experience as part of an autobiography unit. Or you might be asked to write a book review in which you must evaluate some part of a book you've read. (See "Book Review," for an example.) In your social studies class, you might be asked to evaluate an important idea or event. Also, any time you plan a panel discussion or debate for any of your classes, you are thinking and writing at this level.

Let's say as part of a unit on world hunger in your social studies class you are asked to evaluate the Live Aid project. After studying your notes and reading about this project, you feel you have enough information to evaluate its value. The model which follows is an example of what you might have written for this assignment.

644 Assignment: Evaluate the Live Aid project.

Model Evaluating Paragraph

Live Aid has been a project with two main goals: first, to raise money for famine relief and, second, to get relief supplies to the famine victims in Africa. In terms of raising money, the project has been very successful since the Live Aid concert held in the summer of 1985 earned over $70 million for African famine relief. By the end of 1985, $32 million of this money had already been spent for food and medical supplies. But three problems are making it difficult to get these supplies to the famine victims. First, governments in some of the African countries are involved in civil wars and are not interested or able to work with Live Aid officials. Second, some of the worst famine conditions are occurring in hard-to-reach areas where there are few passable roads. Third, outdated railroads and the lack of available trucks make it difficult to even try to transport supplies. Even though these problems have not made things easy for Live Aid officials, they continue to ship supplies to Africa. They also have bought their own fleet of trucks and trailers to help transport the supplies. However, the number of starving people that they will be able to reach with life-saving aid—especially those in the remote areas—is still to be determined.

645 **Persuading**

When your teachers assign a persuasive thinking and writing assignment, they really are asking you to do two things. First, they are asking you to form an opinion—a personal feeling or belief—about some important or controversial subject. Second, they are asking you to judge or evaluate your opinion. You can do this by listing and then studying the important facts and details which you feel support your opinion. When you "know" your opinion is a good one—that is, you have plenty of good facts to support it—you are ready to begin your persuasive writing assignment. If you find that your opinion is not a very strong one—that is, you don't have many facts to support it—modify or change it until you have an opinion which you can support effectively.

646 **Guidelines for Persuasive Writing**

Use the six guidelines which follow to help you with persuasive thinking and writing assignments.

647 **1. Fact vs. Opinion**

Make sure you understand the difference between an opinion and a fact before you start a persuasive writing assignment. An opinion is a view or belief held by a person. A good opinion is based on fact, but it is not a fact itself. A fact is a specific statement which can be checked or proven to be true. Note below the difference between the opinion and the supporting facts. The opinion states a personal view about a teacher. The facts are specific and can be proven; they support the opinion.

Opinion: Mr. Brown might not be a popular teacher, but he has three qualities that make him a good teacher.

Facts: He is well organized for every class.
He is always concerned that we do our best.
He treats everyone fairly.

648   2. Forming an Opinion

Make sure you understand and believe the opinion you are trying to support.   It is difficult to write in a sincere, natural style if you don't really believe in your topic.

Note: Don't be afraid to form an opinion about a controversial issue or topic.   There is not much point in forming an opinion in which everyone already agrees.

649   3. Writing an Opinion Statement

Before an opinion can work well for a writing assignment, it must be well stated.   After you have chosen a specific subject, follow the simple formula given below to help you write a good opinion statement.

Formula: A specific subject (Mr. Brown) + a specific opinion or feeling (might not be a popular teacher, but he has three qualities that make him a good teacher.) = a good opinion statement.

Caution! Opinions including words which are strongly positive or negative like "all," "best," "every," "never," "none," or "worst" may be difficult to support.   For example, an exaggerated opinion statement like "All dogs chase mailmen" would certainly be impossible to support.

650   4. Supporting Your Opinion

When you support or defend an opinion, make sure you do so with clear, provable facts.   Otherwise, your reader probably won't believe your opinion.   Let's say you are supporting the opinion that "The Live Aid concert was a huge success."   Note the difference in the following supporting facts.

Provable Fact: "Twelve television satellites transmitted the Live Aid concert throughout the world."   (You simply have to read different reports of the concert to prove that this statement is true.)

Not a Provable Fact: "Most people who watched the concert donated as much money as they could to Live Aid."   (Certainly an exaggerated statement like this is untrue and impossible to prove.)

651   5. Organizing Your Facts

You can develop a persuasive thinking and writing assignment in two basic ways.   You can state your opinion or belief in the topic sentence (first sentence or two) and then support it with specific facts.   Or, you can start your assignment by presenting a number of specific facts which lead to a believable concluding or ending statement.   Your opinion or belief is made clear in this concluding statement.

Note: In the "Model Persuasive Paragraph," 434, an opinion about a teacher is stated in the topic sentence, and the rest of the paragraph is made up of facts which prove this opinion is a good one.

652 6. **Meaningless and Misleading Ideas**

Make sure that all of your ideas in a persuasive writing assignment are meaningful and well thought out. Often, young writers try to take shortcuts in persuasive thinking and writing assignments, and include meaningless and misleading ideas. Given below are examples of common meaningless and misleading ideas. Avoid these errors in your own writing.

653 a. Avoid statements which jump to a conclusion.

> "Because the Live Aid concert earned over $70 million, thousands of starving people in Africa will be saved."

Discussion: This statement jumps to a conclusion. It suggests that many people will be saved just because a concert earned a lot of money. However, there is much more to saving starving people than simply raising money.

654 b. Avoid statements which are supported with nothing more than the simple fact that the majority of the people also feel this way.

> "Mr. Brown is not a good teacher because most of the guys think he is really hard on them."

Discussion: This type of statement is based on the idea that if more than half the people believe something, it must be true. In other words, Mr. Brown can't possibly be a good teacher because most of the guys think he is hard on them. Certainly, there is more to judging the quality of a teacher than whether the majority of the students like him or not.

655   c. Avoid statements which contain a weak or misleading comparison.

> "Mr. Brown is a good teacher because he is a lot like Vince Lombardi."

Discussion: This statement could be a weak or misleading comparison. Often, a comparison can be helpful in persuasive writing. However, make sure the comparison is a fair one, otherwise it may hurt rather than help your argument. Comparing a teacher to a professional football coach is probably not a fair comparison to make.

656   d. Avoid statements which exaggerate the facts or mislead the reader.

> "Live Aid was a huge success in this country. The American people showed how generous and concerned they are by donating their hard-earned money to help the starving people in Africa."

Discussion: The second statement might be true, but it also could be an exaggeration which tricks us into believing that the majority of Americans donated to Live Aid. It could be that only a small part of the population actually contributed.

657   e. Avoid statements which appeal only to the reader's feelings and contain no factual information.

> "Live Aid was very successful because anything done to help the starving people is a good thing."

Discussion: This statement might appear to be factual, but it actually appeals to our feelings of sadness and pity. It is true that most efforts to fight world hunger are good. However, some efforts might give charities a bad name if they are poorly handled, especially if the money raised ends up in the wrong hands.

658   f. Avoid statements which contain part of the truth, but not the whole truth. These statements are called half-truths.

> "Mr. Brown is not a good teacher because he leaves school the very minute school is out each day."

Discussion: Even though the last portion of this statement is true, it is misleading because it does not contain the whole truth. The statement does not tell the reader the reason Mr. Brown leaves school so quickly. The "whole truth" is that Mr. Brown leaves so that he can travel to the high school where the track team he coaches is waiting for him to arrive.

659 Model Persuasive Paragraph

The "Model Persuasive Paragraph," 434, is an example of a thinking and writing assignment which states an opinion and supports it with provable facts. The writer begins the paragraph with an opinion of his gym teacher and then defends this opinion with three main points.

660 Summary: Thinking and Writing

Prewriting: *Selecting a Subject*

● Normally, your teacher will select the general subject for your essay assignment.

● As in any type of writing assignment, you should select a specific subject which interests you and meets the requirements of the assignment.

Planning: *Preparing the Subject*

● Gather provable facts and details to support your specific subject.

● Write a clear and thoughtful topic sentence (or thesis statement for longer assignments). Make sure this sentence identifies your specific subject and a clear opinion or belief.

● Select a method of organization.

● Write an outline or plan. Consider the different levels of thinking needed for the assignment as you plan your paper.

Writing: *Writing the First Draft*

● Start with your topic sentence or an interesting opening statement.

● Follow with sentences which add clear and provable facts and details.

● Write naturally, and use your outline or plan as a general guide.

● End with an effective concluding sentence.

Revising: *Improving the Writing*

● Make sure the main idea stated in your topic sentence is supported with plenty of good details. Take out details which don't help prove your point.

● If you are persuading or evaluating, make sure your argument is believable and meaningful. (Use the "Guidelines for Persuasive Writing," 459, as a guide when you review the opinion(s) and facts in your paper.)

● Make sure your sentences are clear and smooth reading.

● Check the word choice. Use strong, active words.

● Check the mechanics—the spelling, punctuation, and capitalization—of your paper.

● Write or type a neat final copy.

Using the Library

661   As a student writer, you have two sources of information. The first source is yourself. You should always begin with your own ideas, experiences, and knowledge whenever you write. The second source of information is other people and their ideas, experiences, and knowledge. The best way to collect information from other people is to talk to them directly.

Unfortunately, it is not always possible to sit down and talk to other people, especially people like doctors, lawyers, and scientists who are usually very busy. It is possible, however, to "listen" to these people as they tell about their past experiences. In fact, there is a place you can go nearly any time and share in the past experiences of thousands of people, among them some of the most famous people of all times.

By now you've probably figured out that the place to "listen" to these remarkable people is in your library. Only in your library can you find thousands upon thousands of stories just waiting to be told. Each book contains someone's special story—someone's personal thoughts, memories, ideas, and experiences—which you can use to add life and interest to your writing.

But before you can read these special stories, you have to know how and where to find them. Because there are so many books in your library, you can't simply walk up to the first shelf you come to and begin looking. It would be the same as going from house to house in a big city looking for a friend. You may know the name or subject of the book, but without the book's "address," there is little chance you'll ever find it.

662 Using the Card Catalog

You can find the address or *call number* of each book your library has by looking in the **card catalog.** The card catalog contains cards for each book and nearly all other materials located in the library. Each book is listed in the card catalog by *subject, author,* and *title.* This means you can find a book you are interested in even if you don't know the author or the exact title. All you really need to know is the subject or what the book is about.

The catalog cards will give you the following information: the call number (address), the author, title, subject, publisher, illustrator, copyright date, number of pages, and information about the content (sometimes called an *annotation*) of the book. See the sample catalog cards which follow. These are the same kind of cards you will find in your school's card catalog.

Sample Catalog Cards

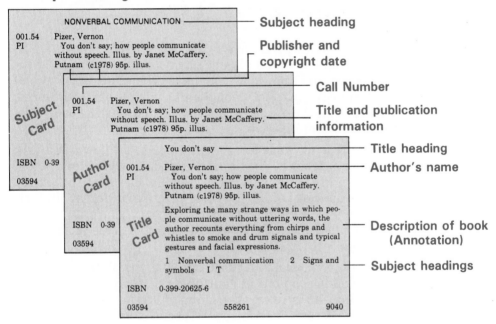

The cards in the card catalog are arranged in alphabetical order and placed in drawers similar to those shown on the next page. Each drawer is labeled clearly so that you can see at a glance which cards are contained in each drawer.

663 Inside the Card Catalog

To find out if your library contains a certain book, simply look in the drawer which covers the letters contained in the title of the book. If you don't know the title, but do know the author, check for the author card. Finally, if you don't know the title or the author, look under the general subject of the book. Also look under the subject if you are interested in finding several books on your topic.

Everything in the card catalog is listed alphabetically. However, certain words, numbers, and abbreviations are handled in a special way when they come first in a book's title. Look carefully at the examples and guidelines below:

McCarthy, Mary
Magnificent Seven (The)
MEDICINE—HISTORY
Medicine Before Physicians
1,000,000's of Everything
Mr. Chips Takes a Vacation

664 Titles

- If the first word in a title is an article *(a, an, the)*, you should skip over the article and begin looking for the title under the second word. **Example:** The title card for *The Magnificent Seven* is placed in the *M* drawer under *Magnificent*.

- If a title begins with a number, the card is placed in alphabetical order as if the number were spelled out. **Example:** The title card for *1,000,000's of Everything* is placed in the *M* drawer under *millions*.

191

- If the title begins with an abbreviation, the title is filed as if the abbreviation were spelled out. **Example:** The title card for *Mr. Chips Takes a Vacation* is placed in the *M* drawer under *Mister*.

665 Authors

- Authors are listed by last name first. **Example:** McCarthy, Mary

- Last names beginning with *Mc* are often filed as if they were written *Mac*.

666 Subjects

- Subject cards are listed alphabetically and are usually placed before titles which begin with the same word. **Example:** The subject card for MEDICINE—HISTORY comes before the title card for *Medicine Before Physicians*.

667 Finding a Book: The Call Number

Once you have found the card you are looking for in the card catalog, you are ready to begin searching for the book. First, copy down the call number of the book. Next, look for that number (or one close to it) on the shelves. Usually each shelf will have a sign listing the numbers of the books it contains. If not, go directly to the shelves and begin reading the numbers.

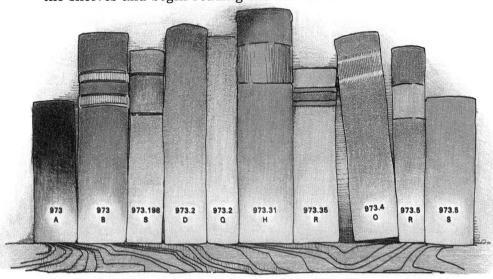

As you continue to look for your book, you must remember to read the call numbers very carefully. Some call numbers contain several decimal points and are much longer than other call numbers. For example, number 973.198 might at first appear to be larger than 973.2. It is, in fact, a "longer" number but not a larger one. You must keep this in mind as you search for your book.

Another point you should know about call numbers is that several books may have the same number on the top line. When this happens, you must look closely at the letters or numbers on the second line of the call number. In the illustration on the preceding page, you will notice that the first two books have the same number on the top line. You should also notice that because of this the books are arranged in order by the letter in the second line. This is why $\frac{973}{A}$ comes before $\frac{973}{B}$.

At this point, you might well ask where the call number for each book comes from and why some books have longer numbers than others. To begin with, most call numbers are assigned according to the Dewey Decimal System, a system set up to help people arrange books more efficiently. Using this system, a librarian can give each book a separate number, a number which tells the reader what that book is about.

A history book, for example, is given a number in the 900's, while a language book is given a number in the 400's. This means that books on the same subject are given similar numbers and are placed together on the shelves. This makes your job of locating several books on the same topic much easier.

In the Dewey Decimal System, all knowledge is divided into ten main classes. Each class is assigned a set of numbers (100's, 200's, 300's, . . . 900's).

668

The Ten Classes of the Dewey Decimal System

000	Generalities	500	Pure Sciences
100	Philosophy	600	Technology (Applied Science)
200	Religion	700	The Arts
300	The Social Sciences	800	Language and Rhetoric
400	Language	900	Geography and History

Each class is further divided into divisions (See the chart which follows.) Each division is then divided into ten sections, each with its own number. These sections are divided into as many subsections as necessary for that particular topic. Together these numbers make up the class number of a book.

669

Understanding the Dewey Decimal Class Number

900	History	Class
970	History of North America	Division
973	History of the United States	Section
973.7	History of the U.S. Civil War	Subsection
973.74	History of Civil War Songs	Subsection

193

In addition to its class number, a call number contains the first letter of the author's last name. It may also contain a cutter number assigned by the librarian to help in shelving the book and the first letter of the title's first significant word. Together these numbers and letters make up the call number or address of the book.

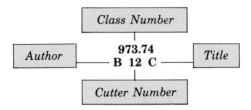

670   *Note:* Fiction books (novels) and individual biographies are not classified by subject as are the rest of the books in the library. Fiction is usually kept in a separate section of the library where the books are arranged by the author's last name. (Classic literature is, however, listed and shelved in the literature class.) Individual biographies and autobiographies are arranged on a separate shelf by the last name of the person written about.

671 **Reader's Guide to Periodical Literature**

The Reader's Guide to Periodical Literature is another useful guide to finding information in the library. The *Reader's Guide* is an organized list of all the latest magazine articles, articles you may find useful for a number of classroom reports or writing assignments.

The *Reader's Guide* is especially useful if you are looking for current information, information which has been reported during the last 12 to 18 months. To use the *Reader's Guide,* simply select the volume which covers the time period (month or year) you are interested in. If, for example, you hope to find a magazine article on a scientific discovery made in November of last year, select the volume covering November and possibly December of that year. You can locate an article by looking up either the author or the subject.

When you find an article you would like to read, fill out a request form *(call slip).* If no forms are available, simply put the title, date, and volume of the magazine on a piece of paper and take it to the librarian. The librarian will get the magazine for you. Look closely at the sample page from the *Reader's Guide.* Notice the following:

• The *Reader's Guide* is cross referenced. This means you will find one or more subject headings listed along with each article. You can go to these other subjects in the *Reader's Guide* to find more information on the same topic.

Sample Reader's Guide Page

ENGLER, PAUL
Oil Shortage today. Beef tomorrow? por Farm J 99:B16 Mr '75

AUTHOR ENTRY

ENGLISH
ENVIRONMENTAL engineering (buildings)
Architecture, energy, economy, and efficiency. G. Soucie. Audubon 77:122 S '75

Autonomous living in the Ouroboros house. S.J. Marcovich. il Pop Sci 207:80-2+ D '75

Conditioned air gets used three times in an energy-conscious design. il Archit Rec 158:133-4 N '75

Energy house from England aims at self-sufficiency. D. Scott. il Pop Sci 207:78-80 Ag '75

NAME OF AUTHOR

Houses designed with nature: their future is at hand; Ouroboros and integral projects. S. Love. bibl il Smithsonian 6:46-53 D '75

DATE

OCF presents awards for energy conservation. il Archit Rec 158:34 D '75

PM visits a house full of energy-saving ideas. J.F. Pearson. il Pop Mech 144:59+ Ag '75

Profession and industry focus on solar energy. il Archit Rec 158:35 Ag '75

NAME OF MAGAZINE

Round table: toward a rational policy for energy use in buildings; with introd by W. F. Wagner, Jr. il Archit Rec 158:8, 92-9 mid-Ag '75

Solar energy systems: the practical side. il Archit Rec 158:128-34 mid-Ag '75

VOLUME

ENVIRONMENTAL health
Environmental hazards and corporate profits. Chr Cent 92: 404 Ap 23 '75
See also
Environmental diseases

"SEE ALSO" CROSS REFERENCE

ENVIRONMENTAL impact statements. See Environmental policy
ENVIRONMENTAL indexes. See Environment—Statistics
ENVIRONMENTAL law
Capitol watch. G. Alderson Liv Wildn 38:60 Wint '74; 39:33 Spr; 42 Jl; 41 O '75

How to save a river; Bellport, N.Y. high students, sponsoring Carmans River bill.
A. Rubin, Sr Schol 105:4-7 Ja 16 '75

PAGE NUMBER

Overview: law. A.W. Reitze Jr and G.L. Reitze. See issues of Environment
See also
Air pollution — Laws and legislation
Land utilization — Laws and regulations

SUBJECT ENTRY

ENVIRONMENTAL movement
After setbacks — new tactics in environmental crusade. J. McWethy. il U.S. News 78:62-3 Je 9 '75

Be a part of Food day every day. Org Gard & Farm 22:32+ Ap '75

TITLE OF ARTICLE

Dialogue: C. Amory versus environmental groups on hunting issue. R.E. Hall. Conservationist 29:1 Ap '75

Ecological view. J. Marshall. Liv Wildn 39: 5-10 Spr '75

Environment, a mature cause in need of a lift. L.J. Carter. Science 187:45-6+ Ja 10 '75

Junior leagues focus on community education; environmental projects. M.D. Poole, por Parks & Rec 10:21+ D '75

Obligation and opportunity. R.F. Hall. Conservationist 29:1 Je '75

"SEE" CROSS REFERENCE

Organic living almanac. See issues of Organic gardening and farming

Prophets of shortage; address, July 11, 1975. D. Hodel. Vital Speeches 41:621-5 Ag 1 '75

What conservationists think about conservation; results of questionnaire. H. Clepper. il Am For 81:28-9+ Ag '75
See also
Canada-United States environmental council
Industry and the environmental movement
Exhibitions

SUBTOPIC

See also
International exposition on the environment. 1974

- Magazine articles are arranged alphabetically by subject and author; the title is listed under both of these entries.

- Each subject entry is divided into subtopics whenever there are a large number of articles on the same subject listed together.

The Reference Section

Another special section of the library is the **reference section.** Students are usually familiar with the reference section because this is the area where the encyclopedias are kept. But there are a number of other reference books which can be just as helpful and often more up-to-date. Some of the most popular titles are listed below:

The *Abridged Reader's Guide to Periodical Literature* is a list of articles from a select group of magazines. These lists are arranged alphabetically by subject in paperbound volumes published monthly during the school year. The monthly issues are bound together in a single volume once a year.

Bartlett's Familiar Quotations contains 20,000 quotations arranged in chronological order from ancient times to the present.

Current Biography is published monthly and annually. Each article includes a photo of the well-known individual, a biographical sketch, and information concerning his or her birth date, address, occupation, and so on.

Facts About the Presidents is a single-volume reference book which contains important facts and dates about all the presidents in chronological order.

The *Junior Authors* books contain biographical information on children's and young adult authors. Each volume is listed in alphabetical order with volumes three through five indexing all previous volumes.

Kane's Famous First Facts is a large, single volume which lists "firsts" in all areas of life by event, year, and date.

Something About the Author: Facts and Pictures About Contemporary Authors and Illustrators of Books for Young People contains about 200 biographical sketches. Each edition contains two volumes, and each volume contains an index.

Webster's Biographical Dictionary is a collection of information about famous people.

Webster's New Geographical Dictionary is a list of all the world's most important places. The names are listed in alphabetical order with important geographical and historical information given about each.

The World Almanac and Book of Facts is published once a year. It contains facts and statistics about the following subjects: entertainment, sports, business, politics, history, religion, education, and social programs. In addition to this information, the book also includes a review of major events of the past year.

674 Other Special Sections

Books, magazines, and reference materials are important sources of information, but they are not the only resources available in the library. Many libraries have *newspapers* with today's news and *vertical files* of older newspaper clippings and current pamphlets. Vertical files are arranged in alphabetical order by subject. Valuable current information can be found there. Records, tapes, slides, picture and photograph files, and numerous other *audio visual materials* may be features of your library. If they are, they are probably color coded in the card catalog. This means each type of audio visual material is on a card with a different color.

Note: Ask your librarian to explain the various resources of your library. *Remember:* The librarian is the best resource you have in the library. Don't be afraid to ask him or her for help in locating material and finding answers to any questions you may have.

Parts of a Book

If the book you have searched for and located in the library is a nonfiction book which you need for a research paper or assignment, it is necessary to understand how to use that book efficiently. Below you will find a brief description of each part of a book. It is especially important, for instance, to make full use of the index when using nonfiction books.

675　The **title page** is usually the first printed page in a book. It gives you (1) the full title of the book, (2) the author's name, (3) the publisher's name, and (4) the place of publication.

676　The **copyright page** is the page right after the title page. Here you will find the year in which the copyright was issued which is usually the same year the book was published.

677　The **preface** (also called **foreword, introduction,** or **acknowledgment**) comes before the table of contents and is there to give you an idea of what the book is about and why it was written.

678　The **table of contents** is one section most of you are familiar with since it shows you the major divisions of the book *(units, chapters,* and *topics).* It comes right before the body of the book and is used to help locate major topics or areas to be studied.

679   The **body** of the book, which comes right after the table of contents, is the main section or *text* of the book.

680   Following the body is the **appendix.** This supplementary section gives extra information, usually in the form of maps, charts, tables, diagrams, letters, or copies of official documents.

681   The **glossary** follows the appendix and is the *dictionary* portion of the book. It is an alphabetical listing of technical terms, foreign words, or special words, with an explanation or definition for each.

682   The **bibliography** is a list of books or articles used by the author when preparing to write the book; the list also serves as a suggestion for further reading.

683   The **index** is probably the most useful part of a book. It is an alphabetical listing of all the important topics appearing in the book. It is similar to the table of contents, except that the index is much more detailed. It will tell you, first, whether the book contains the information you need and, second, on which page that information can be found.

684   # Using the Thesaurus

The **thesaurus** has been a welcome companion to generations of students and writers. A thesaurus is, in a sense, the opposite of a dictionary. You go to a dictionary when you know the word but need the definition. You go to a thesaurus when you know the definition but need the word. For example, you might want a word that means *fear,* the kind of fear that causes a great deal of worry. You need the word to fill in the blank of the following sentence:

> Joan experienced a certain amount of
> _____ over the science exam.

If you have a thesaurus which is in dictionary form, simply look up the word *fear* as you would in a dictionary. If, however, you have a more traditional thesaurus, you must first look up your word in the INDEX at the back of the thesaurus. The index is arranged alphabetically. Let's say you find this entry for *fear* in the index:

> **FEAR 860**
> **fearful** *painful* 830
>   *timid* 862

The numbers after *fear* are GUIDE NUMBERS, not page numbers. (Guide numbers are similar to the topic numbers used in your handbook.) The guide numbers in dark or boldface will always appear next to the key word for that particular group of synonyms. For instance, if you look up number 860 in the body of the thesaurus, you will find (on page 259 in the sample) a long list of synonyms for the word *fear.* These include *timidity, anxiety, care, misgiving, mistrust,* and *suspicion.* For the sample sentence, you select the word *anxiety.* The sentence then becomes:

> Joan experienced a certain amount of *anxiety* over the science exam.

Another feature of the traditional thesaurus is that the synonyms and antonyms for a word are directly before or after each other. Suppose you wanted a word that meant the opposite of *fear.* You could look up *fear* as you did above (guide number 860) and find that guide word 861 is *courage,* the opposite of fear. The guide word is then followed by a list of antonyms of fear such as *boldness, daring, gallantry, heroism,* and *confidence.*

685

> *259*   *PERSONAL AFFECTIONS*   *859-861*
>
> **860. FEAR.** — *N.* **fear,** timidity, diffidence, apprehensiveness, fearfulness, solicitude, anxiety, care, apprehension, misgiving, mistrust, suspicion, qualm; hesitation.
> **trepidation,** flutter, fear and trembling, perturbation, tremor, quivering, shaking, trembling, palpitation, nervousness, restlessness, disquietude, funk *[colloq.]*.
> **fright,** alarm, dread, awe, terror, horror, dismay, consternation, panic, scare; stampede *[of horses]*.
> **intimidation,** bullying; terrorism, reign of terror; terrorist, bully.
> *V.* **fear,** be afraid, apprehend, dread, distrust; hesitate, falter, funk *[colloq.]*, cower, crouch, skulk, take fright, take alarm; start, wince, flinch, shy, shrink, fly.
> **tremble,** shake, shiver, shudder, flutter, quake, quaver, quiver, quail.
> **frighten,** fright, terrify, inspire (*or* excite) fear, bulldoze *[colloq.]*, alarm, startle, scare, dismay, astound; awe, strike terror, appall, unman, petrify, horrify.
> **daunt,** intimidate, cow, overawe, abash, deter, discourage; browbeat, bully, threaten, terrorize.
> **haunt,** obsess, beset, besiege; prey (*or* weigh) on the mind.
> *Adj.* **afraid,** frightened, alarmed, fearful, timid, timorous, nervous, diffident, fainthearted, tremulous, shaky, afraid of one's shadow, apprehensive; aghast, awe-struck, awe-stricken, horror-stricken, panic-stricken.
> **dreadful,** alarming, redoubtable, perilous, dread, fell, dire, direful, shocking, frightful, terrible, terrific, tremendous; horrid, horrible, ghastly, awful, awe-inspiring, revolting.
> **861. [Absence of fear] COURAGE** — *N.* courage, bravery, valor, resoluteness, boldness, spirit, daring, gallantry, intrepidity, prowess, heroism, chivalry, audacity, rashness, dash, defiance, confidence, self-reliance; manhood, manliness, nerve, pluck, mettle, grit, virtue, hardihood, fortitude, firmness, backbone.

Using the Dictionary

Too often a dictionary is used only when someone needs to know the meaning of a word. Even though this is the main reason for using the dictionary, it is only one of several reasons. Below are some of the most important ways a dictionary can help you. *(All are illustrated following this section.)*

687 **Spelling** Not knowing how to spell a word does make it difficult to find that word in the dictionary, but not impossible. You will be surprised at how quickly you can find a word by following its *sounded-out* spelling.

688 **Capital Letters** If you need to know whether a certain word is capitalized, it is probably going to be faster (certainly more accurate) to look it up in the dictionary than to ask a friend who thinks he knows.

689 **Syllabication** The dictionary is often used to check on where you can divide a word. This is especially important when you are typing a paper or when you are working with strict margin requirements.

690 **Pronunciation** Many times people become lost or confused when they look at a word because they don't *hear* the word properly. They may even know the meaning of the word, but without the correct pronunciation they cannot recognize it. To remember a word and its meaning, you must know its correct pronunciation. (The dictionary gives you a **Pronunciation Key** at the bottom of all right-side pages.)

691 The **Parts of Speech** The dictionary uses nine abbreviations for the parts of speech:

n.	noun	v.t.	transitive verb	adj.	adjective
pron.	pronoun	interj.	interjection	adv.	adverb
v.i.	intransitive verb	conj.	conjunction	prep.	preposition

692 **Etymology** (History) Just after the pronunciation and part of speech, you will find [in brackets] the history of each word. Sometimes knowing a little about the history of each word you look up can make it easier to remember the meaning.

693 **Restrictive Labels** There are three main types of labels used in a dictionary: **subject labels,** which tell you that a word has a special meaning when used in a particular field or subject (*mus.* for *music, med.* for *medicine, zool.* for *zoology,* etc.); **usage labels,** which tell you how a word is used (*slang, colloq.* for *colloquial, dial.* for *dialect,* etc.); and **geographic labels,** which tell you the region of the country where that word is mainly used (*N.E.* for *New England, W.* for *West,* etc.).

694 **Synonyms and Antonyms** Even though the best place to look for a selection of synonyms and antonyms is a thesaurus—a dictionary of synonyms and antonyms—a dictionary will quite often list synonyms and antonyms after the meaning.

695 **Illustrations** Whenever a definition is difficult to make clear with words alone, a picture or drawing is used.

696 **Meaning** Even though you probably know how to look up the meaning of a word, it is not quite as easy to figure out what to do with *all those meanings* once you have found them. The first thing to do is to read (or at least skim) all the meanings given. It is important for you to know that most dictionaries list their meanings chronologically. This means the oldest meaning of the word is given first, then the newer or more technical versions. You can see why it is extremely dangerous to simply take the first meaning listed— it is quite possible that this first one is not the meaning you are after at all. Remember to read all the meanings, and then select the one which is best for you.

Spartan

GUIDE WORD

spark² (spärk) *n.* [ON. *sparkr*, lively: for IE. base see prec.] **1.** a gay, dashing, gallant young man **2.** a beau or lover —*vt.*, *vi.* ☆[Colloq.] to court, woo, pet, etc. An old-fashioned term —**spark′er** *n.*

USAGE LABELS

spar·kle (spär′k'l) *vi.* **-kled, -kling** [ME. *sparklen*, freq. of *sparken*, to SPARK¹] **1.** to throw off sparks **2.** to gleam or shine in flashes; glitter or glisten, as jewels, sunlit water, etc. **3.** to be brilliant and lively [*sparkling wit*] **4.** to effervesce or bubble, as soda water and some wines —*vt.* to cause to sparkle —*n.* **1.** a spark, or glowing particle **2.** a sparkling, or glittering **3.** brilliance; liveliness; vivacity — *SYN.* see FLASH

SPELLING OF VERB FORMS

SYNONYM

spar·kler (-klər) *n.* a person or thing that sparkles; specif., *a)* a thin, light stick of pyrotechnic material that burns with bright sparks *b)* [*pl.*] [Colloq.] clear, brilliant eyes *c)* [Colloq.] a diamond or similar gem

☆**spark plug** **1.** a piece fitted into the cylinder of an internal-combustion engine to ignite the fuel mixture within: it carries an electric current into the cylinder, which sparks between two terminals in the presence of the mixture **2.** [Colloq.] a person or thing that inspires, activates, or advances something —**spark′plug′** *vt.* **-plugged′, -plug′ging**

MEANINGS

TERMINAL

INSULATOR

ELECTRODES

GAP

SPARK PLUG (in cross section)

ILLUSTRATION

spark transmitter an early type of radio transmitter that uses the oscillatory discharge of a capacitor through an inductor in series with a spark gap to generate its high-frequency power

spar·ling (spär′liŋ) *n., pl.* **-ling, -lings:** see PLURAL, II, D, 2 [ME. *sperlynge* < MFr. *esperlinge* < MDu. *spirlinc*, orig. dim. of *spīr*, a small point, grass shoot: see SPIRE²] a European smelt (*Osmerus eperlanus*)

SPELLING OF PLURAL FORMS

spar·oid (sper′oid, spar′-) *adj.* [< ModL. *sparoides* < *sparus*, gilthead < L. < Gr. *sparos*: for IE. base see SPEAR] of or pertaining to the sparids —*n.* same as SPARID

PRONUNCIATION

sparring partner any person with whom a prizefighter boxes for practice

spar·row (spar′ō) *n.* [ME. *sparwe* < OE. *spearwa*, akin to MHG. *sparwe* < IE. base *sper-, bird name, esp. for sparrow, whence Gr. *sporgilos*, *psar*, starling] **1.** any of several old-world weaverbirds; esp., any of a genus (*Passer*) including the ENGLISH SPARROW **2.** any of numerous finches native to both the Old and New Worlds; ☆esp., any of various American species, as the SONG SPARROW **3.** any of several other sparrowlike birds

SYLLABICATION AND PARTS OF SPEECH

spar·row·grass (spar′ō gras′, -gräs′) *n.* [altered by folk etym. < ASPARAGUS] *dial. var.* of ASPARAGUS

PRIMARY AND SECONDARY ACCENTS

sparrow hawk [ME. *sparowhawke*: so named from preying on sparrows] **1.** a small European hawk (*Accipiter nisus*) with short, rounded wings ☆**2.** a small American falcon (*Falco sparverius*) with a reddish-brown back and tail

ETYMOLOGY

spar·ry (spär′ē) *adj.* **-ri·er, -ri·est** of, like, or rich in mineral spar

sparse (spärs) *adj.* [L. *sparsus*, pp. of *spargere*, to scatter: see SPARK¹] thinly spread or distributed; not dense or crowded —*SYN.* see MEAGER —**sparse′ly** *adv.* —**sparse′ness, spar′si·ty** (-sə tē) *n.*

SPELLING OF ADJECTIVE FORMS

Spar·ta (spär′tə) city in the S Peloponnesus, Greece, a powerful military city in ancient Laconia

Spar·ta·cus (spär′tə kəs) ?-71 B.C.; Thracian slave & gladiator in Rome: leader of a slave revolt

SPELLING AND CAPITAL LETTERS

spar·te·ine (spär′ti ēn′, -tē in) *n.* [< ModL. *Spartium*, name of the broom genus (< L. *spartum*, broom (see ESPARTO) + -INE⁴] a clear, oily, poisonous, liquid alkaloid, C₁₅H₂₆N₂, obtained from a broom (*Spartium scoparium*)

fur; get; joy; yet; chin; she; thin, *then*; zh, leisure; ŋ, ring; *able* (ā′b'l); Fr. bål; ë, Fr. coeur; ö, Fr. feu; Fr. mon; ô, Fr. coq; cover. ☆ Americanism; ‡foreign; *hypothetical; <derived from

PRONUNCIATION KEY

Reading fast is fine, but reading well is better.

Reading and Study Skills

698   If you want to develop all your interests and talents to their fullest, you must be able to read—and read well. Being able to read well is a key to doing well in school and, later, doing well on the job. Luckily, it's never too late to become a better reader. Some students think the best way to become a better reader is to become a faster reader. Although it is nice to be a fast reader, it is much more important to be an "efficient" reader.

An efficient reader is one who is more concerned about understanding what he reads than he is in how quickly he reads it. To be an efficient reader, you must be a careful, thoughtful reader. You need to have a good vocabulary (or a good dictionary). You need to know how to use "context clues," as well as how to read between the lines. And, perhaps, most importantly, you need to know how to *study* while you read. Only then can you be an efficient reader—a reader who can understand and remember what he has read and put this information to use in the classroom.

699   SQ3R

One of the most popular ways to improve your reading and studying skills is to use the **SQ3R** method. SQ3R is an abbreviation for the five steps in the reading process: *Survey, Question, Read, Recite,* and *Review.* If you follow these five steps each time you read an assignment, you are well on your way to becoming a better reader.

700 Survey: The first step in the SQ3R study method is **survey.** When you "survey" a reading assignment, you try to get a general picture of what the assignment is about. To do this, you must look briefly at each page, paying special attention to the headings, chapter titles, illustrations, and bold-faced type. It is also a good idea to read the first and last paragraphs in the assignment. A survey of this kind will give you a pretty good idea of what the reading material covers.

701 Question: As you do your survey, you should begin to ask yourself **questions** about the reading material. You should ask questions which you hope to find the answers to as you read. One quick way to come up with questions to ask is to turn the headings and sub-headings into questions. These will be questions which might very well come up later in a quiz or class discussion. You should write down any questions that you feel are especially important. Remember, asking questions will make you an "active" rather than "passive" reader. It will keep you involved in the subject and keep you thinking about what may be coming up next.

702 Read: **Read** the assignment carefully from start to finish. Look for main ideas in each paragraph or section. Take notes as you read or stop from time to time to write a brief summary of what you have covered. Read the difficult parts slowly. (Re-read them if necessary.) Use context clues to help you figure out some of the most difficult passages. Use a dictionary or other reference book to look up unfamiliar words or ideas. Use your senses as you read and try to imagine what the subject of your assignment looks, feels, sounds, tastes, or smells like.

703 Recite: One of the most valuable parts of the SQ3R method is the **reciting** step. It is very important that you recite out loud what you have learned from your reading. (Whisper quietly to yourself if you are in a public place.) It is best to stop at the end of each page, section, or chapter depending upon how long the assignment is. Try to answer the *who, what, when, where, why,* and *how* questions. By reciting this information out loud, you can test yourself on how well you understand what you have read. You can go back and re-read if necessary. If you understood the material well, reciting it out loud will help you remember it much longer.

704 Review: The final step in the SQ3R Study Method is the **review** step. You should review or summarize what you have read as soon as you finish. If you have been given some questions to answer about the assignment, do that immediately. The longer you wait, the harder it will be to answer them. If you have no questions to answer, summarize the assignment in a short writing. This will help you remember the information and will also give you something to review later. You can also make an outline, note cards, flash cards, illustrations, etc. to help you review and remember what you have read.

705 Remembering What You Have Read

In addition to using the SQ3R reading method, you can also use a number of memory aids to help you remember the important information you've covered.

706 **Use visual aids:** The best way to remember something is to picture it in your mind. Try to imagine what it looks, sounds, or feels like. Sometimes this is not as easy as it seems. If what you have to remember is an idea rather than an object, you may have to "create" a picture or visual aid. This might be a very simple drawing or map; or it might be a very detailed illustration or diagram. Either way, you will have something to help you remember.

707 **Use acronyms:** Acronyms are words which are made up of the first letters of the words in a group or title. NATO, for example, is an acronym for North Atlantic Treaty Organization. You can create your own acronyms from the words in a group or list you are supposed to memorize. For example, if you have to know the names of the five Great Lakes, you might use the acronym HOMES to help you remember Huron, Ontario, Michigan, Erie, and Superior.

708 **Use rhyming words, phrases, or songs:** Sometimes a simple, even silly, song can help you remember something. Look at the examples which follow. Do any of these look familiar? You can create your own words, phrases, or songs to help you remember what you have read.

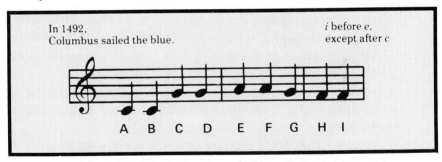

The guidelines which follow will help you understand better all that is involved in the reading and studying process. Read and think about each guideline. Then begin working to improve your skills by following these suggestions.

Study Skills

709 Guidelines to Effective Study Reading

1. Know exactly what the reading assignment is, when it is due, and what you have to do to complete it.

2. Gather all the materials you may need to complete your assignment (notebook, handouts, reference books, etc.).

3. Decide how much time you will need to complete the assignment and when and where (library, study hall, home) you will do it.

4. If you have trouble getting your reading assignments done, try doing them at the same time each day. This will help you control the urge to wait until you are "in the mood" before starting.

5. Try to avoid doing your studying or reading when you are hungry or tired.

6. Take breaks only after completing an assignment or a major part of it.

7. Know your textbooks and what they contain; use the index, glossary, and special sections.

8. Use a specific approach to your study-reading—the SQ3R approach, for example.

9. Preview each chapter or assignment before you begin reading to get an overall picture of what the reading selection is about; if there are questions which go with the assignments, look them over before you begin reading.

10. Read the titles and headings and use them to ask yourself questions about what may be coming up next.

11. Try to figure out the main idea of each paragraph and supporting details which are worth remembering. Notice words or phrases which are in *italics* or **boldface.**

12. Look closely at maps, charts, graphs, and other illustrations to help you understand and remember important information.

13. Take good notes of everything you read—summarize, outline, star, underline, or highlight important information.

14. Use all of your senses when you read. Try to imagine what something looks, feels, and tastes like and draw illustrations in your notes.

15. Remember that some reading assignments are much more difficult than others. Read difficult material slowly; re-read the most difficult parts.

16. Try hard to figure out difficult material by re-reading first; then ask someone for an explanation if necessary.

17. Always summarize difficult material out loud (either to yourself or to someone else).

18. Make out note cards or flash cards of difficult material to study later.

19. Keep a list of things you want to check on or ask your teacher about.

20. Remember that reading is thinking. It often requires a good deal of effort and concentration to do well.

Improving Your Vocabulary

710   One of the best things you can do to improve your reading skills is to improve your vocabulary. Unless you have a good vocabulary, it is very difficult to improve your reading. There are a number of methods which you can use for improving your vocabulary.

711 1. **Use a dictionary.** Rather than guessing what an unfamiliar word means, it is usually a good idea to take some time and "look it up" in the dictionary. When you do, check over *all* the meanings listed, not just the first one. This will give you the best definition and expand your vocabulary at the same time. Also check the pronunciation of the words you look up. It is much easier to remember the definition of a word if you know how to pronounce it.

   2. **Use a thesaurus.** A thesaurus is a dictionary of synonyms and antonyms. It can be a great help to you as you work on your vocabulary improvement. The most efficient time to use a thesaurus is when you are writing a paper which calls for creativity as well as accuracy. Rather than settle for a common, overused word to describe something, use your thesaurus to find a synonym for that word. If, for example, you are using the word *angry* in your paper, and you need a synonym for it, you might be able to think of three or four: *mad, upset, sore,* etc. A quick check in the thesaurus under *angry* would greatly increase that list: *irate, bitter, enraged, fiery,* and so on. Each of these words means *angry,* yet each has a slightly different "shade" of meaning. Depending upon what you are describing, any one of these words could be used in place of *angry* to add color to the writing. Just as important, you will add new words to your working vocabulary.

207

713   3. **Use context clues.** Each word you read or write depends on the other words in the sentence to make sense. These other words are called the *context* of a word. By looking closely at these surrounding words, you can pick up hints or clues which will help you figure out the meaning of a difficult word. Good readers use context clues regularly and are generally aware of the different types of context clues. Knowing something about these different types can help you sharpen your word-attack skills and improve your overall reading ability. In the following chart, you will find seven different types of context clues.

714

Types of Context Clues

1. Clues supplied through **synonyms**:
   Carol is fond of using *trite*, worn-out expressions in her writing. Her favorite is "You can lead a horse to water, but you can't make him drink."
2. Clues contained in **comparisons and contrasts**:
   As the trial continued, the defendant's guilt became more and more obvious. With even the slightest bit of new evidence against him, there would be no chance of *acquittal.*
3. Clues contained in a **definition or description**:
   Peggy is a *transcriptionist*, a person who makes a written copy of a recorded message.
4. Clues through **association** with other words in the sentence:
   Jim is one of the most talented students ever to have attended Walker High. He has won many awards in art, music, and theatre. He also writes poetry and short stories for the school paper and creates video games on his computer. He is on the basketball and football teams and runs marathons in the summer. Jim's talents are *innumerable.*

5. Clues which appear in a **series**:
   The *dulcimer,* fiddle, and banjo are all popular among the Appalachian Mountain people.
6. Clues provided by the **tone and setting**:
   The streets filled instantly with *bellicose* protesters, who pushed and shoved their way through the frantic bystanders. The scene was no longer peaceful and calm as the marchers had promised it would be.
7. Clues derived from **cause and effect**:
   Since nobody came to the first voluntary work session, attendance for the second one is *mandatory* for all the members.

715   As you can see, context clues are made up of synonyms, definitions, descriptions, and other kinds of specific information about the word you are trying to understand.   In addition, clues can help explain how something works, where or when an event takes place, what the purpose or importance of an action is, and so on.   Some context clues are not so direct as those listed above.   They might be simply examples, results, or general statements; still, these indirect clues can be very helpful.   Finally, you should realize that context clues do not always show up immediately.   In a lengthy piece of writing, for example, the clues might not appear until several paragraphs after the word.   Alert readers will be aware of this and continue to look for clues as they read.   The more clues you can find as a reader, the closer you can get to the specific meaning of the word and, in turn, the overall meaning of the passage.

716   Look carefully at the italicized words in the sample passage taken from Jack London's *Call of the Wild.* Then look for direct and indirect context clues which might help the reader understand the meaning of these words. In addition to the clues available in this single paragraph, the reader would also have the advantage of having read the first 46 pages of the novel. Taken together, there is a good chance the reader could figure out the meaning

They made Sixty Miles, which is a fifty-mile run, on the first day; and the second day saw them booming up the Yukon well on their way to Pelly. But such splendid running was achieved not without great trouble and *vexation* on the part of Francois. The revolt led by Buck had destroyed the *solidarity* of the team. It no longer was as one dog leaping in the traces. The encouragement Buck gave the rebels led them into all kinds of petty *misdemeanors.* No more was Spitz a leader greatly to be feared.

of the italicized words. Using context clues regularly can be a reader's most valuable vocabulary-building tool. See how well you can use context clues now that you understand a little better how they work.

717   4. **Use special lists.** You can also benefit greatly from lists of new words which are introduced in your classes. Some students will "learn" these words for a unit exam and then forget them. If you are a good reader, however, you will not let this happen. As long as you need to know these words for even a single day, why not learn these words well enough to remember at least some of them permanently.

718   5. **Use word parts.** By studying the "parts" of a word (the prefix, suffix, and roots which make up a word), it is possible to understand the meaning of that word. Before you can use word parts, however, you must become familiar with the meanings of the most widely used prefixes, suffixes, and roots in our language. For instance, the root *aster* is found in the word *asterisk*, where it means *star;* it is also found in the words *astrology, astronaut, asteroid, astrodome, astrolabe,* and *astronomer* where, in each case, it also means *star.* Not all roots are found in as many as seven different words. Many are, however, and some are found in as many as thirty or forty different words. At the end of this section, you will find a list of the most common prefixes, suffixes, and roots in the English language. Look them over and see if you recognize any. Then learn as many as you can—a few at a time.

Just as you once learned to combine familiar words into new ones . . .

you can now learn a whole new set of word parts to combine.

A Dictionary of Prefixes

a, an [*not, without*] amoral (without a sense of moral responsibility), atypical, atom (not cutable), apathy (without feeling)

ab, abs, a [*from, away*] abnormal, avert (turn away), abduct

acro [*high*] acropolis (high city), acrobat, acronym, acrophobia (fear of height)

ambi, amb [*both, around*] ambidextrous (skilled with both hands), ambiguous, amble

amphi [*both*] amphibious (living on both land and water), amphitheater

ante [*before*] antedate, anteroom, antebellum, antecedent (happening before)

anti, ant [*against*] anticommunist, antidote, anticlimax, antacid

bene, bon [*well*] benefit, bonus, benefactor, benevolent, benediction, bonanza

bi, bis, bin [*both, double, twice*] bicycle, biweekly, binoculars, bilateral, biscuit

by [*side, close, near*] bypass, bystander, by-product, bylaw, byline

circum, circ [*around*] circumference, circumnavigate, circumspect

co (con, col, cor, com) [*together, with*] compose, copilot, conspire, collect, concord

contra, counter [*against*] controversy, contradict, counterpart

de [*from, down*] demote, depress, degrade, deject, deprive

di [*two, twice*] divide, dilemma, diploma

dia [*through, between*] diameter, diagonal, diagram, dialogue (speech between people)

epi [*upon*] epidermis (upon the skin, outer layer of skin), epitaph, epithet

ex, e, ec, ef [*out*] expel (drive out), ex-mayor, exit, exorcism, eccentric (out of the center position), eject, emit

extra, extro [*beyond, outside*] extraordinary (beyond the ordinary), extracurricular, extrovert

fore [*before in time*] forecast, foretell (to tell beforehand), foreshadow, foregone, forefather

hemi, demi, semi [*half*] hemisphere, hemicycle, semicircle (half of a circle), demitasse

homo [*man*] Homo sapiens, homicide (killing man)

hyper [*over, above*] hypersensitive (overly sensitive), hypertensive, hyperactive

hypo [*under*] hypodermic (under the skin), hypothesis

il (ir, in, im) [*not*] incorrect, illegal, immoral, irregular

in (il, im) [*into*] inject, inside, illuminate, impose, illustrate, implant, imprison

inter [*between*] intercollegiate, interfere, intervene, interrupt (break between)

intra [*within*] intramural, intravenous (within the veins)

intro [*into, inward*] introduce, introvert (turn inward)

macro [*large, excessive*] macrodent (having large teeth), macrocosm

mal [*badly, poorly*] maladjusted, malnutrition, malfunction, malady

mis [*incorrect, bad*] misuse, misprint

mono [*one*] monoplane, monotone, monochrome, monocle

multi [*many*] multiply, multiform

non [*not*] nontaxable (not taxed), nontoxic, nonexistent, nonsense

para [*beside, almost*] parasite (one who eats beside or at the table of another), paraphrase, parody, parachute, paramedic, parallel

penta [*five*] pentagon (figure or building having five angles or sides), pentameter, pentathlon

per [*throughout, completely*] pervert (completely turn wrong, corrupt), perfect, perceive, permanent, persuade

peri [*around*] perimeter, (measurement around an area), periphery, periscope, pericardium, period

poly [*many*] polygon (figure having many angles or sides), polygamy, polyglot, polychrome

post [*after*] postpone, postwar, postscript, postseason (after the season)

pre [*before*] prewar, preview, precede, prevent, premonition

pro [*forward, in favor of*] project (throw forward), progress, pro-abortion, promote, prohibition

pseudo [*false*] pseudonym (false or assumed name), pseudo, pseudopodia

re [*back, again*] reclaim, revive, revoke, rejuvenate, retard, reject, return

retro [*backwards*] retrospective (looking backwards), retroactive, retrorocket

se [*aside*] seduce (lead aside), secede, secrete, segregate

self [*by oneself*] self-determination, self-employed, self-service, selfish

sub [*under*] submerge (put under), submarine, subhuman, subject, substitute, subsoil, suburb

super, supr [*above, over, more*] supervise, superman, supreme, supernatural, superior

syn (sym, sys, syl) [*with, together*] sympathy, system, synthesis, symphony, syllable, synchronize (time together), synonym

trans, tra [*across, beyond*] transoceanic, transmit (send across land or sea), transfusion

tri [*three*] tricycle, triangle, tripod, tristate

un [*not, release*] unfair, unnatural, unbutton, unfasten

under [*beneath*] underground, underling

uni [*one, below*] unicycle, uniform, unify, universe, unique (one of a kind)

ultra [*beyond, exceedingly*] ultramodern, ultraviolet, ultraconservative

vice [*in place of*] vice president, vice admiral, viceroy

A Dictionary of Suffixes

able, ible [*able, can do*] capable, agreeable, edible, visible (can be seen)

ade [*result of action*] blockade (the result of a blocking action), lemonade

age [*act of, state of, collection of*] salvage (act of saving), storage, forage

al [*relating to*] sensual, gradual, manual, natural (relating to nature)

algia [*pain*] neuralgia (nerve pain)

an, ian [*native of, relating to*] Canadian (native of Canada), African

211

ance, ancy [*action, process, state*] assistance, allowance, defiance, resistance

ant [*performing, agent*] assistant, servant, defiant

ar, er, or [*one who, that which*] doctor, baker, miller, teacher, racer, amplifier

ard, art [*one who*] drunkard, dullard, braggart (one who brags)

ary, ery, ory [*relating to, quality, place where*] dictionary, dietary, bravery, dormitory (a place where people sleep)

asis, esis, osis [*action, process, condition*] hypnosis, neurosis, osmosis

ate [*cause, make*] liquidate, segregate (cause a group to be set aside)

cian [*having a certain skill or art*] musician, beautician, magician, physician

cide [*kill*] homicide, pesticide, genocide (killing a race of people)

cule, ling [*very small*] molecule, ridicule, duckling (very small duck), sapling

cy [*action, function*] hesitancy, prophecy, normalcy (function in a normal way)

dom [*quality, realm, office*] boredom, freedom, kingdom, stardom, wisdom (quality of being wise)

ee [*one who receives the action*] employee, nominee (one who is nominated), refugee

en [*made of, make*] silken, frozen, oaken (made of oak), wooden, lighten

ence, ency [*action, state of, quality*] difference, conference, urgency (state of being urgent)

er (see *ar*)

ery (see *ary*)

ese [*a native of, the language of*] Japanese, Vietnamese, legalese (language of legal documents)

ess [*female*] actress, goddess, lioness

et, ette [*a small one, group*] midget, octet, baronet, majorette

fic [*making, causing*] scientific, specific

ful [*full of*] frightful, careful, helpful (full of help)

fy [*make*] fortify (make strong), simplify, terrify, amplify

hood [*order, condition, quality*] manhood, womanhood, brotherhood

ible (see *able*)

ic [*nature of, like*] metallic (of the nature of metal), heroic, poetic,
acidic

ice [*condition, state, quality*] justice, malice

ile [*relating to, suited for, capable of*] juvenile, senile (related to being old), missile

ine [*nature of*] feminine, masculine, genuine, medicine

ion, sion, tion [*act of, state of, result of*] action, injection, infection, suspension (state of suspending)

ish [*origin, nature, resembling*] foolish, Irish, clownish (resembling a clown)

ism [*doctrine, system, manner, condition, characteristic*] alcoholism, exorcism, heroism (characteristic of a hero), Communism, realism

ist [*one who, that which*] artist, dentist, violinist, racist

ite [*nature of, quality of, mineral product*] Israelite, dynamite (quality of being powerful), graphite, sulfite

ity, ty [*state of, quality*] captivity, clarity, fraternity

ive [*causing, making*] abusive (causing abuse), exhaustive

ize [*make*] emphasize, publicize (make public), idolize, penalize

less [*without*] baseless, careless (without care), artless, fearless, helpless

ling (see *cule*)

ly [*like, manner of*] carelessly, fearlessly, hopelessly, shamelessly

ment [*act of, state of, result*] contentment, amendment (state of amending), achievement

mony [*a resulting thing*] matrimony, alimony, acrimony

ness [*state of*] carelessness, restlessness, lifelessness

oid [*like, resembling*] asteroid, spheroid, tabloid, anthropoid

ology [*study, science, theory*] biology, anthropology, geology, neurology

or (see *ar*)

ory (see *ary*)

osis (see *asis*)

ous [*full of, having*] gracious, nervous, vivacious (full of life), spacious

ship [*office, state, quality, skill, profession*] friendship, authorship, dictatorship

some [*like, apt, tending to*] lonesome, threesome, gruesome

tude [*state of, condition of*] gratitude, multitude (condition of being many), aptitude, solitude

ure [*state of, act, process, rank*] culture, literature, pressure, rupture (state of being broken)

ward [*in the direction of*] eastward, forward, backward

y [*inclined to, tend to*] cheery, crafty, faulty, dirty, itchy

---

721   A Dictionary of Roots

acer, acid, acri [*bitter, sour, sharp*] acidity (sourness), acrid, acrimony

acu [*sharp*] acute, acupuncture

ag, agi, ig, act [*do, move, go*] agent (doer), agenda (things to do), navigate (move by sea), ambiguous (going both ways, not clear), retroactive, agitate

ali, allo, alter [*other*] alias (a person's other name), alternative, alibi, alien (from another country or planet), alter (change to another form)

altus [*high, deep*] altimeter (a device for measuring heights), altitude

am, amor [*love, liking*] amorous, enamored, amiable

anni, annu, enni [*year*] anniversary, annually (yearly), centennial (occurring once in 100 years)

anthrop [*man*] anthropology (study of mankind), misanthrope (hater of mankind), philanthropic (love of mankind)

arch [*chief, first, rule*] archangel (chief angel), architect (chief worker), archaic (first; very early), archives, monarchy (rule by one person), matriarchy (rule by the mother), patriarchy (rule by the father)

aster, astr [*star*] aster (star flower), asterisk, asteroid, astrology (lit., star-speaking; study of the influence by stars and planets), astronomy (star law), astronaut (lit., star traveler; space traveler)

aud, aus [*hear, listen*] audible (can be heard), auditorium, audio, audition, auditory, audience

aug, auc [*increase*] auction, augur, augment (add to; increase)

auto, aut [*self*] automobile (self-moving vehicle), autograph (self-writing; signature), automatic (self-acting), autobiography (lit., self-life writing)

belli [*war*] rebellion, belligerent (warlike or hostile)

bibl [*book*] Bible, bibliography (writing, list of books), bibliomania (craze for books), bibliophile (book lover)

bio [*life*] biology (study of life), biography, biopsy (cutting living tissue for examination), microbe (small, microscopic living thing)

breve [*short*] abbreviate, brief, brevity

calor [*heat*] calorie (a unit of heat), calorify (to make hot), caloric

cap, cip, cept [*take*] capable, capacity, capture, accept, except, forceps

capit, capt [*head*] decapitate (to remove the head from), capital, captain, caption

carn [*flesh*] carnivorous (flesh eating), incarnate, reincarnation

caus, caut [*burn, heat*] cauterize (to make hot; burn), cauldron, caustic

cause, cuse, cus [*cause, motive*] because, excuse (to attempt to remove the blame or cause), accusation

ced, ceed, cede, cess [*move, yield, go, surrender*] proceed (move forward), cede (yield), accede, concede, intercede, precede, recede, secede (move aside from), success

chrom [*color*] chrome (color purity), chromosome (color body in genetics), Kodachrome, monochrome (one color), polychrome (many colored)

chron [*time*] chronological (in order of time), chronometer (time-measured), chronicle (record of events in time), synchronize (make time with, set time together)

cide [*kill*] suicide (self-killer), homicide (man, human killer), genocide (race killing), pesticide (pest killer), germicide (germ killer), insecticide (insect killer)

cise [*cut*] decide (cut off uncertainty), precise (cut exactly right), concise, incision, scissors

cit [*to call, start*] incite, citation, cite

civ [*citizen*] civic (relating to a citizen), civil, civilian, civvies (civilian clothing), civilization

clam, claim [*cry out*] exclamation, clamor, proclamation, reclamation, acclamation, claim

clud, clus, claus [*shut*] include (to take in), recluse (one who shuts himself away from others), claustrophobia (abnormal fear of being shut up, confined), conclude, include

cognosc, gnosi [*know*] prognosis (forward knowing), diagnosis (thorough knowledge), recognize (to know again), incognito (not known)

cosm [*universe, world*] cosmos (the universe), cosmic, cosmology, cosmopolitan (world citizen), cosmonaut, microcosm, macrocosm

cord, cor, card [*heart*] cordial (hearty, heartfelt), accord, concord, discord, record, courage, encourage (put heart into), discourage (take heart out of), core, coronary, cardiac

corp [*body*] corporation (a legal body), corpse, corpulent

crat [*rule, strength*] autocracy, democratic

cresc, cret, crease, cru [*rise, grow*] crescendo (growing in loudness or intensity), crescent (growing, like the moon in first quarter), concrete (grown together, solidified), increase, decrease, accrue (to grow, as interest on money)

crea [*create*] creature (anything created), recreation, creation, creator

cred [*believe*] creed (statement of beliefs), credo (a creed), credence (belief), credit (belief, trust), credulous (believing too readily, easily deceived), credentials (statements that promote belief, trust), incredible

crit [*separate, choose*] critical, criterion (that which is used in choosing), hypocrisy

cur, curs [*run*] current (running or flowing), concurrent, concur (run together, agree), curriculum (lit., a running, a course), incur (run into), precursor (forerunner), recur, occur, courier

cura [*care*] manicure (caring for the hands), curator, curative

cus, cuse (see *cause*)

cycl, cyclo [*wheel, circular*] Cyclops (a mythical giant with one eye in the middle of his forehead), cyclone (a wind blowing circularly; a tornado), unicycle, bicycle

deca [*ten*] decade, decalogue, decathlon

dem [*people*] democracy (people-rule), demography (vital statistics of the people: deaths, births, etc.), epidemic (on or among the people; general)

dent, dont [*tooth*] dental (relating to teeth), orthodontist, denture, dentifrice

derm [*skin*] hypodermic (under skin; injected under the skin), dermatology (skin study), epidermis (on skin; outer layer), taxidermy (arranging skin; mounting animals)

dic, dict [*say, speak*] diction (how one speaks, what one says), dictionary, dictate, dictator, dictaphone, dictatorial, edict, predict, verdict, contradict, benediction

domin [*master*] dominate, dominion, domain, predominant

don [*give*] donate (make a gift), condone

dorm [*sleep*] dormant, dormitory

dox [*opinion, praise*] doxy (belief, creed or ism), orthodox (having the correct, commonly accepted opinion), heterodox (differing opinion; contrary, self-contradictory), doxology (statement or song of praise), paradox

drome [*to run, step*] syndrome (run together; symptoms) hippodrome (a place where horses run)

duc, duct [*lead*] duke (leader), induce (lead into, persuade), seduce (lead aside), aquaduct (water leader, artificial channel), subdue, viaduct, conduct, conduit, produce, reduce, educate

dura [*hard, lasting*] durable, duration, duramen, endurance

dynam [*power*] dynamo (power producer), dynamic, dynamite, hydrodynamics (lit., water power)

end, endo [*within*] endoral (within the mouth), endocardial (within the heart), endoskeletal, endoplasm

erg [*work*] energy, erg (unit of work), allergy, ergophobia (morbid fear of work), ergometer, ergograph

equi [*equal*] equinox, equilibrium

fac, fact, fic, fect [*do, make*] factory (the place where workmen are employed in making goods of various kinds), fact (a thing done, a deed), manufacture, faculty, amplification, affect

fall, fals [*deceive*] falsify, fallacy

fer [*bear, carry*] ferry (carry by water), coniferous (bearing cones, as a pine tree), fertile (bearing richly), defer, infer, refer, referee, referendum, circumference

213

fic, fect (see *fac*)

fid, fide, feder [*faith, trust*] fidelity, confident, confidante, infidelity, infidel, federal, confederacy, Fido

fila, fili [*thread*] filament (a threadlike conductor heated by electrical current), filter, filet

fin [*end, ended, finished*] final, finite, infinite, finish, confine, fine, refine, define, finale

fix [*fix*] fix, fixation (the state of being attached), -fixture, affix, prefix, suffix

flex, flect [*bend*] flex (bend), reflex (bending back), flexible, flexor (muscle for bending), inflexibility, reflect, deflect, genuflect (bend the knee)

flu, fluc, fluv [*flowing*] influence (to flow in), fluctuate (to wave in an unsteady motion), fluviograph (instrument for measuring the flow of rivers), fluid, flue, flush, fluently

form [*form, shape*] form, uniform, conform, deform, reform, perform, formative, formation, formal, formula

fort, forc [*strong*] fort, fortress (a strong point, fortified), fortify (make strong), forte (one's strong point), forte (strong, loud in music), fortitude (strength for endurance), force, effort

fract, frag [*break*] fracture (a break), infraction, fragile (easy to break), fraction (result of breaking a whole into equal parts), refract (to break or bend, as a light ray), refractive, fragment

fum [*smoke*] fume (smoke; odor), fumigate (destroy germs by smoking them out), perfume

gam [*marriage*] bigamy (two marriages), monogamy, polygamy (lit., many marriages)

gastro [*stomach*] gastric, gastronomic, gastritis (inflammation of the stomach)

gen [*birth, race, produce*] genesis (birth, beginning), genus, genetics (study of heredity), eugenics (lit., well-born), genealogy (lineage by race, stock), generate, genitals (the reproductive organs), congenital (existing as such at birth), indigenous (born, growing or produced naturally in a region or country), genetic

geo [*earth*] geometry (earth measurement), geography (lit., earth-writing), geocentric (earth centered), geology

germ [*vital part*] germination (to grow), germ (seed; living substance, as the germ of an idea), germane

gest [*carry, bear*] congest (bear together, clog), suggestion (mental process by which one thought leads to another), congestive (causing congestion), gestation, suggestion, gesture

gloss, glot [*tongue*] polyglot (many tongues), epiglottis, glossary

glu, glo [*lump, bond, glue*] glue, conglomerate (bond together), agglutinate (make to hold in a bond)

grad, gress [*step, go*] grade (step, degree), gradual (step by step), graduate (make all the steps, finish a course), graduated (in steps or degrees), aggressive (stepping toward, pushing), congress (a going together, assembly)

graph, gram [*write, written*] graph, graphic (written; vivid), autograph (self-writing; signature), photography (light-writing), graphite (carbon used for writing), phonograph (sound-writing), bibliography, telegram (far writing)

grat [*pleasing*] congratulate (express pleasure over success), gratuitous (gratis), gratuity (mark of favor, a tip), grateful, gracious, ingrate (not thankful; hence, unpleasant)

grav [*heavy, weighty*] grave, gravity, aggravate, gravitate

greg [*herd, group, crowd*] gregarian (belonging to a herd), congregation (a group functioning together), segregative (tending to group aside or apart)

hab, habit [*have, live*] habitat (the place in which one lives), inhabit (to live in; to establish as residence), rehabilitate, habitual

helio [*sun*] heliograph (as instrument for using the sun's rays), heliotrope (a plant which turns to the sun)

hema, hemo [*blood*] hematid (red blood corpuscle), hemotoxic (causing blood poisoning), hemorrhage, hemoglobin, hemophilia

here, hes [*stick*] adhere, cohere, cohesion

hetero [*different*] heterogeneous (different in birth), heterosexual (with interest in opposite sex)

homo [*same*] homogeneous (of same birth or kind), homonym (word with same name or pronunciation as another), homogenize

hum, human [*earth, ground, man*] humility (quality of lowliness), humane (marked by sympathy, compassion for other human beings and animals), humus, exhume (to take out of the ground)

hypn [*sleep*] hypnosis, Hypnos (god of sleep), hypnotherapy (treatment of disease by hypnosis)

hydr, hydro, hydra [*water*] dehydrate (take water out of; dry), hydrant (water faucet), hydraulic (pertaining to water or to liquids), hydraulics, hydrogen, hydrophobia (fear of water)

ignis [*fire*] ignite, igneous, ignition

ject [*throw*] deject, inject, project (throw forward), eject, object

join, junct [*join*] junction (act of

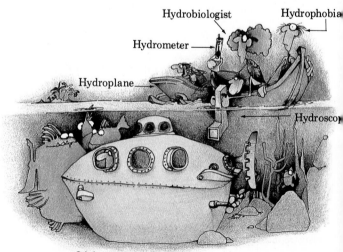

Hydrobiologist · Hydrophobia · Hydrometer · Hydroplane · Hydroscope

joining), enjoin (to lay an order upon; to command), juncture, conjunction, adjoining, injunction

jud, judi, judic [*judge, lawyer*] judge (a public officer who has the authority to give a judgement), judicial (relating to administration of justice), judicious, prejudice

jur, jus [*law*] justice (a just judgement), conjure (to swear together), juror, jurisdiction

juven [*young*] juvenile, rejuvenate (to make young again)

later [*side, broad*] lateral, latitude

laut, lav, lot, lut [*wash*] dilute (to make a liquid thinner and weaker), launder (to wash and iron clothes), lavatory, laundry, lotion, deluge

leg [*law*] legal (lawful; according to law), legislate (to enact a law), legislature (a body of persons who can make laws), legitimize (make legal)

levis [*light*] alleviate (lighten a load), levitate, levity (light conversation; humor)

lic, licit [*permit*] license (freedom to act), licit (permitted; lawful), illicit (not permitted)

lit, liter [*letters*] literary (concerned with books and writing), literature, literal, alliteration, obliterate

lith [*stone*] monolith (one stone, a single mass), lithography (stone writing, printing from a flat stone or metal plate), neolithic (new stone, of the layer stone age)

liver, liber [*free*] liberal (relating to liberty), delivery (freedom; liberation), liberalize (to make more free: as, to liberalize the mind from prejudice), deliverance

loc, loco [*place*] locomotion (act of moving from place to place), locality (locale; neighborhood), allocate (to assign; to place), relocate (to put back into place)

log, logo, ology [*word, study, speech*] zoology (animal study), psychology (mind study), logic (orig., speech; then reasoning), prologue, epilogue, dialogue, catalogue, logorrhea (a flux of words; excessively wordy)

loqu, locut [*talk, speak*] eloquent (speaking out well and forcefully), loquacious (talkative), colloquial (talking together; conversational or informal), circumlo-cution (talking around a subject), soliloquy

luc, lum, lus, lun [*light*] Luna (the moon goddess), lumen (a unit of light), luminary (a heavenly body; someone who shines in his profession), translucent (letting light come through), luster (sparkle; gloss; glaze)

lude [*play*] ludicrous, prelude (before play), interlude

magn [*great*] magnify (make great, enlarge), magnificent, magnanimous (great of mind or spirit), magnate, magnitude, magnum

man [*hand*] manual, manage, manufacture, manacle, manicure, manifest, maneuver, emancipate

mand [*command*] mandatory (commanded), remand (order back), writ of mandamus (written order from a court), countermand (order against, cancelling a previous order), mandate

mania [*madness*] mania (insanity; craze), monomania (mania on one idea), kleptomania (thief mania; abnormal tendency to steal), pyromania (insane tendency to set fires), maniac

mar, mari, mer [*sea, pool*] mermaid (fabled marine creature, half fish), marine (a sailor serving on shipboard), marsh (wet land, swamp), maritime (relating to the sea and navigation)

matri, matro, matric [*mother*] matrimony (state of wedlock), maternal (relating to the mother), matriarchate (rulership of a woman, matron

medi [*half, middle, between, halfway*] mediate (come between, intervene), medieval (pertaining to the middle ages), mediterranean (lying between lands), medium (a person having the faculty to make contact with the supernatural), mediocre

mega [*great*] megaphone (great sound), megalopolis (great city; an extensive urban area including a number of cities), megacycle (a million cycles), megaton (force of a million tons of TNT), omega (great)

mem [*remember*] memorandum (a note; a reminder), commemoration (the act of remembering by a memorial or ceremony), memento, memoir, memo, memorable

meter [*measure*] meter (a measure), voltameter (instrument to measure volts in an electric circuit), barometer, thermometer

micro [*small*] microscope, microfilm, microcard, microwave, micrometer (device for measuring very small distance), micron (a millionth of a meter), microbe (small living thing), omicron (small)

migra [*wander*] migrate (to wander), emigrant (one who leaves a country), immigrate (to come into the land to settle)

mit, miss [*send*] emit (send out, give off), remit (send back, as money due), submit, admit, commit, permit, transmit (send across), omit, intermittent (sending between, at intervals), mission, missile

mob, mot, mov [*move*] mobile (capable of moving), motionless (without motion), motor (that which imparts motion; source of mechanical power), emotional (moved strongly by feelings), motivate, promotion, demote

mon [*warn, remind*] monument (a reminder or memorial of a person or event), admonish (warn), monitor, premonition (forewarning)

monstr, mist [*show*] demonstrate (to display; show) muster (to gather together; collect; put on display) demonstration, monstrosity

morph [*form*] amorphous (with no form, shapeless), Morpheus (the shaper, god of dreams), metamorphosis (a change of form, as a caterpillar into a butterfly), morphidite

mori, mort, mors [*mortal, death*] mortal (causing death or destined for death), immortal (not subject to death), mortality (rate of death), immortality, mortician (one who buries the dead), mortuary (place for the dead, a morgue)

multi, multus [*many, much*] multifold (folded many times), multilinguist (one who speaks many languages), multiped (an organism with many feet), multiply (to increase a number quickly by multiplication)

nasc, nat [*to be born, to spring forth*] nature (the essence of a person or a thing), innate (inborn, inherent in), renascence (a rebirth; a revival), natal, native, nativity

neur [*nerve*] neuritis (inflammation of a nerve), neuropathic (having a nerve disease), neurologist (one who practices neurology), neural, neurosis, neurotic

nom [*law, order*] autonomy (self-law, self-government), astronomy, gastronomy (lit., stomach law; art of good eating), economy (household law, management)

nomen, nomin [*name*] nomenclature, nominate (name someone for an office)

nounce, nunci [*warn, declare*] announcer (one who makes announcements publicly), enunciate (to declare carefully), pronounce (declare; articulate), renounce (retract; revoke), denounce

nov [*new*] novel (new; strange; not formerly known), renovate (to make like new again), novice, nova, innovate

nox, noc [*night*] nocturnal, equinox (equal nights), noctiluca (something which shines by night)

number, numer [*number*] numeral (a figure expressing a number), numeration (act of counting), enumerate (count out, one by one), innumerable

omni [*all, every*] omnipotent (all powerful), omniscient (all knowing), omnipresent (present everywhere), omnivorous (all eating)

onym [*name*] anonymous (without a name), pseudonym (false name), antonym (against name; word of opposite meaning), synonym

oper [*work*] operate (to labor; function), opus (a musical composition or work), cooperate (work together)

ortho [*straight, correct*] orthodox (of the correct or accepted opinion), orthodontist (tooth straightener), orthopedic (originally pertaining to straightening a child), unorthodox

pac [*peace*] pacifist (one for peace only; opposed to war), pacify (make peace, quiet), Pacific Ocean (peaceful ocean)

pan [*all*] Pan American, panacea (cure-all), pandemonium (place of all the demons; wild disorder), pantheon (place of all the gods)

pater, patr [*father*] patriarch (head of the tribe, family), patron (a wealthy person who supports as would a father), paternity (fatherhood, responsibility, etc.), patriot

path, pathy [*feeling, suffering*] pathos (feeling of pity, sorrow), pathetic, sympathy, antipathy (against feeling), apathy (without feeling), empathy (feeling or identifying with another), telepathy (far feeling; through transference)

ped, pod [*foot*] pedal (lever for a foot), impede (get the feet in a trap, hinder), pedestal (foot or base of a statue), pedestrian (foot traveler), centipede, tripod (three-footed support), podiatry (care of the feet), antipodes (opposite feet; parts of the earth diametrically opposed)

Tripod   Pedometer
Podium   Pedestal

pedo [*child*] orthopedic, pedagogue (child leader; teacher), pediatrics (medical care of children)

pel, puls [*drive, urge*] compel, dispel, expel, repel, propel, pulse, impulse, pulsate, compulsory, expulsion, repulsive

pend, pens, pond [*hang, weigh*] pendant (a hanging object), pendulum, depend, impend, suspend, perpendicular, pending, dispense, pensive (weighing thought), appendage

phil [*love*] philosophy (love of wisdom), philanthropy, philharmonic, bibliophile, Philadelphia (city of brotherly love)

phobia [*fear*] claustrophobia (fear of closed spaces), acrophobia (fear of high places), aquaphobia (fear of water)

phon [*sound*] phonograph, phonetic (pertaining to sound), symphony (sounds with or together)

photo [*light*] photograph (light-writing), photoelectric, photogenic (artistically suitable for being photographed), photometer

(light meter), photosynthesis (action of light on chlorophyll to make carbohydrates)

plac, plais [*please*] placid (calm, peaceful), placebo, placate, complacent (self-satisfied)

plenus [*full*] replenish (to fill again), plentiful, plenteous, plenary

plu, plur, plus [*more*] plus (indicating that something is to be added), plural (more than one), plurisyllabic (having more than one syllable)

pneuma, pneumon [*breath*] pneumatic (pertaining to air, wind or other gases), pneumonia (disease of the lungs)

pod (see *ped*)

poli [*city*] metropolis (mother city; main city), police, politics, Indianapolis, megalopolis, Acropolis (high city, fortified upper part of Athens)

pon, pos, pound [*place, put*] postpone (put afterward), component, opponent (one put against), proponent, expose, impose, deposit, posture (how one places himself), position

pop [*people*] population (the number of people in an area), populous (full of people), popular

port [*carry*] porter (one who carries), portable, transport (carry across), report, export, import, support, transportation, port

portion [*part, share*] portion (a part; a share, as a portion of pie), proportion (the relation of one share to others)

posse, potent [*power*] posse (an armed band; a force of legal authority), possible, potent, omnipotent, impotent

prehend [*seize*] apprehend (seize

a criminal), comprehend (seize with the mind), comprehensive (seizing much, extensive)

prim, prime [*first*] primacy (state of being first in rank), prima donna (the first lady of opera), primitive (from the earliest or first time), primary, primal

proto [*first*] prototype (the first model made), protocol, protagonist, protozoan

psych [*mind, soul*] psyche (soul, mind), psychic (sensitive to forces of the mind or soul), psychiatry (hearing of the mind), psychology, psychosis (serious mental disorder), psychotherapy (mind treatment)

punct [*point, dot*] punctual (being exactly on time), punctuation, puncture, acupuncture

put [*think*] computer (a computing or thinking machine), dispute, repute

quies [*be at rest*] quiet, acquiesce, quiescent

reg, recti [*straighten*] correct, direct, regular, rectify (make straight), regiment, rectangle

ri, ridi, risi [*laughter*] ridicule (laughter at the expense of another; mockery), deride (make mock of; jeer at), risible (likely to laugh at), ridiculous

rog, roga [*ask*] prerogative (privilege; asing before), interrogation (questioning; the act of questioning), derogatory

rupt [*break*] rupture (break), interrupt (break into), abrupt (broken off), disrupt (break apart), erupt (break out), incorruptible (unable to be broken down)

salv, salu [*safe, healthy*] salvation (act of being saved), salvage (that which is saved after appearing to be lost), salutary (promoting health), salute (wish health to)

sat, satis [*enough*] satisfy (to give pleasure to; to give as much as is needed), satient (giving pleasure, satisfying), saturate

sci [*know*] science (knowledge), conscious (knowing, aware), omniscient (knowing everything)

scope [*see, watch*] telescope, microscope, kaleidoscope (instrument for seeing beautiful forms), periscope, stethoscope

scrib, script [*write*] scribe (a writer), scribble, inscribe, describe, subscribe, prescribe, manuscript (written by hand)

sed, sess, sid [*sit*] preside (sit before), president, reside, subside, sediment (that which sits or settles out of a liquid), session (a sitting), obsession (an idea that sits stubbornly in the mind), possess

sent, sens [*feel*] sentiment (feeling), consent, resent, dissent, sentimental (having strong feeling or emotion), sense, sensation, sensitive, sensory, dissension

sen [*old*] senior, senator, senile (old; showing the weakness of old age)

sequ, secu, sue [*follow*] sequence (following of one thing after another), sequel, consequence, subsequent, prosecute, execute, consecutive (following in order), ensue, pursue, second (following first)

serv [*save, serve*] servant, service, subservient, servitude, reservation, preserve, conserve, deserve, observe, conservation

sign, signi [*sign, mark, seal*] signal (a gesture or sign to call attention), signature (the mark of a person written in his own handwriting), design, insignia (distinguishing marks), signify

simil, simul [*like, resembling*] similar (resembling in many respects), simulate (pretend; put on an act to make a certain impression), assimilate (to make similar to), simile

sist, sta, stit, stet [*stand*] assist (to stand by with help), circumstance, stamina (power to withstand, to endure), persist (stand firmly; unyielding; continue), substitute (to stand in for another), status (standing), state, static, stable, stationary

solus [*alone*] solo, soliloquy, solitaire, solitude

solv, solu [*loosen*] solvent (a loosener, a dissolver), solve, absolve (loosen from, free from), resolve, soluble, solution, resolution, resolute, dissolute (loosened morally)

somnus [*sleep*] insomnia (not being able to sleep), somnambulist (a sleepwalker)

soph [*wise*] sophomore (wise fool), philosophy (love of wisdom), sophisticated (worldly wise)

sphere [*ball, sphere*] sphere (a planet; a ball), stratosphere (the upper portion of the atmosphere), hemisphere (half of the earth), spheroid

spec, spect, spic [*look*] specimen (an example to look at, study), specific, spectator (one who looks), spectacle, speculate, aspect, expect, inspect, respect, prospect, retrospective (looking backwards), introspective, conspicuous, despicable

spir [*breath*] spirit (lit., breath), conspire (breathe together; plot), inspire (breathe into), aspire (breathe toward), expire (breathe out; die), perspire, respiration

spond, spons [*pledge, answer*] sponsor (one who pledges responsibility to a project), correspond (to communicate by letter; sending and receiving answers), irresponsible, respond

string, strict [*draw, tight*] strict, restrict, stringent (draw tight; rigid), constrict (draw tightly together), boa constrictor (snake that constricts its prey)

stru, struct [*build*] structure, construct, instruct, obstruct, construe (build in the mind, interpret), destroy, destruction

sume, sump [*take, use, waste*] consume (to use up), assume (to take; to use), presume (to take upon oneself before knowing for sure), sump pump (a pump which takes up water)

tact, tang, tag, tig, ting [*touch*] contact (touch), contagious (transmission of disease by touching), intact (untouched, uninjured), intangible (not able to be touched), tangible, tactile

tele [*far*] telephone (far sound), telegraph (far writing), telegram, telescope (far look), television (far seeing), telephoto (far photograph), telecast, telepathy (far feeling)

tempo [*time*] tempo (rate of speed), temporary, pro tem (for the time being), extemporaneously, contemporary (those who live at the same time)

ten, tin, tain [*hold*] contain, tenacious (holding fast), tenant, tenure, untenable, detention, retentive, content, pertinent, continent, obstinate, abstain, pertain, detain, obtain, maintain

tend, tent, tens [*stretch, strain*] tension (a stretching, strain), tendency (a stretching; leaning), extend, intend, contend, pretend, superintend, tender, tent

terra [*earth*] territory, terrestrial, terrain, terrarium

test [*to bear witness*] testament (a will; bearing witness to someone's wishes), detest, attest (certify; affirm; bear witness to), testimony, contest

therm [*heat*] thermometer, therm (heat unit), thermal, thermos bottle, thermostat (heat plus stationary; a device for keeping heat constant), hypothermia (subnormal body temperature)

tom [*cut*] atom (not cutable; smallest particle of matter), appendectomy (cutting out an appendix), tonsillectomy, dichotomy (cutting in two; a division), anatomy (cutting, dissecting to study structure)

tort, tors [*twist*] torsion (act of twisting, as a torsion bar), torture (twisting to inflict pain), retort (twist back, reply sharply), extort (twist out), distort (twist out of shape), contort, tortuous (full of twists)

tox [*poison*] toxic (poisonous), intoxicate, antitoxin

tract, tra [*draw, pull*] tractor, attract, subtract, tractable (can be handled), abstract (to draw away), subtrahend (the number to be drawn away from another)

trib [*pay, bestow*] tribute (to pay honor to), contribute (to give money to a cause), attribute, retribution, tributary

tui, tuit, tut [*guard, teach*] tutor (one who teaches a pupil), tuition (payment for instruction or teaching fees), intuition

turbo [*disturb*] turbulent, turmoil, disturb, turbid

typ [*print*] type, prototype (first print, model), typical, typography, typewriter, typology (study of types, symbols), typify

uni [*one*] unicorn (a legendary creature with one horn), unify (make into one), university, unanimous, universal

vac [*empty*] vacate (to make empty), vacuum (a space entirely devoid of matter), evacuate (to remove troops or people), vacation, vacant

vale, vali, valu [*strength, worth*] valor (value; worth), validity (truth; legal strength), equivalent (of equal worth), evaluate (find out the value; appraise actual worth), valiant, value

ven, vent [*come*] convene (come together, assemble), intervene (come between), circumvent (coming around), invent, convent, venture, venue, event, avenue, advent, convenient, prevent

vert, vers [*turn*] avert (turn away), divert (turn aside, amuse), invert (turn over), introvert (turn inward, one interested in his own reactions), extrovert (turn outward, one interested in what is happening outside himself), controversy (a turning against; a dispute), reverse

vict, vinc [*conquer*] victor (conqueror, winner), evict (conquer out, expel), convict (prove guilty), convince (conquer mentally, persuade), invincible (not able to be conquered), eviction

vid, vis [*see*] video (television), vision, evident, provide, providence, visible, revise, supervise (oversee), vista, visit

viv, vita, vivi [*alive, life*] revive (make live again), survive (live beyond, outlive), vivid (full of life), vivisection (surgery on a living animal), vitality, vivacious (full of life)

voc [*call*] vocation (a calling), avocation (occupation not one's calling), convocation (a calling together), invocation (calling in), evoke, provoke, revoke, advocate, provocative, vocal, vocabulary

vol [*will*] malevolent, benevolent (one of good will), volunteer, volition

volcan, vulcan [*fire*] Vulcan (Roman god of fire), volcano (a mountain erupting fiery lava), volcanize (to undergo volcanic heat)

vor [*eat greedily*] voracious, carnivorous (flesh-eating), herbivorous (plant-eating), omnivorous (eating everything), devour (eating greedily)

zo [*animal*] zoo (short for zoological garden), zoology (study of animal life), zoomorphism (attributing animal form to God), zodiac (circle of animal constellations), protozoa (first animals; one-celled animals)

zo [*animal*] zoo (short for zoological garden), zoology (study of animal life), protozoa (first animals; one-celled animals)

722   # Improving Note-Taking Skills

Isn't it easier to remember something you have actually done than something you have only heard about?   Taking notes is doing something.   It changes information you have only heard about into information you have done something with.   You not only hear the information, you also "see" it as you write it down.   This makes the information become much easier to remember and use.

The most important thing to know about note-taking is that it's not simply writing down what you hear someone say: it's listening, thinking, questioning, summarizing, organizing, listing, illustrating—and writing.

723   ## Guidelines for Improving Note-Taking Skills

The guidelines which follow will help you understand better what you must do to improve your note-taking skills.   Read and follow each suggestion carefully.

1. Listen for and follow the special rules or guidelines your classroom teacher wants you to follow when it comes to note-taking.

2. Place the date and the topic of each lesson at the top of each page of notes.

3. Write your notes in ink, on one side of the paper, and as neatly as time will allow; leave space in the margin for revising or adding to your notes later.

4. Remember, taking good notes does not mean writing down everything; it means summarizing the main ideas and listing only the important supporting details.

219

5. Write as concisely as you can. Leave out words that are not necessary; write your notes in phrases rather than complete sentences.

6. Use as many abbreviations, acronyms, and symbols (U.S., avg., in., ea., lb., vs., @, #, $, %, &, +, -, ⅔, etc.) as you can.

7. Always copy down (or summarize) what the teacher puts on the board or on an overhead projector.

8. Draw simple illustrations in your notes whenever it helps make a point clearer.

9. Write a title or heading for each new topic covered in your notes.

10. Listen for transitions or signal words to help you organize your notes.

11. Number all items presented in a list or in a time order.

12. Circle those words or ideas which you will need to ask about or look up later.

13. Read over the notes you have taken and recopy, highlight, or summarize them as needed. (Consider using a colored marker or pen to highlight those notes which you feel are especially important.)

Listening Skills

724   Listening is the easiest of all ways to learn. At the same time, listening is the most difficult of all the learning skills to improve. Why?

First of all, to listen well you have to pay very close attention to the speaker. You have to concentrate on what he or she is saying and not let your mind wander away. You also have to listen "between the lines" and try to figure out what all of the information is adding up to. This isn't easy.

Secondly, listening is not something we do automatically. Most of us were born with the ability to hear, but not with the ability to listen. We have to be taught this and then given a chance to practice our listening skills. Listening is much more than sitting up straight, looking in the direction of the person speaking, and following what is being said with your mind. There are a number of specific things you should know about listening before you begin working to improve this learning skill.

Guidelines for Improving Listening Skills

725   The guidelines which follow will help you understand better all that is involved in the listening process. Read and think about each guideline. Then begin working to improve your listening skills by following these suggestions.

1. Have a positive attitude toward listening and learning; you have to "want" to improve before you can ever expect to.
2. Avoid poor listening habits such as daydreaming, pretending to listen, or giving up when the material becomes difficult.
3. Concentrate on the speaker and his tone of voice, facial expressions, and other gestures. This may help you figure out which points are most important as well as what the speaker is suggesting (saying between the lines).
4. Listen for spoken directions and follow them carefully.
5. Listen for a pattern in the way the speaker presents the main points and important supporting details.
6. Listen for the speaker's use of signal words and phrases like *as a result, next, secondly,* etc. These signals can help you follow the speaker from one point to the next.
7. Think about what is being said. What does this material mean to me? How might I use this information in the future?
8. Listen with pen in hand. Take notes on any information you have to remember for tests or discussions; do not, however, take so many notes that you miss some of the important points or the overall idea of what is being said.
9. Summarize each main point being made and decide why each point is important.
10. Write down questions you would like to ask; ask them as soon as you get the chance.
11. Find out how much of the information you will be expected to know in the future.
12. Summarize the entire talk in one or two sentences as a final test of whether or not you understand what was said.

726 Guidelines for Writing Assignments

727 **Planning Your Work Session**

1. First of all, know exactly what the writing assignment is, when it is due, and what you must do to complete it successfully.

2. Gather any materials you may need to complete your assignment (journal, notebook, handouts, dictionary, handbook, etc.).

3. Decide how much time you will need to complete the assignment and when and where (library, study hall, home) you will do your assignment.

4. If you are having trouble doing your writing assignments as you should, try doing them at the same time and place each day. This will help you control the urge to wait until you are "in the mood" before starting.

5. Try to avoid doing your writing when you are hungry or tired.

6. Plan to take breaks only after completing a certain amount of each assignment and stick to that schedule. If necessary, ask your family not to disturb you and hold any phone calls you may get.

Preparing to Write

7. Go over all the directions your teacher has given you for this assignment. Look up any words you are unsure of and write down the meaning of each.

8. Keep a list of things you need to check on or ask your teacher about. (Remember, all writing is basically an attempt to solve a problem. You must clearly understand a problem before you can solve it.)

Selecting and Supporting Your Topic

9. If you have not been given a specific topic to write about, begin listing possibilities. Try first to think of topics you are interested in or know something about. Consider the suggestions given by your teacher; look in newspapers or magazines for ideas. (See "Selecting a Topic," 351.)

10. When you have a topic you feel will work for this assignment, place a clear statement of that topic at the top of your paper. This statement can serve as your *controlling idea* and will help keep you from wandering off the topic.

11. Next list all your thoughts and ideas about the topic.

12. Continue to gather information (from as many sources as necessary) until you have enough details to support your topic. (It is always a good idea to collect more information than you think you will actually need.)

Arranging Your Information

13. Look carefully at your information and begin arranging it into the best possible order: order of importance, time order, order of location, etc. Even though you may later add details or change their order, it is always a good idea to start with a specific plan.

14. Put your main points into a working outline. This will help you spot any gaps which may exist and make it clear where you must add more details.

Writing Your Assignment

15. Continue writing. Listen to your ideas as you are putting them on paper. Good writing sounds natural and honest. Here are some pointers which may help you keep your writing sincere and clear:

    a. Don't go hunting for a big word when a small one will do—a big word is one you probably wouldn't use in a classroom conversation.

       Do, however, use your thesaurus when you need a "fresh" word or one which is more specific than the word you first used.

    b. Don't use slang or *qualifiers* like *kind of, sort of, quite,* or *a bit* which add nothing to what you have already said.

       Do, however, use contractions if they sound more natural.

    c. Don't use filler or padding—when you have said all that needs to be said, stop writing.

       Do, however, include enough details (examples, reasons, comparisons, etc.) to prove your point or paint a complete picture.

    d. Don't use adverbs or adjectives when they are unnecessary: return *back, more* perfect, screamed *loudly, final* result.

       Do use verbs which are vivid and nouns which are concrete; by doing so, you eliminate the need for additional modifiers:

       sprinted, dashed, scampered—not *ran fast*
       engineer, conductor, porter—not *railroad worker*

16. Work for an ending which gives the reader something to take with him or her and share with others.

Revising and Proofreading

17. Check your writing for fragments and run-ons. (Reading each paragraph backwards one sentence at a time can help you locate these errors.)

18. Revise and proofread your writing carefully. (Use the checklist in the handbook if necessary.) Always check for spelling, usage, and punctuation errors.

Writing Your Final Copy

19. Follow the directions of your teacher when it comes to writing or typing your final copy. Keep your final copy clean and wrinkle free.

20. Turn your writing assignment in on time and welcome any suggestions your teacher may give you for future improvement. The only way to improve your writing is to write, rewrite, and write again.

Test-Taking Skills

728 Organizing and Preparing Test Material

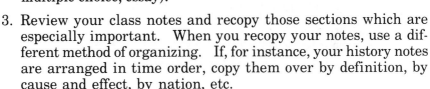

1. Ask the teacher to be as specific as possible about what will be on the test.
2. Ask how the material will be tested (true/false, multiple choice, essay).
3. Review your class notes and recopy those sections which are especially important. When you recopy your notes, use a different method of organizing. If, for instance, your history notes are arranged in time order, copy them over by definition, by cause and effect, by nation, etc.
4. Get any notes or materials you may have missed from the teacher or another student.
5. Set up a specific time to study for an exam and stick to it.
6. Make a list of special terms and study that list carefully.
7. Look over old quizzes and exams.
8. Prepare an outline of everything to be covered on the test.
9. Try to imagine what questions will be on the test and write practice answers for them.
10. Set aside a list of questions to ask the teacher or another student.

729 Reviewing and Remembering Test Material

1. Begin reviewing early. Don't wait until the night before a test.
2. Skim the material in your textbooks.
3. Use maps, lists, diagrams, acronyms, rhymes, or any other special memory aids.
4. Use flash cards or note cards and review with them whenever time becomes available.
5. Recite material out loud whenever possible as you review; also, test yourself by teaching or explaining it to someone else.
6. Study with others only after you have studied well by yourself.
7. Go over your material at least once on the exam day.

730   Taking the Test

1. Check to see that you have all the materials (paper, pens, books, etc.) you need to take the test.

2. Listen carefully to the final instructions of the teacher. How much time do you have to complete the test? Do all the questions count equally? Can you use any aids such as a dictionary or handbook? Are there any corrections, changes, or additions to the test?

3. Begin the test immediately and watch the time carefully.

4. Read the directions carefully, underlining or marking special instructions.

5. Follow all special instructions, like showing your work on math tests.

6. Read all questions carefully, paying attention to words like *always, only, all,* and *never.*

7. Answer the questions you are sure of first.

8. Move on to the next question when you get stuck.

731   Taking the Objective Test

732   True/False Test

1. Read the entire question before answering. Often the first half of a statement will be true or false, while the second half is just the opposite. For an answer to be true, *the entire statement must be true.*

2. Read each word and number carefully. Pay special attention to names and dates which are similar and could easily be confused. Also, watch for numbers which contain the same numerals but in a different order. (Example: 1619 . . . 1691)

3. Be especially careful of true/false statements which contain words like *all, every, always, never,* etc. Very often these statements will be false simply because there is an exception to nearly every rule.

4. Watch for statements which contain more than one negative word. *Remember:* Two negatives make a positive.

733   Matching Test

1. Read through both lists quickly before you begin answering.

2. When matching word to phrase, *read the phrase first* and look for the word it describes.

3. Cross out each answer as you find it—*unless* you are told that the answers can be used more than once.

4. If you get stuck when matching word to word, figure out the part of speech of each word. If the word is a verb, for example, match it with another verb.

734 Multiple Choice Test

1. Read the directions very carefully to determine whether you are looking for the *correct* answer or the *best* answer. Also check to see if some questions can have more than one correct answer.

2. Read the first part of the question very carefully, looking for negative words like *not, never, except, unless,* etc.

3. Try to answer the question in your mind before looking at the choices.

4. Read all the choices before selecting an answer. This is especially important in tests where you have to select the best answer.

5. As you read through the choices, try to rule out those which are obviously incorrect; then go back and choose from the remaining answers.

735 Fill in the Blanks

1. If the word before the blank is *a,* the word you need *probably* begins with a consonant; if the word before the blank is *an,* your answer should begin with a vowel.

2. If the missing word is the subject of the sentence, the verb *should* tell you whether your answer should be singular or plural.

3. The length of the blank will *sometimes* tell you how long your answer should be.

4. If there are several blanks in a row, they *could* represent the number of words which are needed in your answer.

Literary Terms

736 An **abstract** word is one that refers to an idea instead of a real object or thing. *Friendship, pride, competition,* and *kindness* are examples of abstract words.

737 **Action** refers to everything that goes on or happens in a story.

738 An **allegory** is a story in which the characters and action represent an idea or truth about life; often, a strong moral or lesson is taught in this type of story.

739 An **allusion** in literature is a reference to a well-known person, place, thing, or event.

740 An **analogy** is a comparison of two or more similar objects; the analogy implies that since these objects are alike in some ways, they will probably be alike in other ways as well.

741 An **anecdote** is a brief story used to make a point. The story about Abraham Lincoln walking more than two miles to return several pennies he had accidentally overcharged a customer is an example of an anecdote which shows how honest Abe was.

742 The **antagonist** is the person or thing fighting against the hero of a story. If the antagonist is a person, he is usually called the villain.

743 **Antithesis** is a contrasting of ideas in the same or neighboring sentences. *Example:* "We decided to have the bear for supper before he decided to have us!"

744 An **autobiography** is the writer's story of his own life.

745 A **biography** is the writer's story or account of some other person's life.

746 **Caricature** is a description of a character in which his features or characteristics are exaggerated and distorted to the point of being funny or ridiculous. (See illustration.)

747 A **character** is a person in a story or poem.

748 **Characterization** is the author's special way of explaining the people in his story—telling us about their personalities and their reasons for doing things.

749 A **cliche** is a familiar word or phrase which has been used so much that it is no longer a good, effective way of saying something—as in "sharp as a tack" or "fresh as a daisy."

750 The **climax** is the highest point (turning point) in the action of a story.

751 **Comedy** is writing which deals with life in a light, humorous way, often poking fun at the mistakes people make during their lives.

752 A **concrete** word is one that refers to a real object or thing which can be heard, seen, felt, tasted, or smelled. *Pizza, book, tree,* and *tulip* are examples of concrete words.

753 **Conflict** refers to the problems and complications in a story.

754 **Connotation** is the feeling or emotion a word brings to your mind. For example, the word *sparkle* brings a good feeling to mind, while the word *mud* brings a not-so-good feeling.

755 The **context** of a particular word refers to the other words around it. These other words can be used to help you figure out the meaning of the particular word.
      Example: It was a clear, sunny day, and the sky was a pretty shade of *azure.* (By looking at the other words in the sentence, you can figure out that *azure* means *blue.)*

756 **Denotation** is the dictionary meaning of a word, without the emotion or feeling *(connotation)* connected with the word.
      A *denotation of mud:* soft, wet earth or dirt
      A *connotation of mud:* an icky, slimy mixture of dirt and water to be avoided—especially when wearing new shoes

757 The **denouement** is the satisfying end of a play or story—that part of the story in which the problems are solved.

758 **Description** is a type of writing that creates a clear picture in your mind—a clear picture of a person, place, or thing.

759 **Dialogue** refers to the talking that goes on between characters in a story.

760 **Diction** is a writer's choice of words. There are many ways to describe the different kinds of words a writer can use. Below are some examples:

Diction

761 **Archaic** words are old-fashioned words which sound odd to us today.
      Archaic: Hast thou enjoyed thy repast?
      Modern: Have you enjoyed your meal?

762 A **colloquialism** is a common, everyday expression like *"What's happenin'?"* or *"How's it goin'?"*. These expressions are used when talking to each other or when writing dialogue.

763 **Profanity** is language used to degrade someone or something considered to be holy or sacred.

764 **Slang** is language used by a certain group of people when they are talking to each other. For example, "He's *totally awesome"* is a slang expression used by some people today. Many years ago, the slang expression "He's the *cat's pajamas"* would have meant the same thing.

765 **Trite** expressions are like cliches. They are used too much to be a very good way of saying something, especially in writing.
Examples: true blue, red as a beet, hotter than blazes

766 **Vulgarity** is language which is generally crude, gross, and offensive.

767 **Didactic** writing is intended to teach you something, especially a moral lesson.

768 **Drama** is the form of literature commonly known as *plays*. The word *drama* often refers to serious plays written about man and his relationship to society.

769 A **dramatic monologue** is a poem in which a character tells a lot about himself by speaking either to himself or to another character.

770 **Empathy** is putting yourself in someone else's place and imagining how that person must feel. A writer must imagine how each character would feel or react to whatever is happening in a story.

771 An **epigram** is a short, clever poem or saying.
Early to bed and early to rise,
Makes a man healthy, wealthy, and wise.
(Ben Franklin)

772 An **epitaph** is a short poem or verse written in memory of someone.

773 An **epithet** is a word or phrase which describes a certain person and is used in place of (or along with) that person's name. *Examples:* Richard the Lionhearted (a courageous king), Mr. Goodwrench (someone who is good with a wrench), Minnesota Fats (a hefty pool player from Minnesota)

774 An **essay** is a piece of writing which gives the author's ideas or point of view about a subject. Usually, an essay contains several paragraphs and has an introduction, body, and conclusion.

775 **Exaggeration** is stretching the truth. This can be used effectively in some instances in your writing. For example, a frightened character in a story might say, "I thought that dog was going to bite my leg off!"

776 The **exposition** is that part of a play or novel (usually the beginning) which explains the background and setting of the story; the characters are often introduced in the exposition. (See *plot line*.)

777 **Falling action** is that part of a story which follows the climax or turning point; it contains the action or dialogue necessary to lead the story to a resolution or ending.

778 **Farce** is literature (stories or plays) written for one purpose: to make the reader laugh.

779 **Figurative language** is language used in a special way to create a special effect. It is made up of words and phrases which don't mean what they first appear to mean. *Example:* You three *put your*

heads together and plan the class party. (This does not mean *bump your heads together;* it means *share the ideas you have in your heads.*) (See *figures of speech.*)

780 A **figure of speech** is a device used by authors to create a special meaning for their readers. (See the Poetry section of this handbook for explanations of *metaphor, personification,* and *simile.*)

Personification: The rock stubbornly refused to move.

781 In a **flashback**, the author goes back to an earlier time in the story and explains something that will help the reader understand the whole story better.

782 **Foreshadowing** is the writer's hints and clues about what is going to happen in the story.

783 **Form** is the way a piece of writing is put together or organized.

784 **Genre** is the French word for the *form* or *type* of literature. The novel, short story, and poem are three of many *genres.*

785 A **gothic novel** is a special type of book in which a mysterious, sometimes scary story is told. The action usually takes place in a large, old mansion or castle and may include a ghost or two. *Frankenstein* by Mary Shelley is a well-known gothic novel.

786 **Impressionism** is writing which contains impressions about an event or situation instead of only the facts about the event. It is writing which gives the reader a general impression or picture (much like a painting) rather than a true-to-life picture (like a photograph).

787 **Irony** is using a word or phrase to mean the exact opposite of its normal meaning. *Example:* "My *favorite* pastime is cleaning my room."

788 **Local color** is the use of details which are common in a certain place (a *local* area). For example, a story taking place on the western seacoast would probably contain some details about the ocean and the life and people near it.

789   A malapropism is a "mistake" which happens when a character mixes up two words in his mind and then uses the wrong word, creating a *pun* or *play on words*. *Example:* A young student, who had the word *watt* confused with *what*, wrote on a science report, "I know a lot about electricity, but I still can't figure out those *whats!*"

790   Melodrama is drama written in an exaggerated way to produce strong feeling or excitement in the reader or viewer. TV soap operas are examples of modern melodrama.

791   Mood is the feeling(s) a reader gets from a piece of writing: happy, sad, peaceful, etc.

792   The moral is the lesson an author is trying to teach in his story. Children's stories often have rather obvious morals. *"Don't take or use what doesn't belong to you"* is a lesson taught in the story of "The Three Bears."

793   The motif is a repeated incident or idea in literature. *"The forces of good fighting against the forces of evil"* is a common motif in the *Superman* and *Star Wars* stories.

794   A myth is a story that tries to explain a certain belief, especially a belief having to do with nature or religion. *Hercules* is a famous character in Greek mythology.

795   The narrator is the person or character who is telling the story. For example, Black Beauty tells his own story in the book *Black Beauty* by Anna Sewell; so in this instance, the narrator is a horse.

796   A narration is a story. It tells you about an event or a series of events.

797   A novel is a book-length, prose story. It is also fictional, which means it is made up or created by the author's imagination.

798   A parable is a short, descriptive story which explains a certain belief or moral.

799   A paradox is a statement that seems to go against common sense but is actually true. A construction worker or farmer may say, *"My muscles ache from working hard all day, but it's a good feeling."* (Because they are happy to have done a hard day's work, they are able to appreciate their sore muscles.)

800   Parallelism is the repeating of phrases or sentences that are written or constructed in the same way. *Example:* "On our vacation we will *lie on the beach, swim in the ocean,* and *sleep under the stars."* Each verb *(lie, swim,* and *sleep)* is followed by a prepositional phrase.

801   Pathos describes that part of a story that makes you feel sorry for the characters.

802   Plagiarism is copying someone else's writing or ideas and then us-

ing them as if they were your own.

803 The **plot** is the action of the story. This action is usually made up of a series of events called the *plot line.*

804 The **plot line** shows the action or series of events in the story. It has five parts: *exposition, rising action, climax, falling action,* and *resolution.*

805 **Poetry** is writing which is imaginative and emotional. Poetry is written with words that are vivid and colorful. These words are then arranged so that they have pleasing sound and rhythm.

806 The **point of view** is the angle from which a story is told. This depends upon who is telling the story. A *first-person* point of view means that one of the characters is telling the story: *"I walked slowly, wishing I could turn and run instead of facing Mrs. Grunch."* A third-person point of view means that someone outside of the story is telling it: *"She walked slowly, wishing she could turn and run instead of facing Mrs. Grunch."*

807 There are three basic **third-person points of view:**

808 The **unlimited (omniscient)** point of view allows the narrator or storyteller to write about the thoughts and feelings of all the characters as if he were able to read their minds.

233

809 The **limited (limited omniscient)** point of view allows the narrator to relate the thoughts and feelings of one character.

810 The **camera view (objective view)** allows the narrator to see and record the action from a neutral or unemotional point of view. The narrator can write about what the characters are doing but not what they are thinking.

811 The **protagonist** is the hero of the story.

812 A **pseudonym** is the name an author may use in place of his real name. For example, *Mark Twain* was a pseudonym for the author's real name, which was *Samuel Clemens*.

813 A **pun** is a word or phrase used in a way that gives it a funny twist. The words used in a pun sound the same, but they have different meanings. **Example:** *"I scream, you scream, we all scream for ice cream!" (I scream sounds like ice cream.)*

814 **Realism** is writing that *shows life as it really is* rather than as the author or reader might like it to be. This kind of writing often includes the everyday, ordinary happenings of life — like spilling milk at breakfast or trying to get a knot out of your shoelaces.

815 The **resolution** is the satisfying end of a play or story — that part in which the problems are solved.

816 The **rising action** is the central part of a story during which various problems arise, leading up to the climax.

817   **Romance** is writing that *shows life as the author or reader might like it to be* rather than as it really is.   Often, a romance is full of adventure and excitement—like secret agents chasing evil spies or superheroes saving damsels in distress.

818   **Sarcasm** is the use of praise to ridicule or "put down" someone or something.   The praise is not sincere and is actually intended to mean the opposite thing.   Calling a turtle-like person *a real go-getter* would be sarcasm.

819   **Satire** is writing that ridicules or makes fun of people's mistakes and weaknesses.   Satire is often used to raise questions about a current trend or political decision.

820   The **setting** is the time and place in which the action of a story takes place.

821   **Slapstick** comedy uses exaggerated, sometimes violent action to make the audience laugh, as when someone is hit in the face with a pie.

822   A **slice of life** describes the kind of writing the author of a realistic story is trying to give to his readers.   He wants them to see a part or slice of "real everyday life," not "romantic or pretend life."

823   A **soliloquy** is a speech given in a play by a character who is alone on stage.

824   A **stereotype** is a pattern that does not change.   When a character is "stereotyped," it means he is exactly like a certain *type* of person and has no individuality.   For example, athletes are sometimes stereotyped as being big, dumb, and having no other talents than being good at a sport.   Stereotyping creates characters who are so predictable they are not very interesting to read about in a story.

825   **Stream of consciousness** is a style of writing in which the author records his exact thoughts and feelings as they come and go.   The author writes about whatever is on his mind at the time.

826   **Structure** means much the same thing as *form* in writing.   When an author has something to say, he must fit his words into a form or pattern in order to get his point across to the reader.   If a piece of writing has no form or structure, it will probably be difficult to read.   One writer may use a *poem* to organize his words, another may use an *essay*, another a *romantic novel*, and so on.

827   **Style** is *how* the author writes *(his choice and arrangement of words)* rather than *what* he writes *(his message to the readers)*.

828   A **symbol** is a concrete or real object used to represent an idea.   *Examples:* A *bird*, because it can fly, has often been used as a *symbol for freedom*.   Our *flag* is a *symbol of our nation*, the United States of America.   Each star represents one of the fifty states and each stripe represents one of the thirteen original colonies.

829   The **theme** is the *subject or message* being written about or discussed.

830   The **tone** is the author's attitude or feeling about a piece of writing. The author's tone may be *serious, humorous* (funny), *satiric,* and so on.

831   The **total effect** of a piece of writing is the overall influence it has on you, the reader—the way it makes you feel and the ideas it gives you.

832   **Understatement** is the opposite of exaggeration. The author restrains himself or holds back in his writing, thereby bringing special attention to an object or idea. The author Mark Twain once described Tom Sawyer's Aunt Polly as being "prejudiced against snakes." Since she hated snakes, this way of saying so is called *understatement.*

Understatement: Aunt Polly was
prejudiced against snakes.

Speech Skills

833 Determining the Purpose

The purpose behind all speaking is the same. It is to pass on ideas or feelings and get a favorable response in return. When you have to give a speech or an oral report, you must remember that the purpose is still the same.

834   There are a number of questions which you can ask yourself as you prepare your speech or report:

1. What is the purpose of my speech? Is it to share information? Is it to show my classmates how to do something? Is it to persuade my audience?
2. Who am I giving this speech for? My classmates? My teacher? Another class?
3. Does my speech have to be about a particular topic or can I select a topic I like and one which I think my audience will like as well?
4. How long should the speech be?
5. Can I use visual aids?

Once these questions have been answered, you are ready to begin searching for a topic.

835 Selecting and Narrowing the Topic

If your speech can be on any subject, select a person, place, thing, or event which you are familiar with. This could be anything from taking photographs to a trip you took last summer. What's most important is that you like the topic, and you're pretty sure your audience will too.

If your speech has to be on a current topic, you will need to find help from some other source. Possibly one of your teachers or a close friend will have some suggestions for you. If not, the next best place for you to look is in the library. There you will find many sources for possible topics.

1. The *vertical file,* which is a file of newspaper clippings, brochures, pamphlets, etc., contains hundreds of articles on current topics. Look through some of the articles and see if one would work as a speech topic.
2. The *Reader's Guide to Periodical Literature,* which is a publication listing magazine articles by author and subject, can offer dozens of possible current topics.
3. A *newspaper* or *magazine* can remind you of the major issues in the world today.
4. *Encyclopedias* and other reference books can be very helpful tools when it comes to finding a speech topic. Even a textbook from another class can give you some good topic ideas.

Once you have found a possible topic, decide just how much of that topic you can cover in the time limit you've been given. You should now have a specific topic that will interest your audience and will also fit your time limit.

836 Researching and Analyzing the Topic

After you have selected your topic, you are ready to gather details. You can begin by writing down your own thoughts on the topic, along with any personal experiences you've had which relate to the topic. You can also ask friends and family members what their feelings or memories are about this topic and use these details to help you write your speech. If you need factual details, go to your library and use the material which is available there. (See the "Library Skills" section of this handbook for a detailed description of the card catalog, *Reader's Guide,* and other helpful reference materials.)

Writing a Speech

Writing a speech is much the same as writing a paragraph or an essay. You must write in a clear, natural way so that your speech moves smoothly from one point to the next. Your information should be arranged into a beginning, a middle, and an end. But a speech is not exactly the same as other forms of writing. A speech is written to be *heard* rather than read. It must, therefore, *sound* good as well as look good on paper. It must be written using vivid, concrete words which create a clear, colorful picture for the audience. It must also be written with words that bounce and glide rather than plod along. This means your speech must be written even more carefully than other writing assignments.

838 ## The Introduction, Body, and Conclusion

839 The Introduction: After you have collected enough information for your speech, you should arrange these details into an introduction, body, and conclusion. You should, for example, use one of your most interesting details in your opening or **introduction.**

Your introduction should do the following:
- Gain the attention of your audience.
- Make it clear what your talk is going to be about.
- Get your audience to want to hear more about your topic.
- Lead into the main part of your speech.

You can use one of the following ideas in your introduction:
- an amazing fact
- a series of interesting questions
- a humorous story
- a short demonstration
- a colorful illustration or visual aid
- a short history of the topic
- a personal reason for picking the topic

840 The Body: In the body of the speech, you should move smoothly from one point to the next. You should cover the topic in an easy, natural way. You should use your own language—language which lets your audience feel like you're talking to each one of them personally. Don't use big words just to try to impress them. They'd rather hear the real you, not some talking machine reciting facts, figures, and dates. You should, however, try to include enough "new" or little-known information to make your speech interesting.

Arrange your details in the best possible order—order of importance, chronological order, comparison, cause and effect, and so on.   Explain or describe each part of your topic clearly so that your audience can follow along easily and enjoy what you have to say.   If you are giving your opinion about something, make sure you support your point with enough reasons, facts, and other information to convince your audience.   (See "Guidelines for Persuasive Writing," 646.)

841   End your speech by reminding your audience what the purpose of your speech was.   You might tell them why you feel your topic is important or why it may be important in the future.   You can invite them to "get involved," "learn more," or "try it sometime."   However you end your speech, always know *exactly* what your final two or three sentences are going to be—word for word.   This is true even if you "make up" most of your speech as you go along.   Otherwise, you may end up saying something corny like "That's the end of my report," "That's all," or "I guess that's it."

842   Preparing the Speech for Delivery

Once you are satisfied that your speech is well written, you can write your final copy.   Follow the suggestions listed below:

1. Always write or type your copy as neatly as possible and leave an extra-wide margin at the bottom of your card or paper.
2. Never run a sentence from one page to another.
3. Never abbreviate unless you plan to use the abbreviation.   For example, YMCA and FBI may be abbreviated because you will actually read each letter; A.M. and P.M. should not be used.
4. Number each page.

843   Practicing the Delivery

After you have finished writing your speech, practice giving your speech (out loud) as often as you can.   Try to get an audience of family or friends to listen to you.   They can help you get used to "speaking" and can also offer suggestions for improvement.   Practice until you feel comfortable or until you know your speech well enough to put the main points in your own words without looking at your paper or notes.

844 Giving Your Speech

If you have practiced often and well, giving the actual speech should be easy. You may still feel a little nervous at first, but soon you will relax and enjoy sharing your "story" with your audience. Keep the following suggestions in mind as you give your speech:

1. Speak loudly and clearly.
2. Don't rush. Take your time and let your voice add color and interest to your topic.
3. Use your hands. Sometimes you will need your hands to hold a chart or a poster. Other times, your hands will be busy operating part of your demonstration. At the very least, let your hands hold your note cards or paper (if they are allowed). Never leave your hand movements to chance. They'll end up picking lint off your shirt or dangling nervously at your side.
4. Look at your audience as you speak.
5. Keep both feet firmly on the floor. Don't slouch, sway, or teeter.
6. Show enthusiasm for your topic from start to finish.

845 Speech Checklist

1. Choose a topic both you and your audience will like.
2. Make sure your topic fits the assignment and time limit.
3. Do a good job of thinking about and researching your topic. Explore all sides of the topic.
4. Think about the topic information you have gathered and use only the details which will work well for you.
5. Write an introduction which will gain the interest of your audience as well as introduce your topic.
6. Think about how you can move from one point to another smoothly.
7. Use your own language. Write as if you were actually talking to someone.
8. Don't use "big" words when a small one will do.
9. Make sure everything you say is clear and understandable.
10. Speak loudly enough so everyone can hear you.
11. Don't rush.
12. Use your hands to help you in some way.
13. Keep both feet on the floor.
14. Show enthusiasm for your topic.
15. Look at your audience.
16. End with a strong, interesting idea.

Tables, Maps, and Useful Lists

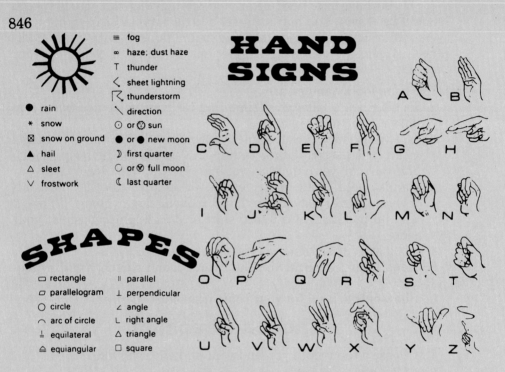

≡	fog
∞	haze; dust haze
T	thunder
⦏	sheet lightning
⦏	thunderstorm
● rain	\ direction
* snow	☉ or ⊛ sun
⊠ snow on ground	● or ● new moon
▲ hail	☽ first quarter
△ sleet	○ or ⊗ full moon
∨ frostwork	☾ last quarter

HAND SIGNS

A B C D E F G H I J K L M N O P Q R S T U V W X Y Z

SHAPES

▭ rectangle	∥ parallel
▱ parallelogram	⊥ perpendicular
○ circle	∠ angle
⌒ arc of circle	∟ right angle
≞ equilateral	△ triangle
≙ equiangular	□ square

Movable Christian and Secular Holidays

Ash Wednesday	Easter	Pentecost	Labor Day	Election Day	Thanksgiving	1st Sunday Advent	
Feb. 20	April 7	May 26	Sept. 2	Nov. 5	Nov. 28	Dec. 1	— 1985
Feb. 12	March 30	May 18	Sept. 1	Nov. 4	Nov. 27	Nov. 30	— 1986
March 4	April 19	June 7	Sept. 7	Nov. 3	Nov. 26	Nov. 29	— 1987
Feb. 17	April 3	May 22	Sept. 5	Nov. 8	Nov. 24	Nov. 27	— 1988
Feb. 8	March 26	May 14	Sept. 4	Nov. 7	Nov. 23	Dec. 3	— 1989
Feb. 28	April 15	June 3	Sept. 3	Nov. 6	Nov. 22	Dec. 2	— 1990
Feb. 13	March 31	May 19	Sept. 2	Nov. 5	Nov. 28	Dec. 1	— 1991
March 4	April 19	June 7	Sept. 7	Nov. 3	Nov. 26	Nov. 29	— 1992

Movable Jewish Holidays

Purim	1st day Passover	1st day Shavuot	1st day Rosh Hashana	Yom Kippur	1st day Sukkot	Simhat Torah	1st day Hanukkah	
March 7	April 6	May 26	Sept. 16	Sept. 25	Sept. 30	Oct. 8	Dec. 8	— 1985
March 25	April 24	June 13	Oct. 4	Oct. 13	Oct. 18	Oct. 26	Dec. 27	— 1986
March 15	April 14	June 3	Sept. 24	Oct. 3	Oct. 8	Oct. 16	Dec. 16	— 1987
March 3	April 2	May 22	Sept. 12	Sept. 21	Sept. 26	Oct. 4	Dec. 4	— 1988
March 21	April 20	June 9	Sept. 30	Oct. 9	Oct. 14	Oct. 22	Dec. 23	— 1989
March 11	April 10	May 30	Sept. 20	Sept. 29	Oct. 4	Oct. 12	Dec. 12	— 1990
Feb. 28	March 30	May 19	Sept. 9	Sept. 18	Sept. 23	Oct. 1	Dec. 2	— 1991
March 14	April 18	June 7	Sept. 28	Oct. 7	Oct. 12	Oct. 20	Dec. 20	— 1992

847

Animal Crackers

Animal	Male	Female	Young	Collective	Gestation	Longevity
Ass	Jack	Jenny	Foal	Herd	340-385	18-20 (63)*
Bear	He-bear	She-bear	Cub	Sleuth	180-240	18-20 (34)
Cat	Tom	Queen	Kitten	Clutter/Clowder	52-65	10-12 (27)
Cattle	Bull	Cow	Calf	Drove/Herd	280	9-12 (25)
Chicken	Rooster	Hen	Chick	Brood/Clutch	21	7-8 (14)
Deer	Buck	Doe	Fawn	Herd	140-250	10-15 (26)
Dog	Dog	Bitch	Pup	Pack	55-70	10-12 (24)
Duck	Drake	Duck	Duckling	Brace/Herd	21-35	10 (15)
Elephant	Bull	Cow	Calf	Herd	515-760	30-40 (98)
Fox	Dog	Vixen	Cub/Kit	Skulk	51-60	8-10 (14)
Goat	Billy	Nanny	Kid	Tribe, Trip	135-163	12 (17)
Goose	Gander	Goose	Gosling	Flock/Gaggle	30	
Horse	Stallion	Mare	Filly/Colt	Herd	304-419	20-25 (50+)
Lion	Lion	Lioness	Cub	Pride	105-111	10 (29)
Monkey	Male	Female	Boy/Girl	Band/Troop	149-179	12-15 (29)
Rabbit	Buck	Doe	Bunny		27-36	6-8 (15)
Sheep	Ram	Ewe	Lamb	Flock/Drove	121-180	12 (16)
Swan	Cob	Pen	Cygnet	Bevy	30	
Swine	Boar	Sow	Piglet	Litter	101-130	10 (15)
Tiger	Tiger	Tigress	Cub		105	19
Whale	Bull	Cow	Calf	Gam/Pod	276-365	37
Wolf	Dog	Bitch	Pup	Pack	63	10-12 (16)

*( ) Record for oldest animal of this type

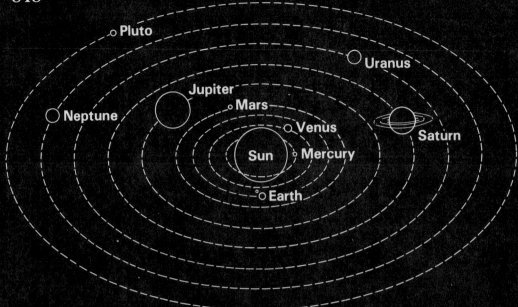

Our solar system is located in the Milky Way Galaxy. Even though this galaxy contains approximately 100 billion stars, our solar system contains only one star—the sun. The sun, which is the center of our solar system, has 9 planets and a myriad of asteroids, meteors, and comets orbiting it. The planets are large, nonluminous bodies which follow fixed elliptical orbits about the sun. (See the illustration above.) The planets are divided into two categories: the terrestrial planets—Mercury, Venus, Earth, Mars, and Pluto—which resemble the Earth in size, chemical composition, and density; and the Jovian planets—Jupiter, Saturn, Uranus, and Neptune—which are much larger in size and have thick, gaseous atmospheres and low densities. (See the table below.)

Planet Profusion

	Sun	Moon	Mercury	Venus	Earth	Mars	Jupiter	Saturn	Uranus	Neptune	Pluto
Orbital Speed (in miles per second)		.6	29.8	21.8	18.5	15.0	8.1	6.0	4.1	3.4	2.9
Rotation on Axis	24 days 16 hr. 48 min.	27 days 7 hr. 38 min.	59 days	243 days	23 hr. 56 min.	1 day 37 min.	9 hr. 50 min.	10 hr. 8 min.	10 hr. 46 min.	18 hr. 12 min.	6 days 9 hr.
Mean Surface Gravity (Earth = 1.00)		0.16	0.33	0.87	1.00	0.37	2.64	1.15	.99	1.27	0.5 (less than)
Density (times that of water)	100	3.3	5.4	5.3	5.5	3.9	1.3	0.7	1.2	1.6	1.0
Mass (times that of earth)	333,000	0.012	0.055	0.8	6×10^{21} metric tons	0.1	318	95	15	17	0.002
Approx. weight of a Human (in pounds)		25	49	130	150	55	396	172	148	190	75
Number of Satellites	9 planets	0	0	0	1	2	16	17	5	2	1
Mean Distance to Sun (in millions of miles)			36.0	67.22	93.0	141.6	483.5	886.5	1,785	2,793	3,664
Revolution around Sun		365.25 days	88.0 days	224.7 days	365.25 days	686.99 days	11.86 years	29.46 years	84.0 years	164.8 years	247.6 years
Approximate Surface Temperature (degrees Fahrenheit)	27,000, 000°	lighted side 200° dark side -230°	lighted side 800° dark side -275°	900°	60°	-60°	-200°	-300°	-355°	-330°	-382°
Diameter (in miles)	867,000	2,155	3,031	7,680	7,921	4,218	88,700	74,940	32,190	30,760	3,600

All About Maps

849   A **map** is a picture of an area.   Special marks and symbols on the picture show where things are located in that area.   Depending on its purpose, a map may show the whole area (a country, for example) or just part of it (a state, county, or city).

850 Kinds of Maps

Maps have many uses.   There are as many different kinds of maps as there are uses.   Your handbook uses one kind of map, the *political map*.   Political maps show how the Earth is divided into countries and states.   Often they also show the capitals and major cities.   The different sizes and styles of the print (or type) used for names on the maps are also important.   These are clues to help make the map information clear.   Usually, the most important names are typed in the largest print.   Different kinds of type are used for countries, cities, rivers, lakes, and other places.

851 Using the Maps

Mapmakers use special marks and symbols to show where things are or to give other useful information.   Among other things, these marks and symbols show direction (north, south, east, and west).   Each can be used to locate direction on a map.

On most maps, north is at the top.   But you should always check the *compass rose* or *directional finder* to make sure you know where north is.   If there is no symbol, you can assume that north is at the top.

852 The Legend

Other important marks and symbols are explained in a box printed on each map.   This box is called the *legend* or *key*.   It is included to make it easier for you to understand and use the map.   Below is the United States map legend   This legend also includes symbols for state capitals and state boundaries.

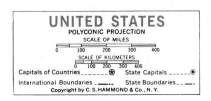

853 The Map Scale

Legends also explain the map scale. The purpose of a map scale is to show how far it really is between places. For example, a scale might show that one inch on the map equals one hundred miles on the Earth. If two cities are shown five inches apart, then they are really five hundred miles apart. A ruler makes using a scale easy, but even an index card or piece of paper will work. Here is the scale from the map of the United States.

SCALE OF MILES
0   100   200   300   400

Line up an index card or piece of paper under it. Put a dot on the card at "0." Now put another dot on your card at the right end of the scale. You've just marked off 400 miles. This can be used to judge the distance between points on the map. Don't forget that scales differ from map to map. Always refer to the scale on the map you are using.

854 Latitude and Longitude

Latitude and longitude lines are another feature of most maps which can be very useful. Latitude and longitude refer to imaginary lines that mapmakers use. When used together, these lines can be used to locate any point on Earth.

The imaginary lines that go from east to west around the Earth are called lines of latitude. The line of latitude that goes around the Earth exactly halfway between the North Pole and the South Pole is called the equator. Latitude is measured in degrees, with the equator being 0 degrees (0°). Above the equator, the lines are called north latitude and measure from 0° to 90° North (the North Pole). Below the equator, the lines are called south latitude and measure from 0° to 90° South (the South Pole). On a map, latitude numbers are printed along the left- and right-hand sides.

Imaginary lines that run from the North Pole to the South Pole are lines of longitude. Longitude is also measured in degrees, beginning with 0 degrees. The north-south line measuring 0° passes through Greenwich, England. This line is called the prime meridian. Lines east of the prime meridian are called east longitude. Lines west of the prime meridian are called west longitude. East and west longitude each go halfway around the Earth. They meet exactly opposite the prime meridian at 180° longitude. On a map, longitude numbers are printed at the top and bottom.

The latitude and longitude number of a place are sometimes called its coordinates. In each set of coordinates, latitude is given first, then longitude. To locate a certain place on a map using its coordinates, find the point where the two lines cross. The place you are looking for will be at or near this point.

INDEX TO WORLD MAPS

Country	Latitude	Longitude	Country	Latitude	Longitude
Afghanistan	33° N	65° E	Guinea	11° N	10° W
Albania	41° N	20° E	Guinea-Bissau	12° N	15° W
Algeria	28° N	3° E	Guyana	5° N	59° W
Andorra	42° N	1° E	Haiti	19° N	72° W
Angola	12° S	18° E	Honduras	15° N	86° W
Antigua and Barbuda	17° N	61° W	Hungary	47° N	20° E
Argentina	34° S	64° W	Iceland	65° N	18° W
Australia	25° S	135° E	India	20° N	77° E
Austria	47° N	13° E	Indonesia	5° S	120° E
Bahamas	24° N	76° W	Iran	32° N	53° E
Bahrain	26° N	50° E	Iraq	33° N	44° E
Bangladesh	24° N	90° E	Ireland	53° N	8° W
Barbados	13° N	59° W	Israel	31° N	35° E
Belgium	50° N	4° E	Italy	42° N	12° E
Belize	17° N	88° W	Ivory Coast	8° N	5° W
Benin	9° N	2° E	Jamaica	18° N	77° W
Bhutan	27° N	90° E	Japan	36° N	138° E
Bolivia	17° S	65° W	Jordan	31° N	36° E
Botswana	22° S	24° E	Kenya	1° N	38° E
Brazil	10° S	55° W	Kiribati	0° N	175° E
Brunei	4° N	114° E	North Korea	40° N	127° E
Bulgaria	43° N	25° E	South Korea	36° N	128° E
Burkina Faso/U.Volta	13° N	2° W	Kuwait	29° N	47° E
Burma	22° N	98° E	Laos	18° N	105° E
Burundi	3° S	30° E	Lebanon	34° N	36° E
Cambodia	13° N	105° E	Lesotho	29° S	28° E
Cameroon	6° N	12° E	Liberia	6° N	10° W
Canada	60° N	95° W	Libya	27° N	17° E
Cape Verde	16° N	24° W	Liechtenstein	47° N	9° E
Central African Rep.	7° N	21° E	Luxembourg	49° N	6° E
Chad	15° N	19° E	Madagascar	19° S	46° E
Chile	30° S	71° W	Malawi	13° S	34° E
China	35° N	105° E	Malaysia	2° N	112° E
Colombia	4° N	72° W	Maldives	2° N	70° E
Comoros	12° S	44° E	Mali	17° N	4° W
Congo	1° S	15° E	Malta	36° N	14° E
Costa Rica	10° N	84° W	Mauritania	20° N	12° W
Cuba	21° N	80° W	Mauritius	20° S	57° E
Cyprus	35° N	33° E	Mexico	23° N	102° W
Czechoslovakia	49° N	17° E	Monaco	43° N	7° E
Denmark	56° N	10° E	Mongolia	46° N	105° E
Djibouti	11° N	43° E	Morocco	32° N	5° W
Dominica	15° N	61° W	Mozambique	18° S	35° E
Dominican Republic	19° N	70° W	Namibia	22° S	17° E
Ecuador	2° S	77° W	Nauru	1° S	166° E
Egypt	27° N	30° E	Nepal	28° N	84° E
El Salvador	14° N	89° W	Netherlands	52° N	5° E
Equatorial Guinea	2° N	9° E	New Zealand	41° S	174° E
Ethiopia	8° N	38° E	Nicaragua	13° N	85° W
Fiji	19° S	174° E	Niger	16° N	8° E
Finland	64° N	26° E	Nigeria	10° N	8° E
France	46° N	2° E	Northern Ireland	55° N	7° W
Gabon	1° S	11° E	Norway	62° N	10° E
The Gambia	13° N	16° W	Oman	22° N	58° E
East Germany	52° N	12° E	Pakistan	30° N	70° E
West Germany	51° N	9° E	Panama	9° N	80° W
Ghana	8° N	2° W	Papua New Guinea	6° S	147° E
Greece	39° N	22° E	Paraguay	23° S	58° W
Greenland	70° N	40° W	Peru	10° S	76° W
Grenada	12° N	61° W	Philippines	13° N	122° E
Guatemala	15° N	90° W	Poland	52° N	19° E

Country	Latitude	Longitude	Country	Latitude	Longitude
Portugal	39° N	8° W	Taiwan	23° N	121° E
Qatar	25° N	51° E	Tanzania	6° S	35° E
Romania	46° N	25° E	Thailand	15° N	100° E
Rwanda	2° S	30° E	Togo	8° N	1° E
St. Christopher & Nevis	17° N	62° W	Tonga	20° S	173° W
Saint Lucia	14° N	61° W	Trinidad/Tobago	11° N	61° W
Saint Vincent			Tunisia	34° N	9° E
and the Grenadines	13° N	61° W	Turkey	39° N	35° E
San Marino	44° N	12° E	Tuvala	8° S	179° E
Sao Tome and Principe	1° N	7° E	Uganda	1° N	32° E
Saudi Arabia	25° N	45° E	USSR	60° N	80° E
Scotland	57° N	5° W	United Arab Emirates	24° N	54° E
Senegal	14° N	14° W	United Kingdom	54° N	2° W
Seychelles	5° S	55° E	United States	38° N	97° W
Sierra Leone	8° N	11° W	Uruguay	33° S	56° W
Singapore	1° N	103° E	Vanuatu	17° S	170° E
Solomon Islands	8° S	159° E	Venezuela	8° N	66° W
Somalia	10° N	49° E	Vietnam North	21° N	105° E
South Africa	30° S	26° E	Vietnam South	13° N	108° E
Spain	40° N	4° W	Wales	53° N	3° W
Sri Lanka	7° N	81° E	Western Samoa	10° S	173° W
Sudan	15° N	30° E	North Yemen	15° N	44° E
Suriname	4° N	56° W	South Yemen	15° N	48° E
Swaziland	26° S	31° E	Yugoslavia	44° N	19° E
Sweden	62° N	15° E	Zaire	4° S	25° E
Switzerland	47° N	8° E	Zambia	15° S	30° E
Syria	35° N	38° E	Zimbabwe	20° S	30° E

856
TOPOGRAPHIC TALLY TABLE

THE CONTINENTS

	Area (Sq Km)	Percent of Earth's Land
Asia	44,026,000	29.7
Africa	30,271,000	20.4
North America	24,258,000	16.3
South America	17,823,000	12.0
Antarctica	13,209,000	8.9
Europe	10,404,000	7.0
Australia	7,682,000	5.2

MAJOR ISLANDS

	Area (Sq Km)
Greenland	2,175,600
New Guinea	792,500
Borneo	725,500
Madagascar	587,000
Baffin	507,500
Sumatra	427,300
Honshu	227,400
Great Britain	218,100
Victoria	217,300
Ellesmere	196,200
Celebes	178,700
South (New Zealand)	151,000
Java	126,700

THE OCEANS

	Area (Sq Km)	Percent of Earth's Water Area
Pacific	166,241,000	46.0
Atlantic	86,557,000	23.9
Indian	73,427,000	20.3
Arctic	9,485,000	2.6

MAJOR LAKES

	Area (Sq Km)	Greatest Depth (Meters)
Caspian Sea, Europe-Asia	371,000	1,025
Superior, North America	82,100	406
Victoria, Africa	69,500	82
Aral Sea, Asia	64,500	67
Huron, North America	59,600	229
Michigan, North America	57,800	281

LONGEST RIVERS

	Length (Km)
Nile, Africa	6,671
Amazon, South America	6,437
Chang Jiang (Yangtze), Asia	6,380
Mississippi-Missouri, North America	5,971
Ob-Irtysk, Asia	5,410
Huang (Yellow), Asia	4,672
Congo, Africa	4,667
Amur, Asia	4,416
Lena, Asia	4,400
Mackenzie-Peace, North America	4,241

MAJOR SEAS

	Area (Sq Km)	Average Depth (Meters)
South China	2,974,600	1,464
Caribbean	2,515,900	2,575
Mediterranean	2,510,000	1,501
Bering	2,261,000	1,491
Gulf of Mexico	1,507,600	1,615
Sea of Okhotsk	1,392,100	973
Sea of Japan	1,012,900	1,667
Hudson Bay	730,100	93

THE WORLD
MERCATOR PROJECTION
Capitals of Countries............ ●

Longitude West of Greenwich

Longitude East of Greenwich

International Date Line

Copyright by C. S. HAMMOND & CO., N.Y.

249

NORTH AMERICA
LAMBERT AZIMUTHAL EQUAL-AREA PROJECTION

SCALE OF MILES

0 200 400 600 800 1000

SCALE OF KILOMETERS

0 200 400 600 800 1000

Capitals of Countries .... ⊙
International Boundaries .... —·—·—
Canals .... ═══

© Copyright HAMMOND INCORPORATED, Maplewood, N.J.

UNITED STATES
POLYCONIC PROJECTION
SCALE OF MILES
0   100   200   300   400
SCALE OF KILOMETERS
0   100 200 300 400
Capitals of Countries . . . . ⊛
International Boundaries . . . . — — —
State Capitals . . . . ⊛
State Boundaries . . . . — — —
Copyright by C. S. HAMMOND & CO., N.Y.

SOUTH AMERICA

LAMBERT AZIMUTHAL
EQUAL-AREA PROJECTION

MILES
0 200 400 600

KILOMETERS
0 200 400 600

Capitals of Countries .... ⊙
International Boundaries .... —·—·—

® Copyright by HAMMOND INCORPORATED, Maplewood, N.J.

252

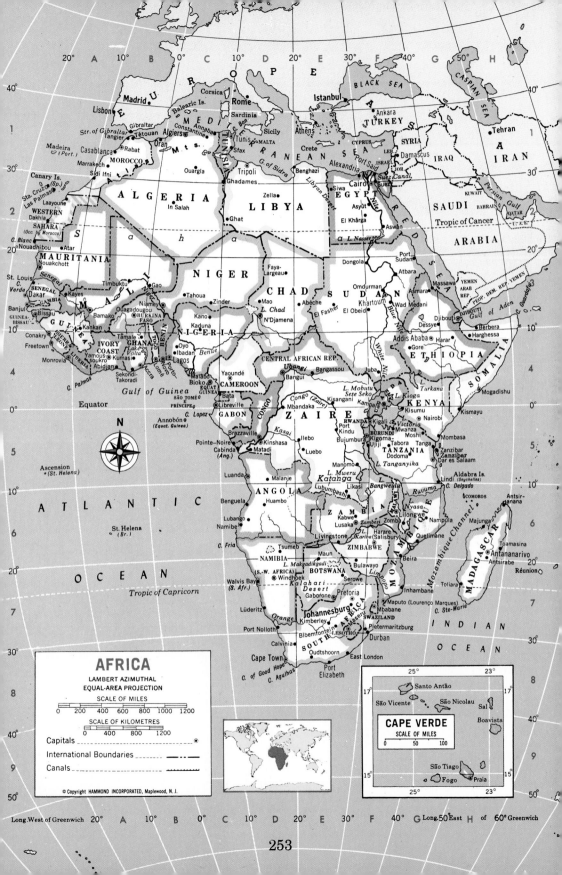

AFRICA
LAMBERT AZIMUTHAL EQUAL-AREA PROJECTION

SCALE OF MILES
0 200 400 600 800 1000 1200

SCALE OF KILOMETRES
0 400 800 1200

Capitals .... ●
International Boundaries _____
Canals ....

© Copyright HAMMOND INCORPORATED, Maplewood, N.J.

CAPE VERDE
SCALE OF MILES
0   50   100

Santo Antão
São Vicente
São Nicolau
Sal
Boavista
São Tiago
Fogo
Praia

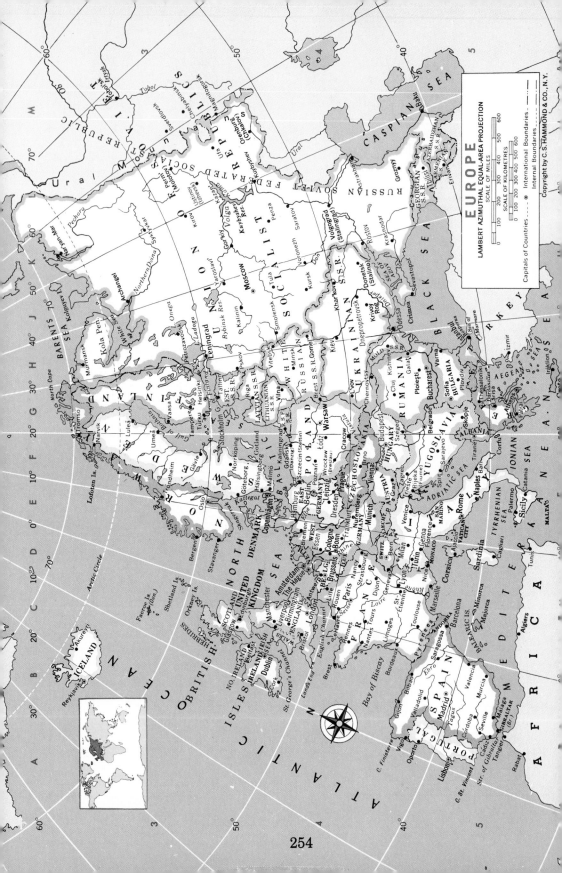

AUSTRALIA and PACIFIC OCEAN
LAMBERT AZIMUTHAL EQUAL-AREA PROJECTION

Improving Math Skills

858 Basic Math Symbols

Mathematics has its own special language. To "speak" or understand the language of mathematics, you must know its symbols or signs. Two lists of mathematical symbols follow. The first list includes common symbols and their meaning. These symbols are used very often in middle school and junior high math classes. The second list includes symbols which are used in more advanced math classes.

Common Math Symbols

+	plus (addition)
−	minus (subtraction)
×	multiplied by
÷	divided by
=	is equal to
≠	is not equal to
<	is less than
>	is greater than
±	plus or minus
%	percent
¢	cents
$	dollars
°	degree
′	minute (also foot)
″	second (also inch)
:	is to (ratio)
π	pi

Advanced Math Symbols

$\sqrt[2]{}$ or $\sqrt{}$	square root
$\sqrt[3]{}$	cube root
≥	is greater than or equal to
≤	is less than or equal to
{ }	set
∩	intersection
∪	union
⊂	is a subset of
∈	is an element of
⊄	is not a subset of
∉	is not an element of
∅	the empty set
≅	is congruent to
∠	angle
⊥	is perpendicular to
‖	is parallel to
∴	therefore
Σ	summation

859 Real Numbers

Numbers which we commonly use are called real numbers. The capital letter R is used to represent real numbers, and a number line is often used to illustrate them.

860 Number Line

$$-5 \quad -4 \quad -3 \quad -2 \quad -1 \quad 0 \quad 1 \quad 2 \quad 3 \quad 4 \quad 5$$

Every real number can be represented (shown) by a point on the number line, and every point on the number line represents (shows) a real number.

There is an infinite number of real numbers. That is, real numbers are endless—they go on forever. All of the following are real numbers: (They come in many shapes and sizes.)

$$0,\ 6,\ 23,\ 1025,\ 2.67,\ 2/3,\ 7\tfrac{1}{8},\ -31,\ -\tfrac{3}{8},\ \sqrt{2}\ \ldots$$

861 Sets of Numbers

There are many sets or special groups of real numbers used in your math classes. All of these sets of numbers are real numbers. Use the following list to help you remember them. *Note:* The three dots (. . .) after each list of numbers means "and so on."

1. **Natural numbers**—counting numbers.
   $\{1, 2, 3, 4, 5, \ldots\}$

2. **Whole numbers**—counting numbers including zero.
   $\{0, 1, 2, 3, 4, 5, \ldots\}$

3. **Integers**—whole numbers and their opposites.
   $\{\ldots -5, -4, -3, -2, -1, 0, 1, 2, 3, 4, 5, \ldots\}$

4. **Even numbers**—0 and whole numbers that are multiples of 2.
   $\{0, 2, 4, 6, 8, 10, \ldots\}$

5. **Odd numbers**—whole numbers that are not even numbers.
   $\{1, 3, 5, 7, 9, 11, 13, \ldots\}$

6. **Rational numbers**—a real number which can be written as a fraction, one integer over another integer. $\left\{\frac{a}{b}\right\}$

7. **Prime numbers**—a whole number greater than one which has only two factors. It is useful to know the prime numbers, especially when working with fractions. A chart of the prime numbers through 500 is given on the next page.

862

| A Chart of Prime Numbers Less Than 500 |

2,	3,	5,	7,	11,	13,	17,	19,	23,	29,
31,	37,	41,	43,	47,	53,	59,	61,	67,	71,
73,	79,	83,	89,	97,	101,	103,	107,	109,	113,
127,	131,	137,	139,	149,	151,	157,	163,	167,	173,
179,	181,	191,	193,	197,	199,	211,	223,	227,	229,
233,	239,	241,	251,	257,	263,	269,	271,	277,	281,
283,	293,	307,	311,	313,	317,	331,	337,	347,	349,
353,	359,	367,	373,	379,	383,	389,	397,	401,	409,
419,	421,	431,	433,	439,	443,	449,	457,	461,	463,
467,	479,	487,	491,	499					

Note: A factor divides into a number without giving a remainder. For example, the numbers 1, 2, 4, 5, 10, and 20 are all factors of 20 because they will divide into 20 without giving a remainder. A number like 29 is a prime number because it has only two factors, 1 and 29. They are the only two numbers which will divide into 29 without giving a remainder.

863 **Basic Operations for Whole Numbers**
Numbers are made up of digits. For example, the number 15,263 has five digits: 1, 5, 2, 6, and 3. The value of each digit is known by the place it occupies within the number.

Since the digit 2 is in the hundred's place in 15,263, it has a value of 200. Note the value of the other digits in the number 15,263.

1	5	2	6	3
Ten Thousands	Thousands	Hundreds	Tens	Ones

Multiplication of Whole Numbers

Multiplication is a quick way to add the same number several times. For example, 6 × 4 means 6 added to itself *four* times or 6 + 6 + 6 + 6. Since 6 + 6 + 6 + 6 = 24, then we can conclude that 6 × 4 = 24.

864 **Multiplication Facts:** When you multiply two numbers, such as 9 × 3 = 27, you end up with a multiplication fact. The *table of basic multiplication facts* which follows must be memorized so that you can do multiplication problems. The table lists 121 multiplication facts. For example, the table shows us that 7 × 4 = 28, 8 × 3 = 24, 9 × 10 = 90, and so on.

Table of Basic Multiplication Facts

×	0	1	2	3	4	5	6	7	8	9	10
0	0	0	0	0	0	0	0	0	0	0	0
1	0	1	2	3	4	5	6	7	8	9	10
2	0	2	4	6	8	10	12	14	16	18	20
3	0	3	6	9	12	15	18	21	24	27	30
4	0	4	8	12	16	20	24	28	32	36	40
5	0	5	10	15	20	25	30	35	40	45	50
6	0	6	12	18	24	30	36	42	48	54	60
7	0	7	14	21	28	35	42	49	56	63	70
8	0	8	16	24	32	40	48	56	64	72	80
9	0	9	18	27	36	45	54	63	72	81	90
10	0	10	20	30	40	50	60	70	80	90	100

Very important notes! Notice that 0 times any number is always 0 ($0 \times 3 = 0$, $0 \times 7 = 0$, etc.). Also notice that 1 times any number is equal to the number itself ($1 \times 3 = 3$, $1 \times 7 = 7$, etc.). Finally, notice that $7 \times 4 = 28$ and $4 \times 7 = 28$. This means that the order in which you multiply does not change the answer.

Fractions

866   A fraction is a number which is made up of two numbers, a *numerator* and a *denominator*. Numbers like $\frac{1}{2}$, $\frac{2}{3}$, $\frac{7}{4}$, $\frac{6}{25}$, and $\frac{9}{5}$ are fractions.

$$\text{Fraction} \left\{ \begin{array}{l} 3 \leftarrow \text{numerator} \\ 4 \leftarrow \text{denominator} \end{array} \right.$$

When you write a fraction such as $\frac{3}{4}$, the denominator (4) represents the total number of equal parts, and the numerator (3) represents the number of those equal parts that you are talking about or referring to.

867   **Equal Parts:** Fractions represent equal parts of a unit. When a unit is divided into 2 equal parts, the parts are called *halves*. When a unit is divided into 3 equal parts, the parts are called *thirds*.

    4 equal parts are called *fourths* or *quarters*.
    5 equal parts are called *fifths*.
    6 equal parts are called *sixths* and so on.

Note: If the unit is not divided into equal parts, you cannot use fractions.

For example, this pizza was divided into four equal parts. One of the equal parts has already been eaten. You can say that three-fourths or $\frac{3}{4}$ of the pizza is left. The denominator (4) represents the total number of equal parts. The numerator (3) represents the part of the total number which is left.

This pizza was divided into four parts as well, but all four parts are not equal. You cannot represent the amount of pizza which still remains with a fraction.

Note: A fraction like $\frac{3}{4}$ can be called a *ratio*. A ratio is a comparison of two numbers. In this case, we are comparing 3 to 4.

868   Equivalent Fractions

Two fractions might not look the same, but they might represent the same number and therefore be equal or *equivalent fractions*.

$$\frac{1}{2} \qquad = \qquad \frac{2}{4}$$

Since the shaded area in both rectangles is the same, we can say that $\frac{1}{2}$ is equal or equivalent to $\frac{2}{4}$.

Example:

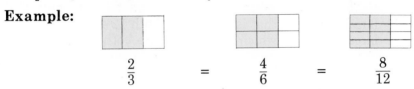

$$\frac{2}{3} \qquad = \qquad \frac{4}{6} \qquad = \qquad \frac{8}{12}$$

The fractions $\frac{2}{3}$, $\frac{4}{6}$, and $\frac{8}{12}$ are all equivalent because they represent the same amount of shaded area.

Making Equivalent Fractions: Equivalent fractions can be made by multiplying the numerator and the denominator of a fraction by the same number.

Example: $\dfrac{2 \times 4}{3 \times 4} = \dfrac{8}{12}$ $\frac{2}{3}$ and $\frac{8}{12}$ are equivalent fractions.

869   Simplifying Fractions

The fractions $\frac{3}{6}$, $\frac{2}{4}$, $\frac{10}{20}$, and $\frac{1}{2}$ are examples of equivalent fractions because they are all equal in value. The simplest form of these four fractions is $\frac{1}{2}$ because it uses the smallest numerator and denominator. The following fractions are **also** equivalent: $\frac{12}{15}$, $\frac{16}{20}$, $\frac{4}{5}$, $\frac{28}{35}$.

The fraction $\frac{4}{5}$ is in simplest form because its numerator of 4 and its denominator of 5 are smaller than the others.

When working with fractions, you will often want to write them as equivalent fractions in their simplest form. For example, instead of writing $\frac{4}{6}$, it is better to write the equivalent fraction $\frac{2}{3}$ because it is easier to work with. Renaming $\frac{4}{6}$ as $\frac{2}{3}$ is called simplifying the fraction or reducing the fraction to its lowest terms.

870 Steps in Simplifying: To simplify a fraction such as $\frac{4}{6}$, you should follow three steps:

Step 1: Find the greatest common factor (GCF) of the numerator and denominator. The GCF of 4 and 6 is 2. (See the explanation which follows.)

Step 2: $\dfrac{4 \div 2}{6 \div 2}$ — Divide the numerator and denominator by the GCF.

Step 3: $\dfrac{4 \div 2}{6 \div 2} = \dfrac{2}{3}$ — Write the simplest form of the fraction.

871

Greatest Common Factor

In order to simplify a fraction, you must understand how to find the **Greatest Common Factor** (GCF). To find the GCF of two numbers such as 12 and 18, you must find the largest number that is a factor of both 12 and 18. That is, the largest number which will divide into both 12 and 18.

If the numbers are small, you can usually figure out the GCF quite easily. For example the GCF of 12 and 18 is 6. This means that 6 is the largest number which will divide into 12 and 18. If you cannot figure out the GCF of numbers like 12 and 18 in your head, follow these steps:

Step 1: List all of the factors of both 12 and 18.
Factors of 12: 1, 2, 3, 4, 6, 12
Factors of 18: 1, 2, 3, 6, 9, 18

Step 2: Circle the common factors in each list.

①②③ 4 ⑥ 12

①②③⑥ 9 18

Step 3: Then, pick the largest number circled. This number is the Greatest Common Factor: 6

872

Common Divisibility Tests

To help you find the factors of a certain number, you can use *divisibility tests*. These are especially helpful when you are simplifying fractions with large numerators and denominators like $\frac{144}{840}$. The chart which follows includes eight common divisibility tests.

DIVISIBILITY TESTS

A number will be divisible by:	if the number has the following characteristics:	Example:
2	The number is even.	654 is divisible by 2 because 654 is an even number. $$\frac{327}{2\overline{)654}}$$
3	The sum of the digits of the number is divisible by 3.	465 is divisible by 3 because 4 + 6 + 5 = 15 and 15 is divisible by 3. $$\frac{155}{3\overline{)465}}$$
4	The number formed by the last two digits is divisible by 4.	2712 is divisible by 4 because 12 is divisible by 4. $$\frac{678}{4\overline{)2712}}$$
5	The number ends in either 0 or 5.	7230 is divisible by 5 because 7230 ends in 0. $$\frac{1446}{5\overline{)7230}}$$
6	The number is divisible by both 2 and 3.	738 is divisible by 6 because 738 is divisible by 2 and 3. $$\frac{123}{6\overline{)738}}$$
8	The number formed by the last 3 digits is divisible by 8.	45864 is divisible by 8 because 864 (the last three digits) is divisible by 8. $$\frac{5733}{8\overline{)45864}}$$
9	The sum of the digits of the number is divisible by 9.	67122 is divisible by 9 because 6 + 7 + 1 + 2 + 2 = 18 which is divisible by 9. $$\frac{7458}{9\overline{)67122}}$$
10	The number ends in 0.	45670 is divisible by 10 because 45670 ends in a 0. $$\frac{4567}{10\overline{)45670}}$$

Addition of Fractions

873 Addition of Fractions

To help you understand the operation of addition with fractions, look at the illustration below:

The *pentagon* (a five-sided figure) is cut into five equal parts.

$\frac{1}{5}$ is shaded black.

$\frac{3}{5}$ is shaded red.

How much of the pentagon is shaded?

One way to answer this question would be to count the number of shaded parts. You can clearly see that $\frac{4}{5}$ is shaded. Another way would be to add the black shaded part to the red shaded part. To do this simply add the numerators (1 + 3) and write the denominator (5) unchanged.

$$\frac{1}{5} + \frac{3}{5} = \frac{1+3}{5} = \frac{4}{5}$$

874 Adding Fractions with Common Denominators: When you add fractions with a common denominator, you add the numerators and keep the denominators the same.

Example: $\frac{7}{15} + \frac{4}{15}$

Solution: $\frac{7}{15} + \frac{4}{15} = \frac{7+4}{15} = \frac{11}{15}$ $\underline{\text{Add the numerators.}}$
$\phantom{\frac{7}{15} + \frac{4}{15} = }$ Keep the common denominators the same

$\uparrow \qquad \uparrow$
Common Denominators

875 Adding Fractions without Common Denominators: If the fractions do not have common denominators, then you must change the fractions to equivalent fractions that have common denominators before you can add them. (See "Finding the Least Common Multiple.")

876 ## Finding the Least Common Multiple (LCM)

To add fractions, you must be able to find the *Least Common Multiple (LCM)*, a number which you will use as the common denominator of the fractions you are adding. The LCM is the smallest multiple shared by two or more numbers.

Multiples are found by multiplying a number by 0, 1, 2, 3, 4, 5 and so on. For example, the multiples of the number 4 are given below in the bold print.

$$0 \times 4 = \mathbf{0} \qquad 3 \times 4 = \mathbf{12}$$
$$1 \times 4 = \mathbf{4} \qquad 4 \times 4 = \mathbf{16}$$
$$2 \times 4 = \mathbf{8} \qquad 5 \times 4 = \mathbf{20}. . .$$

Sometimes you can figure out the LCM in your head if the numbers are small. For example, to add the fractions $\frac{1}{4} + \frac{5}{6}$, it is not too difficult to find the LCM of 4 and 6, the denominators of the two fractions. The LCM is 12. That is, 12 is the smallest multiple shared by both 4 and 6: $4 \times 3 = 12$ and $6 \times 2 = 12$. Twelve is the common denominator of the two fractions.

If you cannot figure out the LCM in your head, follow the three steps given next.

Step 1: List several multiples of each denominator of the fractions you are adding.
Multiples of 6:

6, 12, 18, (24,) 30, 36, 42, (48.) . .

Multiples of 8:

8, 16, (24,) 32, 40, (48,) 56. . .

(Use the "Multiplication Table" for help in finding multiples of numbers.)

Step 2: Circle the multiples shared by the two numbers. (These are called *common multiples.*)

Step 3: Pick the smallest circled number. The LCM of 6 and 8 is 24. This number would be the common denominator if you were adding two fractions with 6 and 8 as denominators.

Division of Fractions

877 **Reciprocals:** To divide with fractions, you need to use *reciprocals.* Reciprocals are numbers whose product is 1. Since $\frac{2}{3} \times \frac{3}{2} = \frac{6}{6} = 1$, then $\frac{2}{3}$ and $\frac{3}{2}$ are reciprocals of one another. Since $\frac{1}{5} \times \frac{5}{1} = 1$, then $\frac{1}{5}$ and 5 are reciprocals of one another.

The following chart lists some numbers and their reciprocals.

Number	$\frac{1}{2}$	$\frac{2}{5}$	1	$\frac{75}{8}$	0	7	$\frac{2}{9}$
Reciprocal	2	$\frac{5}{2}$	1	$\frac{8}{75}$	None	$\frac{1}{7}$	$\frac{9}{2} = 4\frac{1}{2}$

Note: The number 0 does not have a reciprocal because 0 times any number equals 0.

878 The Division Process: Dividing by a number is the same as multiplying by its reciprocal. For example, dividing 6 by $\frac{1}{3}$ is the same as multiplying 6 by 3 because $\frac{1}{3}$ and 3 are reciprocals.

$$6 \div \frac{1}{3} = 6 \times 3 = 18$$

reciprocals

The division problem $\frac{5}{8} \div \frac{2}{3}$ can be figured out by following the steps given below.

Example: $\frac{5}{8} \div \frac{2}{3}$
Solution:

Step 1: $\quad \frac{5}{8} \times$ 　　Copy the first fraction and change the division sign to a multiplication sign.

Step 2: $\quad \frac{5}{8} \times \frac{3}{2}$ 　　Write the reciprocal of the second fraction.

Step 3: 　　Simplify (if possible) and multiply the
$\frac{5}{8} \div \frac{2}{3} = \frac{5}{8} \times \frac{3}{2} = \frac{15}{16}$ 　　two numbers.

879 Decimal Numbers

Numbers such as .2, 5.86, 0.0062, 215.097, and $7.98 are examples of **Decimal Numbers.**

A decimal number contains a decimal point and has two parts. The **whole part** is the number to the left of the decimal point, and the **fractional part** is the number to the right of the decimal point.

2 1 7 . 0 9 2 3

Whole 　　　 *Fractional*
Part 　　　　 *Part*

Decimal numbers give us a quick and easy way to write fractions and mixed numbers.

880 Writing a Decimal as a Fraction:

The decimal .3 means $\frac{3}{10}$.

The decimal 2.8 means $2\frac{8}{10}$ or $2\frac{4}{5}$.

The decimal .73 means $\frac{73}{100}$.

The decimal 19.327 means $19\frac{327}{1000}$.

The denominator of the fraction is determined by the number of digits to the right of the decimal point. For example, in the decimal .3, there is only one digit to the right of the decimal point, so you would use a denominator of 10 in writing the decimal .3 as the fraction $\frac{3}{10}$.

In the decimal .73, there are two digits to the right of the decimal point so you would use a denominator of 100 in writing .73 as the fraction $\frac{73}{100}$.

881 Looking at Decimals: The following chart shows the place value of the digits in several decimal numbers. It also includes an equivalent fraction or mixed number for each decimal number. The correct way to read a decimal number is given as well. Read the decimal point as "and."

Thousands	Hundreds	Tens	Ones		Tenths	Hundredths	Thousandths	Ten-Thousandths	Equivalent fraction	Word Name
			5	.	7				$5\frac{7}{10}$	five and seven tenths
				.	5	9			$\frac{59}{100}$	fifty-nine hundredths
		1	2	.	0	0	3		$12\frac{3}{1000}$	twelve and three thousandths
	5	7	6	.	7	0			$576\frac{70}{100}$	five hundred seventy-six and seventy hundredths
			0	.	0	0	6	9	$\frac{69}{10000}$	sixty-nine ten-thousandths
		2	7	.	2	7			$27\frac{27}{100}$	twenty-seven and twenty-seven hundredths
			$4	.	7	5			$\$4\frac{75}{100}$	four and seventy-five hundredths dollars or four dollars and seventy-five cents

Solving Word Problems

Solving word problems requires careful reading, thinking, and planning. If you try to take shortcuts, you will probably not solve them correctly. Given in the following guidelines are the important steps you should follow when you carefully work on word problems. With enough practice and with the help of these guidelines, you can train yourself to work through even the most difficult word problems.

Guidelines for Solving Word Problems

1. Read the problem very carefully. This means that you might have to read each word and phrase many times before you understand all parts of the problem. (One way to check your understanding of a word problem is to restate the problem in your own words.)

2. Decide which information you will need to use to solve a problem. Sometimes there is information given which isn't really important to the problem. At other times, there is not enough information given to solve the problem.

3. Pay special attention to the key words and phrases in the problem. These words tell you what you have to figure out. For example, a phrase like *in total* in a sentence like "How much did he pay *in total*" tells you that you'll probably have to *add*. The word *more* in a sentence like "How much *more* did John make this month than last month" tells you that you'll have to *subtract* to solve the problem.

4. Study carefully any illustrations—maps, charts, graphs, etc.—which go along with the problem. These illustrations often contain information which you need to know to solve a word problem.

5. Organize the information in the problem so that you solve it correctly. Sometimes making your own chart or graph from the information in the problem will help you solve a difficult problem.

6. Identify all of the basic operations—addition, subtraction, multiplication, division—you will have to use to figure out the problem. You will often solve a word problem in steps. To complete each step you might have to use different basic operations.

7. As you solve the problem, show all of your work so that you can check your answer later. Make sure that you perform all of the basic operations in the right way. Also, if there is more than one step in the problem, make sure that you solve each step in the correct order.

8. **Check** your answer.

883 Sample Word Problems

Six sample word problems follow. Each of the first four problems deals with one of the basic operations—addition, subtraction, multiplication, and division. The last two problems deal with mixed numbers and fractions. Take special note of the discussion or explanation which goes along with the planning and solving of each word problem.

884 Addition

Example: A shirt costs $8.79, a pair of pants costs $13.47, and a sweater costs $12.50. What would be the total cost if someone bought all three items?

Solution:

Step 1: Set up the problem

$ 8.79
13.47
+12.50

Discussion: This is a one-step problem in which you must add three numbers. (The word "total" is a key word which tells you to add.)

Step 2: Solve the problem

$ 8.79
13.47
+12.50
$ 34.76

Discussion: Drop the decimal point which separates the dollars from the cents down to your answer.

Step 3: Check your answer

$12.50
8.79
+13.47
$ 34.76

Discussion: Check your answer by adding the three numbers in a different order. Make sure that you have copied the numbers correctly and that your answer makes sense.

Answer: $34.76 is the amount of money to pay for the three items of clothing.

885   **Subtraction**

Example: The student council bought 48 chocolate donuts, 36
          sugared donuts, and 36 powdered donuts for the school
          bake sale.   Only 42 of the donuts were sold.   How
          many donuts were left?

Solution:
    Step 1: **Set up the**   *Discussion:* This is really a two-step
            problem   problem. Before you can find out
                               how many donuts were left, you have
            48   120   to find out how many donuts there
            36   − 42   were to begin with.   Then subtract
           +36   ‾‾‾‾‾   the 42 donuts sold in order to find out
           ‾‾‾‾   the number of donuts remaining.
           120

    Step 2: **Solve the**
            problem

                 ¹ ¹⁰
               120
             − 42
             ‾‾‾‾‾
                78

    Step 3: **Check your**   *Discussion:* Check all of your calcu-
            answer   lating. You can check a subtraction
                               problem by adding your answer to the
                78   second number in the subtraction
               +42   problem.   Also, make sure that your
               ‾‾‾‾   answer makes sense.
               120

Answer: 78 donuts were left.

886   **Multiplication**

Example: Rent-A-Junker, a "new" car rental company, repaired
          13 junkers each day in July in preparation for its grand
          opening in August.   How many cars in total did this
          company prepare for its grand opening?

Solution:
    Step 1: **Set up the**   *Discussion:* This problem has some
            problem   missing information. In order to
                               solve the problem, you would need to
                               know the number of days in July
                31   (31).   Then, since the company re-
               ×13   paired the same number of cars each
               ‾‾‾‾   day, you can multiply that number
                               (13) times the number of days in July
                               (31).

Step 2: **Solve the problem**

$$
\begin{array}{r}
31 \\
\times 13 \\
\hline
93 \\
31 \\
\hline
403
\end{array}
$$

Step 3: **Check your answer**

$$
\begin{array}{r}
13 \\
31\overline{)403} \\
31 \\
\hline
93 \\
93 \\
\hline
0
\end{array}
$$

Discussion: To check, divide the product, 403, by one of the numbers in the multiplication problem. Your answer should be the other number in the multiplication problem. Also, make sure your answer makes sense.

Answer: Rent-A-Junker fixed up 403 cars in July.

887

Division

Example: The eighth grade class at Pilgrim Junior High School wants to go to a new amusement park for a class trip. The total cost for this trip—transportation, tickets, lunch—would be $1,164.00 if all 97 students in the class decide to go. How much would each student have to pay if they equally shared the total cost?

Solution:

Step 1: **Set up the problem**

$$97\overline{)1164}$$

Discussion: This is a one-step problem in which you must divide. (The phrase "each student" is a key phrase which tells you to divide.) Divide the total cost for the trip by the number of students in the class to solve the problem. You might want to round the numbers off to get an idea of what your answer might be—$1,100 \div 100 = 11.$

Step 2: **Solve the problem**

$$
\begin{array}{r}
12 \\
97\overline{)1164} \\
97 \\
\hline
194 \\
194 \\
\hline
0
\end{array}
$$

Step 3: **Check your answer**

$$\begin{array}{r} 97 \\ \times 12 \\ \hline 194 \\ 97 \\ \hline 1164 \end{array}$$

Discussion: To check your answer, multiply the divisor by the quotient of the division problem. Also, make sure that your answer makes sense. Compare it to the estimate you made with simpler numbers.

Answer: Each student would have to pay $12.00.

888

Mixed Numbers

Example: A carpenter needs to cut an eight-foot board into pieces that are each 2⅔ feet long. How many pieces will the carpenter be able to cut from the eight-foot board?

Solution:

Step 1: **Set up the problem**

$$8 \div 2\frac{2}{3} = 8 \div \frac{8}{3}$$

Discussion: Since you are asked to find how many smaller pieces you can get from a large piece, you will need to divide. To divide eight by 2⅔, you should first change the mixed number into a fraction. Remember that dividing fractions is done by multiplying the reciprocal of the divisor.

Step 2: **Solve the problem**

$$\frac{\cancel{8}^{1}}{1} \times \frac{3}{\cancel{8}_{1}} = \frac{3}{1}$$

Discussion: You can simplify before you multiply.

Step 3: **Check your answer**

$$\begin{array}{r} 2\frac{2}{3} \\ 3\overline{)8} \\ \underline{6} \\ 2 \end{array}$$

Discussion: To check your answer, divide the eight by the three to see if it equals 2⅔. Also, make sure your answer makes sense.

Answer: The carpenter can cut three pieces of wood from the eight-foot board.

Fractions

Example: One-quarter of the actors from the community play attend Park High School. One-third of the actors attend Jefferson Junior High School. What fraction of the entire cast for the spring play attends the two schools?

Solution:

Step 1: **Set up the problem**

$$\frac{1}{4} + \frac{1}{3} =$$

Discussion: To solve this problem, you will have to add the two fractions. You might want to draw a picture which illustrates the information given in the problem. (A picture can help you to understand the problem.)

Step 2: **Solve the problem**

$$\frac{1 \times 3}{4 \times 3} = \frac{3}{12}$$

$$+ \frac{1 \times 4}{3 \times 4} = \frac{4}{12}$$

$$\frac{7}{12}$$

Discussion: To add fractions, you must have common denominators. As a result, you must find the least common multiple (LCM) of the numbers 3 and 4—the denominators of the two fractions. The LCM is 12.

Step 3: **Check your answer**

$$\frac{7}{12}$$

Discussion: Check your answer to make sure it is written in its simplest terms. ($\frac{7}{12}$ cannot be simplified any further.) Also, check your answer to see if it makes sense when you compare it to your picture. Since $\frac{7}{12}$ and the picture both represent a little more than half, the answer makes sense.

Answer: 7/12 of the cast attend the two schools.

Table of Weights and Measures

Linear Measure

1 inch		=	2.54 centimeters
1 foot	= 12 inches	=	0.3048 meter
1 yard	= 3 feet	=	0.9144 meter
1 rod (or pole or perch)	= 5½ yards or 16½ feet	=	5.029 meters
1 furlong	= 40 rods	=	201.17 meters
1 (statute) mile	= 8 furlongs or 1,760 yards or 5,280 feet	=	1,609.3 meters
1 (land) league	= 3 miles	=	4.83 kilometers

Square Measure

1 square inch		=	6.452 square centimeters
1 square foot	= 144 square inches	=	929 square centimeters
1 square yard	= 9 square feet	=	0.8361 square meter
1 square rod	= 30¼ square yards	=	25.29 square meters
1 acre	= 160 square rods or 4,840 square yards or 43,560 square feet	=	0.4047 hectare
1 square mile	= 640 acres	=	259 hectares or 2.59 square kilometers

Cubic Measure

1 cubic inch		=	16.387 cubic centimeters
1 cubic foot	= 1,728 cubic inches	=	0.0283 cubic meter
1 cubic yard	= 27 cubic feet	=	0.7646 cubic meter
1 cord foot	= 16 cubic feet		
1 cord	= 8 cord feet	=	3.625 cubic meters

Chain Measure
(Gunter's or surveyor's chain)

1 link	= 7.92 inches	=	20.12 centimeters
1 chain	= 100 links or 66 feet	=	20.12 meters
1 furlong	= 10 chains	=	201.17 meters
1 mile	= 80 chains	=	1,609.3 meters

(Engineer's chain)

1 link	= 1 foot	=	0.3048 meter
1 chain	= 100 feet	=	30.48 meters
1 mile	= 52.8 chains	=	1,609.3 meters

Surveyor's (Square) Measure

1 square pole	= 625 square links	=	25.29 square meters
1 square chain	= 16 square poles	=	404.7 square meters
1 acre	= 10 square chains	=	0.4047 hectare
1 square mile or 1 section	= 640 acres	=	259 hectares or 2.59 square kilometers
1 township	= 36 square miles	=	9,324 hectares or 93.24 square kilometers

Nautical Measure

1 fathom	= 6 feet	=	1.829 meters
1 cable's length (ordinary)	= 100 fathoms		

(In the U. S. Navy 120 fathoms or 720 feet = 1 cable's length; in the British Navy 608 feet = 1 cable's length)

1 nautical mile (6,076.10333 feet, by international agreement in 1954)	= 10 cables' lengths	=	1 nautical mile = 1.852 kilometers
1.1508 statute miles (length of a minute of longitude at the equator)			
1 marine league (3.45 statute miles)	= 3 nautical miles	=	5.56 kilometers
1 degree of a great circle of the earth	= 60 nautical miles		

Dry Measure

1 pint		= 33.60 cubic inches	= 0.5505 liter
1 quart	= 2 pints	= 67.20 cubic inches	= 1.1012 liters
1 peck	= 8 quarts	= 537.61 cubic inches	= 8.8096 liters
1 bushel	= 4 pecks	= 2,150.42 cubic inches	= 35.2383 liters

Liquid Measure

1 gill		= 7.219 cubic inches	= 0.1183 liter
(see next table)			
1 pint	= 4 gills	= 28.875 cubic inches	= 0.4732 liter
1 quart	= 2 pints	= 57.75 cubic inches	= 0.9463 liter
1 gallon	= 4 quarts	= 231 cubic inches	= 3.7853 liters

Apothecaries' Fluid Measure

1 minim		= 0.0038 cubic inch	= 0.0616 milliliter
1 fluid dram	= 60 minims	= 0.2256 cubic inch	= 3.6966 milliliters
1 fluid ounce	= 8 fluid drams	= 1.8047 cubic inches	= 0.0296 liter
1 pint	= 16 fluid ounces	= 28.875 cubic inches	= 0.4732 liter

Circular (or Angular) Measure

60 seconds ('')	=	1 minute (')
60 minutes	=	1 degree (°)
90 degrees	=	1 quadrant or 1 right angle
4 quadrants or 360 degrees	=	1 circle

Avoirdupois Weight
(The grain, equal to 0.0648 gram, is the same in all three tables of weight)

1 dram or 27.34 grains		=	1.772 grams
1 ounce	= 16 drams or 437.5 grains	=	28.3495 grams
1 pound	= 16 ounces or 7,000 grains	=	453.59 grams
1 hundredweight	= 100 pounds	=	45.36 kilograms
1 ton	= 2,000 pounds	=	907.18 kilograms

Troy Weight
(The grain, equal to 0.0648 gram, is the same in all three tables of weight)

1 carat	= 3.086 grains	=	200 milligrams
1 pennyweight		=	1.5552 grams
1 ounce	= 20 pennyweights or 480 grains	=	31.1035 grams
1 pound	= 12 ounces or 5,760 grains	=	373.24 grams

Apothecaries' Weight
(The grain, equal to 0.0648 gram, is the same in all three tables of weight)

1 scruple	= 20 grains	=	1.296 grams
1 dram	= 3 scruples	=	3.888 grams
1 ounce	= 8 drams or 480 grains	=	31.1035 grams
1 pound	= 12 ounces or 5,760 grains	=	373.24 grams

Miscellaneous

3 inches	=	1 palm
4 inches	=	1 hand
6 inches	=	1 span
18 inches	=	1 cubit
21.8 inches	=	1 Bible cubit
2½ feet	=	1 military pace

Handy Conversion Factors

To change	to	multiply by	To change	to	multiply by
acres	hectares	.4047	liters	quarts (liquid)	1.0567
acres	square feet	43,560	meters	feet	3.2808
acres	square miles	.001562	meters	miles	.0006214
Celsius	Fahrenheit	**9/5	meters	yards	1.0936
* (then add 32)			metric tons	tons (long)	.9842
centimeters	inches	.3937	metric tons	tons (short)	1.1023
centimeters	feet	.03281	miles	kilometers	1.6093
cubic meters	cubic feet	35.3145	miles	feet	5280
cubic yards	cubic meters	1.3079	miles (nautical)	miles (statute)	1.1516
degrees	radians	.01745	miles (statute)	miles (nautical)	.8684
Fahrenheit	Celsius	*5/9	miles/hr.	feet/min.	88
* (after subtracting 32)			millimeters	inches	.0394
feet	meters	.3048	ounces avdp.	grams	28.3495
feet	miles (nautical)	.0001645	ounces	pounds	.0625
feet	miles (statute)	.0001894	ounces (troy)	ounces (avdp.)	1.09714
feet/sec.	miles/hr.	.6818	pecks	liters	8.8096
furlongs	feet	660.0	pints (dry)	liters	.5506
furlongs	miles	.125	pints (liquid)	liters	.4732
gallons (U. S.)	liters	3.7853	pounds ap or t	kilograms	.3782
grains	grams	.0648	pounds avdp.	kilograms	.4536
grams	grains	15.4324	pounds	ounces	16
grams	ounces avdp.	.0353	quarts (dry)	liters	1.1012
grams	pounds	.002205	quarts (liquid)	liters	.9463
hectares	acres	2.4710	rods	meters	5.029
horsepower	watts	745.7	rods	feet	16.5
hours	days	.04167	square feet	square meters	.0929
inches	millimeters	25.4000	square kilometers	square miles	.3861
inches	centimeters	2.5400	square meters	square feet	10.7639
kilograms	pounds avdp or t	2.2046	square meters	square yards	1.1960
kilograms	miles	.6214	square miles	square kilometers	2.5900
kilowatts	horsepower	1.341	square yards	square meters	.8361
knots	nautical miles/hr.	1.0	tons (long)	tons (short)	1.1060
knots	statute miles/hr.	1.151	tons (long)	metric tons	1.0160
liters	gallons (U. S.)	.2642	tons (short)	metric tons	.9072
liters	pecks	.1135	tons (long)	pounds	2240
liters	pints (dry)	1.8162	tons (short)	pounds	2000
liters	pints (liquid)	2.1134	watts	BTU/hr.	3.4129
liters	quarts (dry)	.9081	watts	horsepower	.001341
			yards	meters	.9144
			yards	miles	.0005682

Decimal Equivalents of Common Fractions

1/2	.5000	1/32	.0313	3/11	.2727	6/11	.5455
1/3	.3333	1/64	.0156	4/5	.8000	7/8	.8750
1/4	.2500	2/3	.6667	4/7	.5714	7/9	.7778
1/5	.2000	2/5	.4000	4/9	.4444	7/10	.7000
1/6	.1667	2/7	.2857	4/11	.3636	7/11	.6364
1/7	.1429	2/9	.2222	5/6	.8333	7/12	.5833
1/8	.1250	2/11	.1818	5/7	.7143	8/9	.8889
1/9	.1111	3/4	.7500	5/8	.6250	8/11	.7273
1/10	.1000	3/5	.6000	5/9	.5556	9/10	.9000
1/11	.0909	3/7	.4286	5/11	.4545	9/11	.8182
1/12	.0833	3/8	.3750	5/12	.4167	10/11	.9091
1/16	.0625	3/10	.3000	6/7	.8571	11/12	.9167

The Metric System

Linear Measure

1 centimeter	= 10 millimeters	=	0.3937 inch
1 decimeter	= 10 centimeters	=	3.937 inches
1 meter	= 10 decimeters	=	39.37 inches or 3.28 feet
1 decameter	= 10 meters	=	393.7 inches
1 hectometer	= 10 decameters	=	328 feet 1 inch
1 kilometer	= 10 hectometers	=	0.621 mile
1 myriameter	= 10 kilometers	=	6.21 miles

Square Measure

1 square centimeter	= 100 square millimeters	=	0.15499 square inch
1 square decimeter	= 100 square centimeters	=	15.499 square inches
1 square meter	= 100 square decimeters	=	1,549.9 square inches or 1.196 square yards
1 square decameter	= 100 square meters	=	119.6 square yards
1 square hectometer	= 100 square decameters	=	2.471 acres
1 square kilometer	= 100 square hectometers	=	0.386 square mile

Capacity Measure

1 centiliter	= 10 milliliters	=	.338 fluid ounce
1 deciliter	= 10 centiliters	=	3.38 fluid ounces
1 liter	= 10 deciliters	=	1.0567 liquid quarts or 0.9081 dry quart
1 decaliter	= 10 liters	=	2.64 gallons or 0.284 bushel
1 hectoliter	= 10 decaliters	=	26.418 gallons or 2.838 bushels
1 kiloliter	= 10 hectoliters	=	264.18 gallons or 35.315 cubic feet

Land Measure

1 centare	= 1 square meter	=	1,549.9 square inches
1 are	= 100 centares	=	119.6 square yards
1 hectare	= 100 ares	=	2.471 acres
1 square kilometer	= 100 hectares	=	0.386 square mile

Volume Measure

1 cubic centimeter	= 1,000 cubic millimeters	=	.06102 cubic inch
1 cubic decimeter	= 1,000 cubic centimeters	=	61.02 cubic inches
1 cubic meter	= 1,000 cubic decimeters	=	35.314 cubic feet

Weights

1 centigram	= 10 milligrams	=	0.1543 grain
1 decigram	= 10 centigrams	=	1.5432 grains
1 gram	= 10 decigrams	=	15.432 grains
1 decagram	= 10 decagrams	=	0.3527 ounce
1 hectogram	= 10 decagrams	=	3.5274 ounces
1 kilogram	= 10 hectograms	=	2.2046 pounds
1 myriagram	= 10 kilograms	=	22.046 pounds
1 quintal	= 10 myriagrams	=	220.46 pounds
1 metric ton	= 10 quintals	=	2,204.6 pounds

Roman Numerals

I	1	VIII	8	LX	60
II	2	IX	9	LXX	70
III	3	X	10	LXXX	80
IV	4	XX	20	XC	90
V	5	XXX	30	C	100
VI	6	XL	40	D	500
VII	7	L	50	M	1,000

$\bar{V}$	5,000
$\bar{X}$	10,000
$\bar{L}$	50,000
$\bar{C}$	100,000
$\bar{D}$	500,000
$\bar{M}$	1,000,000

Computer Introduction

If you haven't had any experience using a computer, it might seem like a very complex or difficult machine which knows more than you do. Well, nothing could be further from the truth. A computer doesn't know anything. All it can do is help you use and organize information in new and creative ways. Those of you who have worked with computers already know this. You also know that it is necessary to know the basic computer vocabulary to use one effectively. (Since a computer offers so many new ways to use information, it has a vocabulary of its own.) A glossary of basic computer terms follows. Use this list to help you operate and program a computer.

Also, a basic computer keyboard is illustrated. Use this illustration to help you practice typing. Knowing how to use a keyboard properly is important when you use a word processing program in your computer. Notice the illustration of the left and right hand which identifies the keys each finger can and should hit when you keyboard. Keep your fingers right above the home row (shaded in this illustration) as you practice.

Computer Terms

Address: A number used to identify where a piece of information is located in the computer's memory.

Algorithm: The computer programmer's "plan of attack" showing each step used in the solution of a problem.

Array: A group of variables called by the same name, but having different subscripts.

Back-up: A copy of data or programs used to protect the original copy if it is lost, stolen, or destroyed.

BASIC: *(Beginners All-purpose Symbolic Instruction Code)* A computer language specifically designed to be easy to learn and use. It is commonly used with smaller computers.

Binary: The number system commonly used by computers because the values 0 and 1 can easily be represented electronically in the computer.

Bit: *(BInary digiT)* The smallest piece of information understood by a computer consisting of either a 0 or a 1.

Boot: To start up a computer system by loading a program into the memory.

Bug: An error in a computer program.

Byte: A string of eight bits commonly acting as a single piece of information.

Character: A letter or digit used to display information.

Chip: A small piece of silicon containing thousands of electrical elements. Also referred to as an integrated circuit.

Command: An instruction to a computer to perform a special task.

Compiler: A program which translates an instruction written in a high-level language into machine language so that the instruction can be understood by the computer.

Computer: An electronic device for performing programmed computations quickly and accurately. A computer is made up of five basic blocks: memory, control, the arithmetic logic unit (ALU), input, and output.

Computer program: A list of statements, commands, and instructions written in computer language which, when executed correctly, will perform a task or function.

Control character: A character that is entered by holding down the control key while hitting another key. The control character "controls" or changes information which is printed or displayed.

CPU: *(Central Processing Unit)* The hardware portion of a computer which executes instructions. The "brain" of the computer which controls all other devices.

CRT: *(Cathode Ray Tube)* An electronic vacuum tube, such as that found in a TV, which is used to display information.

Cursor: A symbol on a computer screen which points out where the next character typed from the keyboard will appear.

Data: Information used or produced by a computer program.

Data base: A collection of information which is organized in such a way that a computer can process it efficiently.

Debug: Removing errors from a computer program.

Device: A hardware component of a computer system designed to perform a certain task. A CRT, printer, or disk drive are examples of computer devices.

Digit: A character used to express numbers in a number system. For instance, 0 and 1 are digits in base 2; 0 to 7 are digits in base 8; 0 to 9 are digits in base 10; and 0 to 9, A, B, C, D, E, and F are digits in base 16.

Digital: A class of computers which process information which is in binary form. It is also used to describe information which is in binary form.

Dimension: A statement in a program which tells a computer how large an array is and to set aside memory for that array.

Disk: A magnetic storage device used to record computer information. Each disk appears flat and square on the outside; inside, the disk is circular and rotates so that information can be stored on its many circular tracks.

Disk drive: The device that writes and reads information onto the disk.

Documentation: A practice used by all good programmers in which comments are inserted into a computer program so that someone else can look at the program and understand what a program is supposed to do and how it does it.

DOS: *(Disk Operating System)* A software system that allows a computer to communicate with and control one or more disk drives.

Edit: To change an original document or program by adding, deleting, or replacing parts of it, thus creating a new document or program.

Error: A programming mistake which will cause the program to run incorrectly or not run at all.

Error message: A message, displayed or printed, which tells you an error or problem is in a program.

Execute: To run a computer program.

File: A collection of information stored on a computer device.

Floppy disk: A storage device made of a thin, magnetically coated plastic.

Flowchart: A diagram which shows the steps in a computer program.

Format: To prepare a blank disk for use (also *initialize*).

Graphics: Information which is displayed as pictures or images rather than by characters.

Hardcopy: A printed copy of a program, data, or results.

Hardware: The actual electronic and mechanical components of a computer system. A floppy disk is *hardware,* while a program stored on it is *software.*

Input: Information taken from a disk drive, keyboard, or other device and transported into a computer.

Instruction: Machine language which commands an action to be taken by the CPU *(central processing unit)* of a computer.

Interactive: A computer system in which the operator and computer frequently exchange information.

Interface: The hardware, software, and firmware which is used to link one computer or computer device to another.

K: A term used when describing the capacity of a computer memory or storage device. For example, 16K equals 16x1024 or 16,384 memory addresses.

Keyboard: An input device used to enter information into a computer by striking keys which are labeled much like those on a typewriter.

Letter-quality printer: A printer that produces type quality similar to that of an electric typewriter.

Library: A collection of programs which may be referred to often.

List: A display or printout of a computer program or file.

Load: To take information from an external storage device and *load* it into a computer's memory.

LOGO: A language which combines pictures and words to teach programming to children.

Loop: A series of instructions which is repeated, usually with different data on each pass.

Machine language: The language used to directly instruct computer hardware. The computer uses this language to process data and instructions in binary form.

Mainframe computer: A large computer generally with many operators using it at one time.

Main memory: The memory that is built into a computer.

Memory: The part of the computer which stores information and program instructions until they are needed.

Menu: A detailed list of choices presented in a program from which a user can select.

Microcomputer: A small, inexpensive computer using a microprocessor as its processing unit.

Minicomputer: A computer larger than a microcomputer whose CPU cannot be contained on a single chip; generally used in small business, science, and engineering.

Modem: *(MOdulator DEModulator)* A device which allows computers to communicate over telephone lines.

Monitor: A video screen on which information from a computer can be displayed. By viewing the displayed information, the user can visualize and control the operation of a program.

Output: Information sent from a computer to a disk drive, monitor, printer, or any other external device.

PASCAL: A high-level language designed to teach the principles of structured programming. (Named after Blaise Pascal, a 17th century mathematician.)

Peripheral device: An external device such as a plotter, disk drive, or printer added to a computer system to increase the capabilities of the system.

PILOT: *(Programmed Inquiry, Learning, Or Teaching)* A high-level language used for computer aided instruction.

Printed circuit board: A flat, rigid board commonly made of fiberglass. It is used to hold and electronically connect computer chips and other electrical elements.

Printer: A peripheral device (similar to a typewriter) used to produce printed copies of computer data or programs.

Printout: A copy of computer output produced on paper by a printer.

Processor: The portion of computer hardware that performs machine-language instructions and controls all other parts of the computer.

Program: A step-by-step list of instructions which a computer will follow in order to accomplish a specific task.

Programmer: A person involved in the writing, editing, and production of a computer program.

Programming language: A set of guidelines and rules for writing a program which will perform a task on a computer.

Prompt: A question which asks the user to input information to be processed or to tell the computer which part of a program to branch to.

Resolution: Describes the quality of a video image displayed on a computer monitor or graphics screen.

Save: To take a program or file from main memory and store it on a device (disk, cassette, etc.) for later use.

Sector: A fraction of the recording surface on a disk; a sector is a fraction of a *track*.

Software: Programs which instruct a computer how to perform a desired task.

Spreadsheet: A program used to organize numbers and figures into a worksheet form.

Statement: An instruction in a program which will perform a desired operation.

Storage: Describes the main memory or external devices where information or programs can be stored.

String: A group of consecutive letters, numbers, and characters which are not used for computational purposes.

Subroutine: A group of statements which can be found and used from several different places in a main program.

System: The collection of hardware, software, and firmware that forms a functioning computer.

Telecommunications: Sending and receiving information from one computer to another over long distances via phone lines, satellites, or other forms of communication equipment.

Terminal: A peripheral device which contains a keyboard for putting information into a computer and a monitor to receive output from a computer.

Text: Information in the form of characters which can be read by an individual.

Track: A fraction of the recording surface on a disk. (A track can be compared to the space used by each song on an album.) The number of tracks on a disk varies.

User: A person *using* a computer system.

Variable: A place in the computer's memory which can be assigned a value or have that value read, changed, or deleted from memory by the programmer.

Word: A string of bits treated as a single unit by a computer.

Word processor: A program designed to assist a user in writing letters, memos, and other kinds of text.

Write-enable notch: The small, rectangular cutout in the edge of a disk's jacket used to protect the contents of a disk. If the notch is not present, or is covered by a write-protect tab, information cannot be written on the disk.

Write-protect: To apply a write-protect tab to a disk, making it impossible for new information to be written on the disk. The information on the disk is now protected from being overwritten.

Write-protect tab: A sticker used to cover the write-enable notch on a disk.

Computer Keyboard

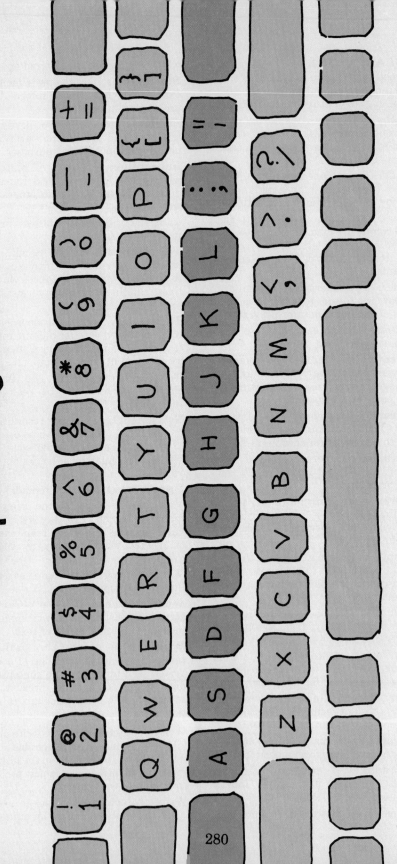

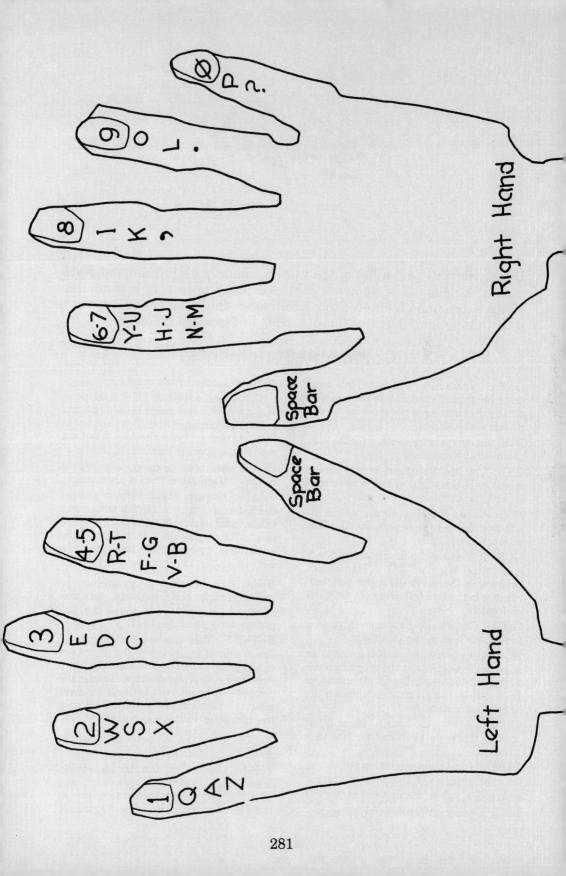

Right Hand

Left Hand

Space Bar

Space Bar

281

Below you will find a list of the most commonly used command statements. Command statements are used when operating a computer. When a command is entered into a computer, the computer will perform a certain action. Each of those actions is described below.

Command Statements

DATA: Allows data to be stored in a computer program. This data can be retrieved during the running of the program by the READ statement.

DIM: Saves space in memory for the size of an array you select.

END: The last statement in a program which stops the program and returns control of the computer to the user.

FOR: Allows the programmer to set up a loop which is to be repeated a specified number of times.

GOSUB: Causes the program to go to a subroutine. When a RETURN statement is made in the subroutine, the program returns to the line following the GOSUB statement.

GOTO: Causes the computer to go to a particular line in the program.

IF: A statement which tells the computer to go to the next line in the program if the argument following the IF statement is false or to go to a given line number if the argument is true.

INPUT: Allows the user to input information from the keyboard for use in a program.

LET: An optional instruction which can be used when a variable in a program is assigned a value. (Example: Let A=25.)

LIST: Displays or prints a copy of the program presently in the computer.

NEXT: Used with the FOR statement. When a NEXT statement is used in a program, the computer branches back to the FOR statement until the loop has been repeated a specific number of times.

PRINT: Instructs the computer to type or display information from a program.

READ: Instructs the computer to read the information in a DATA statement; takes information from a DATA statement and assigns the information to the variable(s) immediately following the READ statement.

REM: Allows the programmer to insert remarks and comments into a program which are used to make the program easier to understand.

RETURN: This command will instruct the computer to go back to the main part of the program. When encountered in a subroutine, this statement will cause the computer to branch to the first statement after the GOSUB command which sent the computer to the subroutine.

RUN: Causes the computer to "run" the program in memory.

THEN: Used with the IF statement. When the argument between the IF and THEN is true, the statements following the THEN statement are performed.

Constitution of the United States of America

Note: The original text of the Constitution has been edited to conform to contemporary American usage. The bracketed words have been added to help you locate information more quickly; they are not part of the Constitution.

The oldest federal constitution in existence was framed by a convention of delegates from twelve of the thirteen original states in Philadelphia in May, 1787, Rhode Island failing to send a delegate. George Washington presided over the session, which lasted until September 17, 1787. The draft (originally a preamble and seven Articles) was submitted to all thirteen states and was to become effective when ratified by nine states. It went into effect on the first Wednesday in March, 1789, having been ratified by New Hampshire, the ninth state to approve, on June 21, 1788. The states ratified the Constitution in the following order:

Delaware	December 7, 1787	South Carolina	May 23, 1788
Pennsylvania	December 12, 1787	New Hampshire	June 21, 1788
New Jersey	December 18, 1787	Virginia	June 25, 1788
Georgia	January 2, 1788	New York	July 26, 1788
Connecticut	January 9, 1788	North Carolina	November 21, 1789
Massachusetts	February 6, 1788	Rhode Island	May 29, 1790
Maryland	April 28, 1788		

[Preamble]

We the people of the United States, in order to form a more perfect Union, establish justice, insure domestic tranquility, provide for the common defense, promote the general welfare, and secure the blessings of liberty to ourselves and our posterity, do ordain and establish this Constitution for the United States of America.

Article I

Section 1

[Legislative powers vested in Congress] All legislative powers herein granted shall be vested in a Congress of the United States, which shall consist of a Senate and House of Representatives.

Section 2

1. **[Make-up of the House of Representatives]** The House of Representatives shall be composed of members chosen every second year by the people of the several States, and the electors in each State shall have the qualifications requisite for electors of the most numerous branch of the State Legislature.

2. **[Qualifications of Representatives]** No person shall be a Representative who shall not have attained to the age of twenty-five years, and been seven years a citizen of the United States, and who shall not, when elected, be an inhabitant of that State in which he shall be chosen.

3. **[Apportionment of Representatives and direct taxes—census]** (Representatives and direct taxes shall be apportioned among the several States which may be included within this Union, according to their respective numbers, which shall be determined by adding to the whole number of free persons, including those bound to service for a term of years, and excluding Indians not taxed, three-fifths of all other persons.—*Amended by the 14th Amendment, section 2.)* The actual enumeration shall be made within three years after the first meeting of the Congress of the United States, and within every subsequent term of ten years, in such manner as they shall by law direct. The number of Representatives shall not exceed one for every thirty thousand, but each State shall have at least one Representative; and until such enumeration shall be made, the State of New Hampshire shall be entitled to choose three; Massachusetts, eight; Rhode Island and Providence Plantations, one; Connecticut, five; New York, six; New Jersey, four; Pennsylvania, eight; Delaware, one; Maryland, six; Virginia, ten; North Carolina, five; South Carolina, five; and Georgia, three.

4. **[Filling of vacancies in representation]** When vacancies happen in the representation from any State, the Executive Authority thereof shall issue writs of election to fill such vacancies.

5. **[Selection of officers; power of impeachment]** The House of Representatives shall choose their Speaker and other officers; and shall have the sole power of impeachment.

Section 3

1. **[The Senate]** (The Senate of the United States shall be composed of two Senators from each State, chosen by the Legislature thereof, for six years; and each Senator shall have one vote.—*Amended by the 17th Amendment, section 1.)*

2. **[Classification of Senators; filling of vacancies]** Immediately after they shall be assembled in consequence of the first election, they shall be divided as equally as may be into three classes. The seats of the Senators of the first class shall be vacated at the expiration of the second year, of the second class at the expiration of the fourth year, and of the third class at the expiration of the sixth year, so that one-third may be chosen every second year; and if vacancies happen by resignation, or otherwise, (during the recess of the Legislature of any State,) the Executive thereof may make temporary appointments (until the next meeting of the Legislature, which shall then fill such vacancies.—*Amended by the 17th Amendment.)*

3. **[Qualification of Senators]** No person shall be a Senator who shall not have attained to the age of thirty years, and been nine years a citizen of the United States, and who shall not, when elected, be an inhabitant of that State for which he shall be chosen.

4. **[Vice President to be President of Senate]** The Vice President of the United States shall be President of the Senate, but shall have no vote, unless they be equally divided.

5. **[Selection of Senate officers; President pro tempore)** The Senate shall choose their other officers, and also a President pro tempore, in the absence of the Vice President, or when he shall exercise the office of President of the United States.

6. **[Senate to try impeachments]** The Senate shall have the sole power to try all impeachments. When sitting for that purpose, they shall be on oath or affirmation. When the President of the United States is tried, the Chief Justice shall preside: and no person shall be convicted without the concurrence of two-thirds of the members present.

7. **[Judgment in cases of impeachment]** Judgment in cases of impeachment shall not extend further than to removal from office, and disqualification to hold and enjoy any office of honor, trust, or profit under the United States; but the party convicted shall nevertheless be liable and subject to indictment, trial, judgment, and punishment, according to Law.

Section 4

1. **[Control of congressional elections]** The times, places, and manner of holding elections for Senators and Representatives shall be prescribed in each State by the Legislature thereof; but the Congress may at any time by law make or alter such regulations, except as to the places of choosing Senators.

2. **[Time for assembling of Congress]** The Congress shall assemble at least once in every year, (and such meeting shall be on the first Monday in December, unless they shall by law appoint a different day.—*Amended by the 20th Amendment, section 2.)*

Section 5

1. **[Each House to be the judge of the election and qualifications of its members; regulations as to quorum]** Each House shall be the judge of the elections, returns, and qualifications of its own members, and a majority of each shall constitute a quorum to do business; but a smaller number may adjourn from day to day, and may be authorized to compel the attendance of absent members, in such manner, and under such penalties as each House may provide.

2. **[Each House to determine its own rules]** Each House may determine the rules of its proceedings, punish its members for disorderly behavior, and, with the concurrence of two-thirds, expel a member.

3. **[Journals and yeas and nays]** Each House shall keep a journal of its proceedings, and from time to time publish the same, excepting such parts as may in their judgment require secrecy; and the yeas and nays of the members of either House on any question shall, at the desire of one-fifth of those present, be entered on the journal.

4. **[Adjournment]** Neither House, during the session of Congress, shall, without the consent of the other, adjourn for more than three days, nor to any other place than that in which the two Houses shall be sitting.

Section 6

1. **[Compensation and privileges of members of Congress]** The Senators and Representatives shall receive a compensation for their services, to be ascertained by law, and paid out of the Treasury of the United States. They shall in all cases, except treason, felony, and breach of the peace, be privileged from arrest during their attendance at the session of their respective Houses, and in going to and returning from the same; and for any speech or debate in either House, they shall not be questioned in any other place.

2. **[Incompatible offices; exclusions]** No Senator or Representative shall, during the time for which he was elected, be appointed to any civil office under the authority of the United States, which shall have been created, or the emoluments whereof shall have been increased during such time; and no person holding any office under the United States shall be a member of either House during his continuance in office.

Section 7

1. **[Revenue bills to originate in House]** All bills for raising revenue shall originate in the House of Representatives; but the Senate may propose or concur with amendments as on other bills.

2. **[Manner of passing bills; veto power of President]** Every bill which shall have passed the House of Representatives and the Senate, shall, before it becomes a law, be presented to the President of the United States; if he approve, he shall sign it, but if not he shall return it, with his objections to that House in which it shall have originated, who shall enter the objections at large on their journal, and proceed to reconsider it. If after such reconsideration two-thirds of that House shall agree to pass the bill, it shall be sent, together with the objections, to the other House, by which it shall likewise be reconsidered, and if approved by two-thirds of that House, it shall become a law. But in all such cases the votes of both Houses shall be determined by yeas and nays, and the names of the persons voting for and against the bill shall be entered on the journal of each House, respectively. If any bill shall not be returned by the President within ten days (Sundays excepted) after it shall have been presented to him, the same shall be a law, in like manner as if he had signed it, unless the Congress by their adjournment prevent its return, in which case it shall not be a law.

3. **[Concurrent orders or resolutions to be passed by President]** Every order, resolution, or vote to which the concurrence of the Senate and House of Representatives may be necessary (except on a question of adjournment) shall be presented to the President of the United States; and before the same shall take effect, shall be approved by him, or being disapproved by him, shall be repassed by two-thirds of the Senate and House of Representatives, according to the rules and limitations prescribed in the case of a bill.

Section 8

[General powers of Congress] The Congress shall have the power:

1. **[Taxes, duties, imposts, and excises]** To lay and collect taxes, duties, imposts, and excises, to pay the debts and provide for the common defense and general welfare of the United States; but all duties, imposts, and excises shall be uniform throughout the United States; *(See the 16th Amendment.)*

2. **[Borrowing of money]** To borrow money on the credit of the United States;

3. **[Regulation of commerce]** To regulate commerce with foreign nations, and among the several States, and with the Indian tribes;

4. **[Naturalization and bankruptcy]** To establish a uniform rule of naturalization, and uniform laws on the subject of bankruptcies throughout the United States;

5. **[Money, weights, and measures]** To coin money, regulate the value thereof, and of foreign coin, and fix the standard of weights and measures;

6. **[Counterfeiting]** To provide for the punishment of counterfeiting the securities and current coin of the United States;

7. **[Post offices]** To establish post offices and post roads;

8. **[Patents and copyrights]** To promote the progress of science and useful arts, by securing for limited times to authors and inventors the exclusive right to their respective writings and discoveries;

9. **[Inferior courts]** To constitute tribunals inferior to the Supreme Court;

10. **[Piracies and felonies]** To define and punish piracies and felonies committed on the high seas, and offenses against the law of nations.

11. **[War; marque and reprisal]** To declare war, grant letters of marque and reprisal, and make rules concerning captures on land and water;

12. **[Armies]** To raise and support armies, but no appropriation of money to that use shall be for a longer term than two years;

13. **[Navy]** To provide and maintain a navy;

14. **[Land and naval forces]** To make rules for the government and regulation of the land and naval forces;

15. **[Calling out militia]** To provide for calling forth the militia to execute the laws of the Union, suppress insurrections, and repel invasions.

16. **[Organizing, arming, and disciplining militia]** To provide for organizing, arming, and disciplining the militia, and for governing such part of them as may be employed in the service of the United States, reserving to the States, respectively, the appointment of the officers, and the authority of training the militia according to the discipline prescribed by Congress;

17. **[Exclusive legislation over District of Columbia]** To exercise exclusive legislation in all cases whatsoever, over such district (not exceeding ten miles square) as may, by cession of particular States, and the acceptance of Congress, become the seat of the Government of the United States, and to exercise like authority over all places purchased by the consent of the Legislature of the State in which the same shall be, for the erection of forts, magazines, arsenals, dock-yards, and other needful buildings;—And

18. **[To enact laws necessary to enforce Constitution]** To make all laws which shall be necessary and proper for carrying into execution the foregoing powers, and all other powers vested by this Constitution in the Government of the United States, or in any department or officer thereof.

Section 9

1. **[Migration or importation of certain persons not to be prohibited before 1808]** The migration or importation of such persons as any of the States now existing shall think proper to admit, shall not be prohibited by the Congress prior to the year one thousand eight hundred and eight, but a tax or duty may be imposed on such importation, not exceeding ten dollars for each person.

2. **[Writ of habeas corpus not to be suspended; exception]** The privilege of the writ of habeas corpus shall not be suspended, unless when in cases of rebellion or invasion the public safety may require it.

3. **[Bills of attainder and ex post facto laws prohibited]** No bill of attainder or ex post facto law shall be passed.

4. **[Capitation and other direct taxes]** No capitation, or other direct, tax shall be laid, unless in proportion to the census or enumeration herein before directed to be taken. *(See the 16th Amendment.)*

5. **[Exports not to be taxed]** No tax or duty shall be laid on articles exported from any State.

6. **[No preference to be given to ports of any State; interstate shipping]** No preference shall be given by any regulation of commerce or revenue to the ports of one State over those of another: nor shall vessels bound to, or from, one State, be obliged to enter, clear, or pay duties in another.

7. **[Money, how drawn from treasury; financial statements to be published]** No money shall be drawn from the Treasury, but in consequence of appropriations made by law; and a regular statement and account of the receipts and expenditures of all public money shall be published from time to time.

8. **[Titles of nobility not to be granted; acceptance by government officers of favors from foreign powers]** No title of nobility shall be granted by the United States: and no person holding any office of profit or trust under them, shall, without the consent of the Congress, accept of any present, emolument, office, or title, of any kind whatever, from any king, prince, or foreign state.

Section 10

1. **[Limitations of the powers of the several States]** No state shall enter into any treaty, alliance, or confederation; grant letters of marque and reprisal; coin money; emit bills of credit; make anything but gold and silver coin a tender in payment of debts; pass any bill of attainder, ex post facto law, or law impairing the obligation of contracts, or grant any title of nobility.

2. **[State imposts and duties]** No State shall, without the consent of the Congress, lay any imposts or duties on imports or exports, except what may be absolutely necessary for executing its inspection laws: and the net produce of all duties and imposts, laid by any State on imports or exports, shall be for the use of the Treasury of the United States; and all such laws shall be subject to the revision and control of the Congress.

3. **[Further restrictions on powers of States]** No State shall, without the consent of Congress, lay any duty of tonnage, keep troops, or ships of war in time of peace, enter into any agreement or compact with another state, or with a foreign power, or engage in war, unless actually invaded, or in such imminent danger as will not admit of delay.

Article II
Section 1

1. **[The President; the executive power]** The executive power shall be vested in a President of the United States of America. He shall hold his office during the term of four years, and together with the Vice President, chosen for the same term, be elected, as follows:

2. **[Appointment and qualifications of presidential electors]** Each State shall appoint, in such manner as the Legislature thereof may direct, a number of electors, equal to the whole number of Senators and Representatives to which the State may be entitled in the Congress: but no Senator or Representative, or person holding an office of trust or profit under the United States, shall be appointed an elector.

3. **[Original method of electing the President and Vice President]** (The electors shall meet in their respective States, and vote by ballot for two persons, of whom one at least shall not be an inhabitant of the same State with themselves. And they shall make a list of all the persons voted for, and of the number of votes for each; which list they shall sign and certify, and transmit sealed to the seat of the Government of the United States, directed to the President of the Senate. The President of the Senate shall, in the presence of the Senate and House of Representatives, open all the certificates, and the votes shall then be counted. The person having the greatest number of votes shall be the President, if such number be a majority of the whole number of electors appointed; and if there be more than one who have such majority, and have an equal number of votes, then the House of Representatives shall immediately choose by ballot one of them for President; and if no person have a majority, then from the five highest on the list the said House shall in like manner choose the President. But in choosing the President, the votes shall be taken by States, the representation from each State having one vote; a quorum for this purpose shall consist of a member or members from two-thirds of the States, and a majority of all the states shall be necessary to a choice. In every case, after the choice of the President, the person having the greatest number of votes of the electors shall be

Constitution

the Vice President. But if there should remain two or more who have equal votes, the Senate should choose from them by ballot the Vice President.—*Replaced by the 12th Amendment.)*

4. [Congress may determine time of choosing electors and day for casting their votes] The Congress may determine the time of choosing the electors, and the day on which they shall give their votes; which day shall be the same throughout the United States.

5. [Qualifications for the office of President] No person except a natural born citizen, or a citizen of the United States, at the time of the adoption of this Constitution, shall be eligible to the office of President; neither shall any person be eligible to that office who shall not have attained to the age of thirty-five years, and been fourteen years a resident within the United States. *(For qualifications of the Vice President, see the 12th Amendment.)*

6. [Filling vacancy in the office of President] (In case of the removal of the President from office, or of his death, resignation, or inability to discharge the powers and duties of the said office, the same shall devolve on the Vice President, and the Congress may by law provide for the case of removal, death, resignation or inability, both of the President and Vice President, declaring what officer shall then act as President, and such officer shall act accordingly, until the disability be removed, or a President shall be elected.—*Amended by the 20th and 25th Amendments.)*

7. [Compensation of the President] The President shall, at stated times, receive for his services, a compensation, which shall neither be increased nor diminished during the period for which he shall have been elected, and he shall not receive within that period any other emolument from the United States, or any of them.

8. [Oath to be taken by the President] Before he enter on the execution of his office, he shall take the following oath or affirmation:—"I do solemnly swear (or affirm) that I will faithfully execute the office of President of the United States, and will to the best of my ability, preserve, protect, and defend the Constitution of the United States."

Section 2

1. [The President to be Commander-in-Chief of army and navy and head of executive departments; may grant reprieves and pardons] The President shall be Commander-in-Chief of the Army and Navy of the United States, and of the militia of the several States, when called into the actual service of the United States; he may require the opinion, in writing, of the principal officer in each of the executive departments, upon any subject relating to the duties of their respective offices, and he shall have power to grant reprieves and pardons for offenses against the United States, except in cases of impeachment.

2. [President may, with concurrence of Senate, make treaties, appoint ambassadors, etc.; appointment of inferior officers, authority of Congress over] He shall have power, by and with the advice and consent of the Senate, to make treaties, provided two-thirds of the Senators present concur; and he shall nominate, and by and with the advice and consent of the Senate, shall appoint ambassadors, other public ministers and consuls, judges of the Supreme Court, and all other officers of the United States, whose appointments are not herein otherwise provided for, and which shall be established by law: but the Congress may by law vest the appointment of such inferior officers, as they think proper, in the President alone, in the courts of law, or in the heads of departments.

3. [President may fill vacancies in office during recess of Senate] The President shall have power to fill up all vacancies that may happen during the recess of the Senate, by granting commissions which shall expire at the end of their session.

Section 3

[President to give advice to Congress; may convene or adjourn it on certain occasions; to receive ambassadors, etc.; have laws executed and commission all officers] He shall from time to time give to the Congress information of the state of the Union, and recommend to their consideration such measures as he shall judge necessary and expedient; he may, on extraordinary occasions, convene both Houses, or either of them, and in case of disagreement between them, with respect to the time of adjournment, he may adjourn them to such time as he shall think proper; he shall receive ambassadors and other public ministers: he shall take care that the laws be faithfully executed, and shall commission all the officers of the United States.

Section 4

[All civil officers removable by impeachment] The President, Vice President, and all civil officers of the United States shall be removed from office on impeachment for, and conviction of, treason, bribery, or other high crimes and misdemeanors.

Article III
Section 1

[Judicial powers; how vested; term of office and compensation of judges] The judicial power of the United States, shall be vested in one Supreme Court, and in such inferior courts as the Congress may from time to time ordain and establish. The judges, both of the supreme and inferior courts, shall hold their offices during good behavior, and shall, at stated times, receive for their services, a compensation, which shall not be diminished during their continuance in office.

Section 2

1. [Jurisdiction of Federal courts] (The judicial power shall extend to all cases, in law and equity, arising under this Constitution, the laws of the United States, and treaties made, or which shall be made, under their authority; to all cases affecting ambassadors, other public ministers and consuls; to all cases of admiralty and maritime jurisdiction; to controversies to which the United States, shall be a party; to controversies between two or more States; between a State and citizens of another State; between citizens of different States, between citizens of the same State claiming lands under grants of different states, and between a State, or the citizens thereof, and foreign states, citizens, or subjects.—*Amended by the 11th Amendment.)*

2. [Original and appellate jurisdiction of Supreme Court] In all cases affecting ambassadors, other public ministers and consuls, and those in which a State shall be party, the Supreme Court shall have original jurisdiction. In all the other cases before mentioned, the Supreme Court shall have appellate jurisdiction, both as to law and fact, with such exceptions, and under such regulations, as the Congress shall make.

3. [Trial of all crimes, except impeachment, to be by jury] The trial of all crimes, except in cases of impeachment, shall be by jury; and such trial shall be held in the State where the said crimes shall have been committed; but when not committed within any State, the trial shall be at such place or places as the Congress may by law have directed.

286

Section 3

1. **[Treason defined; conviction of]** Treason against the United States, shall consist only in levying war against them, or, in adhering to their enemies, giving them aid and comfort. No person shall be convicted of treason unless on the testimony of two witnesses to the same overt act, or on confession in open court.

2. **[Congress to declare punishment for treason; proviso]** The Congress shall have power to declare the punishment of treason, but no attainder of treason shall work corruption of blood, or forfeiture except during the life of the person attainted.

Article IV

Section 1

[Each State to give full faith and credit to the public acts and records of other States] Full faith and credit shall be given in each State to the public acts, records, and judicial proceedings of every other State. And the Congress may by general laws prescribe the manner in which such acts, records, and proceedings shall be proved, and the effect thereof.

Section 2

1. **[Privileges of citizens]** The citizens of each State shall be entitled to all privileges and immunities of citizens in the several States.

2. **[Extradition between the several States]** A person charged in any State with treason, felony, or other crime, who shall flee from justice, and be found in another State, shall on demand of the Executive authority of the State from which he fled, be delivered up, to be removed to the State having jurisdiction of the crime.

3. **[Persons held to labor or service in one State, fleeing to another, to be returned]** (No person held to service or labor in one State, under the laws thereof, escaping into another, shall, in consequence of any law or regulation therein, be discharged from such service or labor, but shall be delivered up on claim of the party to whom such service or labor may be due.—*Eliminated by the 13th Amendment.)*

Section 3

1. **[New States]** New States may be admitted by the Congress into this Union; but no new State shall be formed or erected within the jurisdiction of any other State; nor any State be formed by the junction of two or more States, or parts of States, without the consent of the Legislatures of the States concerned as well as of the Congress.

2. **[Regulations concerning territory]** The Congress shall have power to dispose of and make all needful rules and regulations respecting the territory or other property belonging to the United States; and nothing in this Constitution shall be so construed as to prejudice any claims of the United States, or of any particular State.

Section 4

[Republican form of government and protection guaranteed the several States] The United States shall guarantee to every State in this Union a Republican form of government, and shall protect each of them against invasion; and on application of the Legislature, or of the Executive (when the Legislature cannot be convened) against domestic violence.

Article V

[Ways in which the Constitution can be amended] The Congress, whenever two-thirds of both Houses shall deem it necessary, shall propose amendments to this Constitution, or, on the application of the Legislatures of two-thirds of the several States shall call a convention for proposing amendments, which, in either case, shall be valid to all intents and purposes, as part of this Constitution, when ratified by the Legislatures of three-fourths of the several States, or by conventions in three-fourths thereof, as the one or the other mode of ratification may be proposed by the Congress; provided that no amendment which may be made prior to the year one thousand eight hundred and eight shall in any manner affect the first and fourth clauses in the ninth Section of the first Article; and that no State, without its consent, shall be deprived of its equal suffrage in the Senate.

Article VI

1. **[Debts contracted under the confederation secured]** All debts contracted and engagements entered into, before the adoption of this Constitution, shall be as valid against the United States under this Constitution, as under the Confederation.

2. **[Constitution, laws, and treaties of the United States to be supreme]** This Constitution, and the laws of the United States which shall be made in pursuance thereof; and all treaties made, or which shall be made, under the authority of the United States, shall be the supreme law of the land; and the judges in every State shall be bound thereby, anything in the Constitution or laws of any State to the contrary notwithstanding.

3. **[Who shall take constitutional oath; no religious test as to official qualification]** The Senators and Representatives before mentioned, and the members of the several State Legislatures, and all executive and judicial officers, both of the United States and of the several States, shall be bound by oath or affirmation, to support this Constitution; but no religious test shall ever be required as a qualification to any office or public trust under the United States.

Article VII

[Constitution to be considered adopted when ratified by nine States] The ratification of the conventions of nine States shall be sufficient for the establishment of this Constitution between the States so ratifying the same.

Amendments to the Constitution of the United States

Note: Amendments I to X, popularly known as the Bill of Rights, were proposed and sent to the states by the first session of the First Congress. They were ratified Dec. 15, 1791.

Amendment 1

[Freedom of religion, speech, of the press, and right of petition] Congress shall make no law respecting an establishment of religion, or prohibiting the free exercise thereof; or abridging the freedom of speech, or of the press; or the right of the people peaceably to assemble, and to petition the Government for a redress of grievances.

Amendment 2

[Right of people to bear arms not to be infringed] A well-regulated militia, being necessary to the security of a free State, the right of the people to keep and bear arms, shall not be infringed.

Amendment 3

[Quartering of troops] No soldier shall, in time of peace be quartered in any house, without the consent of the owner, nor in time of war, but in a manner to be prescribed by law.

Amendment 4

[Persons and houses to be secure from unreasonable searches and seizures] The right of the people to be secure in their persons, houses, papers, and effects, against unreasonable searches and seizures, shall not be violated, and no warrants shall issue, but upon probable cause, supported by oath or affirmation, and particularly describing the place to be searched, and the persons or things to be seized.

Amendment 5

[Trials for crimes; just compensation for private property taken for public use] No person shall be held to answer for a capital, or otherwise infamous crime, unless on a presentment or indictment of a Grand Jury, except in cases arising in the land or naval forces, or in the militia, when in actual service in time of war or public danger; nor shall any person be subject for the same offense to be twice put in jeopardy of life or limb; nor shall be compelled in any criminal case to be a witness, against himself, nor be deprived of life, liberty, or property, without due process of law; nor shall private property be taken for public use, without just compensation.

Amendment 6

[Right to speedy trial, witnesses, counsel] In all criminal prosecutions, the accused shall enjoy the right to a speedy and public trial, by an impartial jury of the State and district wherein the crime shall have been committed, which district shall have been previously ascertained by law, and to be informed of the nature and cause of the accusation; to be confronted with the witnesses against him; to have compulsory process for obtaining witnesses in his favor, and to have the assistance of counsel for his defense.

Amendment 7

[Right of trial by jury] In suits at common law, where the value in controversy shall exceed twenty dollars, the right of trial by jury shall be preserved, and no fact tried by a jury, shall be otherwise re-examined in any court of the United States, than according to the rules of the common law.

Amendment 8

[Excessive bail, fines, and punishments prohibited] Excessive bail shall not be required, nor excessive fines imposed, nor cruel and unusual punishments inflicted.

Amendment 9

[Reserved rights of people] The enumeration in the Constitution, of certain rights, shall not be construed to deny or disparage others retained by the people.

Amendment 10

[Rights of States under Constitution] The powers not delegated to the United States by the Constitution, nor prohibited by it to the States, are reserved to the States, respectively, or to the people.

Amendment 11

(The proposed amendment was sent to the states March 5, 1794, by the Third Congress. It was ratified Feb. 7, 1795. It changes Article III, Sect. 2, Para. 1.)

[Judicial power of United States not to extend to suits against a State] The judicial power of the United States shall not be construed to extend to any suit in law or equity, commenced or prosecuted against one of the United States by citizens of another State, or by citizens or subjects of any foreign state.

Amendment 12

(The proposed amendment was sent to the states Dec. 12, 1803, by the Eighth Congress. It was ratified July 27, 1804. It replaces Article II, Sect. 1, Para. 3.)

[Manner of electing President and Vice President by electors] (The electors shall meet in their respective states, and vote by ballot for President and Vice President, one of whom, at least, shall not be an inhabitant of the same state with themselves; they shall name in their ballots the person voted for as President, and in distinct ballots the person voted for as Vice President, and they shall make distinct lists of all persons voted for as President, and of all persons voted for as Vice President, and of the number of votes for each, which lists they shall sign and certify, and transmit sealed to the seat of the government of the United States, directed to the President of the Senate; the President of the Senate shall, in the presence of the Senate and House of Representatives, open all the certificates and the votes shall then be counted; the person having the greatest number of votes for President, shall be the President, if such number be a majority of the whole number of electors appointed; and if no person have such majority, then from the persons having the highest numbers not exceeding three on the list of those voted for as President, the House of Representatives shall choose immediately, by ballot, the President. But in choosing the President, the votes shall be taken by states, the representation from each State having one vote; a quorum for this purpose shall consist of a member or members from two-thirds of the states, and a majority of all the states shall be necessary to a choice. And if the House of Representatives shall not choose a President whenever the right of choice shall devolve upon them, before the fourth day of March next following, then the Vice President shall act as President, as in the case of the death or other constitutional disability of the President. The person having the greatest number of votes as Vice President, shall be the Vice President, if such number be a majority of the whole number of electors appointed, and if no person have a majority, then from the two highest numbers on the list, the Senate shall choose the Vice President; a quorum for the purpose shall consist of two-thirds of the whole number of Senators, and a majority of the whole number shall be necessary to a choice. But no person constitutionally ineligible to the office of President shall be eligible to that of Vice President of the United States.—*Amended by the 20th Amendment, sections 3 and 4.)*

Amendment 13

(The proposed amendment was sent to the states Feb. 1, 1865, by the Thirty-eighth Congress. It was ratified Dec. 6, 1865. It eliminates Article IV, Sect. 2, Para. 3.)

Section 1

[Slavery prohibited] Neither slavery nor involuntary servitude, except as a punishment for crime whereof the party shall have been duly convicted, shall exist within the United States, or any place subject to their jurisdiction.

Section 2

[Congress given power to enforce this article] Congress shall have power to enforce this article by appropriate legislation.

Amendment 14

(The proposed amendment was sent to the states June 16, 1866, by the Thirty-ninth Congress. It was ratified July 9, 1868. It changes Article 1, Sec. 2, Para. 3.)

Section 1

[Citizenship defined; privileges of citizens] All persons born or naturalized in the United States, and subject to the jurisdiction thereof, are citizens of the United States and of the State wherein they reside. No State shall make or enforce any law which shall abridge the privileges or immunities of citizens of the United States; nor shall any State deprive any person of life, liberty, or property, without due process of law; nor deny to any person within its jurisdiction the equal protection of the laws.

Section 2

[Apportionment of Representatives] Representatives shall be apportioned among the several States according to their respective numbers, counting the whole number of persons in each State, excluding Indians not taxed. But when the right to vote at any election for the choice of electors for President and Vice President of the United States, Representatives in Congress, the executive and judicial officers of a State, or the members of the Legislature thereof, is denied to any of the male inhabitants of such State, being twenty-one years of age, and citizens of the United States, or in any way abridged, except for participation in rebellion, or other crime, the basis of representation therein shall be reduced in the proportion which the number of such male citizens shall bear to the whole number of male citizens twenty-one years of age in such State.

Section 3

[Disqualification for office; removal of disability] No person shall be a Senator or Representative in Congress, or elector of President and Vice President, or hold any office, civil or military, under the United States, or under any State, who, having previously taken an oath, as a member of Congress, or as an officer of the United States, or as a member of any State Legislature, or as an executive or judicial officer of any State, to support the Constitution of the United States, shall have engaged in insurrection or rebellion against the same, or given aid or comfort to the enemies thereof. But Congress may by a vote of two-thirds of each House, remove such disability.

Section 4

[Public debt not to be questioned; payment of debts and claims incurred in aid of rebellion forbidden] The validity of the public debt of the United States, authorized by law, including debts incurred for payment of pensions and bounties for services in suppressing insurrection or rebellion, shall not be questioned. But neither the United States nor any State shall assume or pay any debt or obligation incurred in aid of insurrection or rebellion against the United States, or any claim for the loss or emancipation of any slave; but all such debts, obligations, and claims shall be held illegal and void.

Section 5

[Congress given power to enforce this article] The Congress shall have power to enforce, by appropriate legislation, the provisions of this article.

Amendment 15

(The proposed amendment was sent to the states Feb. 27, 1869, by the Fortieth Congress. It was ratified Feb. 3, 1870.)

Section 1

[Right of certain citizens to vote established] The right of citizens of the United States to vote shall not be denied or abridged by the United States or by any State on account of race, color, or previous condition of servitude.

Section 2

[Congress given power to enforce this article] The Congress shall have power to enforce this article by appropriate legislation.

Amendment 16

(The proposed amendment was sent to the states July 12, 1909, by the Sixty-first Congress. It was ratified Feb. 3, 1913.)

[Income taxes authorized] The Congress shall have power to lay and collect taxes on incomes, from whatever source derived, without apportionment among the several States, and without regard to any census or enumeration.

Amendment 17

(The proposed amendment was sent to the states May 16, 1912, by the Sixty-second Congress. It was ratified April 8, 1913. It changes Article 1, Sect. 3, Para. 1 and 2.)

[Election of United States Senators; filling of vacancies; qualifications of electors] The Senate of the United States shall be composed of two Senators from each State, elected by the people thereof, for six years; and each Senator shall have one vote. The electors in each State shall have the qualifications requisite for electors of the most numerous branch of the State Legislatures.

When vacancies happen in the representation of any State in the Senate, the executive authority of such State shall issue writs of election to fill such vacancies: Provided, that the legislature of any State may empower the executive thereof to make temporary appointment until the people fill the vacancies by election as the legislature may direct.

This amendment shall not be so construed as to affect the election or term of any Senator chosen before it becomes valid as part of the Constitution.

Amendment 18

(The proposed amendment was sent to the states Dec. 18, 1917, by the Sixty-fifth Congress. It was ratified by three-quarters of the states by Jan. 16, 1919, and became effective Jan. 16, 1920. It was

repealed by the 21st Amendment.)

Section 1
[Manufacture, sale, or transportation of intoxicating liquors, for beverage purposes, prohibited] After one year from the ratification of this article the manufacture, sale, or transportation of intoxicating liquors within, the importation thereof into, or the exportation thereof from the United States and all territory subject to the jurisdiction thereof for beverage purposes is hereby prohibited.

Section 2
[Congress and the several States given concurrent power to pass appropriate legislation to enforce this article] The Congress and the several States shall have concurrent power to enforce this article by appropriate legislation.

Section 3
[Provisions of article to become operative, when adopted by three-fourths of the States] This article shall be inoperative unless it shall have been ratified as an amendment to the Constitution by the legislatures of the several States, as provided in the Constitution, within seven years from the date of the submission hereof to the States by Congress.

Amendment 19
(The proposed amendment was sent to the states June 4, 1919, by the Sixty-sixth Congress. It was ratified Aug. 18, 1920.)

[The right of citizens to vote shall not be denied because of sex] The right of citizens of the United States to vote shall not be denied or abridged by the United States or by any State on account of sex.

[Congress given power to enforce this article] Congress shall have power to enforce this article by appropriate legislation.

Amendment 20
(The proposed amendment, sometimes called the "Lame Duck Amendment," was sent to the states March 3, 1932, by the Seventy-second Congress. It was ratified Jan. 23, 1933; but, in accordance with Section 5, Sections 1 and 2 did not go into effect until Oct. 15, 1933. It changes Article 1, Sect. 4, Para. 2 and the 12th Amendment.)

Section 1
[Terms of President, Vice President, Senators, and Representatives] The terms of the President and Vice President shall end at noon on the twentieth day of January, and the terms of Senators and Representatives at noon on the third day of January, of the years in which such terms would have ended if this article had not been ratified; and the terms of their successors shall then begin.

Section 2
[Time of assembling Congress] The Congress shall assemble at least once in every year, and such meeting shall begin at noon on the third day of January, unless they shall by law appoint a different day.

Section 3
[Filling vacancy in office of President] If, at the time fixed for the beginning of the term of the President, the President-elect shall have died, the Vice President-elect shall become President. If a President shall not have been chosen before the time fixed for the beginning of his term, or if the President-elect shall have failed to qualify, then the Vice President shall have qualified; and the Congress may by law provide for the case wherein neither a President-elect nor a Vice President-elect shall have qualified, declaring who shall then act as President, or the manner in which one who is to act shall be selected,

and such person shall act accordingly until a President or Vice President shall have qualified.

Section 4
[Power of Congress in Presidential succession] The Congress may by law provide for the case of the death of any of the persons from whom the House of Representatives may choose a President whenever the right of choice shall have devolved upon them, and for the case of the death of any of the persons from whom the Senate may choose a Vice President whenever the right of choice shall have devolved upon them.

Section 5
[Time of taking effect] Sections 1 and 2 shall take effect on the 15th day of October following the ratification of this article.

Section 6
[Ratification] This article shall be inoperative unless it shall have been ratified as an amendment to the Constitution by the legislatures of three-fourths of the several States within seven years from the date of its submission.

Amendment 21
(The proposed amendment was sent to the states Feb. 20, 1933, by the Seventy-second Congress. It was ratified Dec. 5, 1933. It repeals the 18th Amendment.)

Section 1
[Repeal of Prohibition Amendment] The eighteenth article of amendment to the Constitution of the United States is hereby repealed.

Section 2
[Transportation of intoxicating liquors] The transportation or importation into any State, territory, or possession of the United States for delivery or use therein of intoxicating liquors, in violation of the laws thereof, is hereby prohibited.

Section 3
[Ratification] This article shall be inoperative unless it shall have been ratified as an amendment to the Constitution by convention in the several States, as provided in the Constitution, within seven years from the date of the submission thereof to the States by the Congress.

Amendment 22
(The proposed amendment was sent to the states March 21, 1947, by the Eightieth Congress. It was ratified Feb. 27, 1951.)

Section 1
[Limit to number of terms a President may serve] No person shall be elected to the office of the President more than twice, and no person who has held the office of President, or acted as President for more than two years of a term to which some other person was elected President shall be elected to the office of the President more than once. But this article shall not apply to any person holding the office of President when this article was proposed by the Congress, and shall not prevent any person who may be holding the office of President, or acting as President, during the term within which this article becomes operative from holding the office of President or acting as President during the remainder of such term.

Section 2
[Ratification] This article shall be inoperative unless it shall have been ratified as an amendment to the Constitution by the legislatures of three-fourths of the several States within seven years from the date of its submission to the States by the Congress.

Amendment 23

(The proposed amendment was sent to the states June 16, 1960, by the Eighty-sixth Congress. It was ratified March 29, 1961.)

Section 1

[Electors for the District of Columbia] The District constituting the seat of Government of the United States shall appoint in such manner as the Congress may direct:

A number of electors of President and Vice President equal to the whole number of Senators and Representatives in Congress to which the District would be entitled if it were a State, but in no event more than the least populous State; they shall be in addition to those appointed by the States, but they shall be considered, for the purposes of the election of President and Vice President, to be electors appointed by a State; and they shall meet in the District and perform such duties as provided by the twelfth article of amendment.

Section 2

[Congress given power to enforce this article] The Congress shall have the power to enforce this article by appropriate legislation.

Amendment 24

(The proposed amendment was sent to the states Aug. 27, 1962, by the Eighty-seventh Congress. It was ratified Jan. 23, 1964.)

Section 1

[Payment of poll tax or other taxes barred in federal elections] The right of citizens of the United States to vote in any primary or other election for President or Vice President, for electors for President or Vice President, or for Senator or Representative in Congress, shall not be denied or abridged by the United States or any State by reasons of failure to pay any poll tax or other tax.

Section 2

[Congress given power to enforce this article] The Congress shall have the power to enforce this article by appropriate legislation.

Amendment 25

(The proposed amendment was sent to the states July 6, 1965, by the Eighty-ninth Congress. It was ratified Feb. 10, 1967.)

Section 1

[Succession of Vice President to Presidency] In case of the removal of the President from office or of his death or resignation, the Vice President shall become President.

Section 2

[Vacancy in office of Vice President] Whenever there is a vacancy in the office of the Vice President, the President shall nominate a Vice President who shall take office upon confirmation by a majority vote of both Houses of Congress.

Section 3

[Vice President as Acting President] Whenever the President transmits to the President pro tempore of the Senate and the Speaker of the House of Representatives his written declaration that he is unable to discharge the powers and duties of his office, and until he transmits to them a written declaration to the contrary, such powers and duties shall be discharged by the Vice President as Acting President.

Section 4

[Vice President as Acting President] Whenever the Vice President and a majority of either the principal officers of the executive departments or of such other body as Congress may by law provide, transmit to the President pro tempore of the Senate and the Speaker of the House of Representatives their written declaration that the President is unable to discharge the powers and duties of his office, the Vice President shall immediately assume the powers and duties of the office as Acting President.

Thereafter, when the President transmits to the President pro tempore of the Senate and the Speaker of the House of Representatives his written declaration that no inability exists, he shall resume the powers and duties of his office unless the Vice President and a majority of either the principal officers of the executive department or of such other body as Congress may by law provide, transmit within four days to the President pro tempore of the Senate and the Speaker of the House of Representatives their written declaration that the President is unable to discharge the powers and duties of his office. Thereupon Congress shall decide the issue, assembling within forty-eight hours for that purpose if not in session. If the Congress, within twenty-one days after receipt of the latter written declaration, or, if Congress is not in session, within twenty-one days after Congress is required to assemble, determines by two-thirds vote of both Houses that the President is unable to discharge the powers and duties of his office, the Vice President shall continue to discharge the same as Acting President; otherwise, the President shall resume the powers and duties of his office.

Amendment 26

(The proposed amendment was sent to the states March 23, 1971, by the Ninety-second Congress. It was ratified July 1, 1971.)

Section 1

[Voting for 18-year-olds] The right of citizens of the United States, who are 18 years of age or older, to vote shall not be denied or abridged by the United States or by any state on account of age.

Section 2

[Congress given power to enforce this article] The Congress shall have power to enforce this article by appropriate legislation.

---

898 How a Bill Becomes a Law

When a Senator or a Representative introduces a bill, he sends it to the clerk of his house, who gives it a number and title. This is the *first reading,* and the bill is referred to the proper committee.

The committee may decide the bill is unwise or unnecessary and *table* it, thus killing it at once. Or it may decide the bill is worthwhile and hold hearings to listen to facts and opinions presented by experts and other interested persons. After members of the committee have debated the bill and perhaps offered amendments, a vote is taken; and if the vote is favorable, the bill is sent back to the floor of the house.

The clerk reads the bill sentence by sentence to the house; this is known as the *second reading.* Members may then debate the bill and offer amendments. In the House of Representatives, the time for debate is limited by a *cloture rule,* but there is no such restriction in the Senate for cloture. Instead, 60 votes are required to limit debate. This makes possible a *filibuster,* in which one or more opponents hold the floor in an attempt to defeat the bill.

The *third reading* is by title only, and the bill is put to a vote, which may be by voice or roll call, depending on the circumstances and parliamentary rules. Members who must be absent at the time but who wish to record their vote may be paired if each negative vote has a balancing affirmative one.

The bill then goes to the other house of Congress, where it may be defeated or passed with or without amendments. If the bill is defeated, it dies. If it is passed with amendments, a joint Congressional committee must be appointed by both houses to iron out the differences.

After its final passage by both houses, the bill is sent to the President. If he approves, he signs it, and the bill becomes a law. However, if he disapproves, he *vetoes* the bill by refusing to sign it. He then sends the bill back to the house of origin with his reasons for the veto. The objections are read and debated, and a roll-call vote is taken. If the bill receives less than a two-thirds vote, it is defeated and goes no farther. But if it receives a two-thirds vote or greater, it is sent to the other house for a vote. If that house also passes it by a two-thirds vote, the President's veto is *overridden,* and the bill becomes a law.

Should the President desire neither to sign nor to veto the bill, he may retain it for ten days, Sundays excepted, after which time it automatically becomes a law without signature. However, if Congress has adjourned within those ten days, the bill is automatically killed, that process of indirect rejection being known as a *pocket veto.*

---

899 # Emancipation Proclamation

January 1, 1863

By the President of the United
States of America:

A Proclamation

Whereas on the 22d day of September, A.D. 1862, a proclamation was issued by the President of the United States, containing, among other things, the following, to wit:

"That on the 1st day of January, A.D. 1863, all persons held as slaves within any State or designated part of a State the people whereof shall then be in rebellion against the Union States shall be then, thenceforward, and forever free; and the executive government of the United States, including the military and naval authority thereof, will recognize and maintain the freedom of such persons and will do no act or acts to repress such persons, or any of them, in any efforts they may make for their actual freedom.

"That the executive will on the 1st day of January aforesaid, by proclamation, designate the States and parts of States, if any, in which the people thereof, respectively, shall then be in rebellion against the United States; and the fact that any State or the people thereof shall on that day be in good faith represented in the Congress of the United States by members chosen thereto at elections wherein a majority of the qualified voters of such States shall have participated shall, in the absence of strong countervailing testimony, be deemed conclusive evidence that such State and the people thereof are not then in rebellion against the United States."

Now therefore, I, Abraham Lincoln, President of the United States, by virtue of the power in me vested as Commander-in-Chief of the Army and Navy of the United States in time of actual armed rebellion against the authority and government of the United States, and as a fit and necessary war measure for suppressing said rebellion, do, on this 1st day of January, A.D. 1863, and in accordance with my purpose so to do, publicly proclaimed for the full period of one hundred days from the first day above mentioned, order and designate as the States and parts of States wherein the people thereof, respectively, are this day in rebellion against the United States the following, to wit:

Arkansas, Texas, Louisiana (except the parishes of St. Bernard, Plaquemines, Jefferson, St. John, St. Charles, St. James, Ascension, Assumption, Terrebonne, Lafourche, St. Mary, St. Martin, and Orleans, including the city of New Orleans), Mississippi, Alabama, Florida, Georgia, South Carolina, North Carolina, and Virginia (except the forty-eight counties designated as West Virginia, and also the counties of Berkeley, Accomac, Northhampton, Elizabeth City, York, Princess Anne, and Norfolk, including the cities of Norfolk and Portsmouth), and which excepted parts are for the present left precisely as if this proclamation were not issued.

And by virtue of the power and for the purpose aforesaid, I do order and declare that all persons held as slaves within said designated States and parts of States are, and henceforward shall be, free; and that the Executive Government of the United States, including the military and naval authorities thereof, will recognize and maintain the freedom of said persons.

And I hereby enjoin upon the people so declared to be free to abstain from all violence, unless in necessary self-defense; and I recommend to them that, in all cases when allowed, they labor faithfully for reasonable wages.

And I further declare and make known that such persons of suitable condition will be received into the armed service of the United States to garrison forts, positions, stations, and other places, and to man vessels of all sorts in said service.

And upon this act, sincerely believed to be an act of justice, warranted by the Constitution upon military necessity, I invoke the considerate judgment of mankind and the gracious favor of Almighty God.

U.S. Presidents

(* Did not finish term)

1	George Washington	April 30, 1789 - March 3, 1797	.... John Adams	1
2	John Adams	March 4, 1797 - March 3, 1801	...... Thomas Jefferson	2
3	Thomas Jefferson	March 4, 1801 - March 3, 1805	.... Aaron Burr	3
	Thomas Jefferson	March 4, 1805 - March 3, 1809	.... George Clinton	4
4	James Madison	March 4, 1809 - March 3, 1813	.... George Clinton	
	James Madison	March 4, 1813 - March 3, 1817	.... Elbridge Gerry	5
5	James Monroe	March 4, 1817 - March 3, 1825	... Daniel D. Tompkins	6
6	John Quincy Adams	March 4, 1825 - March 3, 1829	.......John C. Calhoun	7
7	Andrew Jackson	March 4, 1829 - March 3, 1833	.......John C. Calhoun	
	Andrew Jackson	March 4, 1833 - March 3, 1837	..... Martin Van Buren	8
8	Martin Van Buren	March 4, 1837 - March 3, 1841	.... Richard M. Johnson	9
9	William Henry Harrison*.	March 4, 1841 - April 4, 1841	...........John Tyler	10
10	John Tyler	April 6, 1841 - March 3, 1845		
11	James K. Polk	March 4, 1845 - March 3, 1849	...... George M. Dallas	11
12	Zachary Taylor*	March 5, 1849 - July 9, 1850	.... Millard Fillmore	12
13	Millard Fillmore	July 10, 1850 - March 3, 1853		
14	Franklin Pierce	March 4, 1853 - March 3, 1857	.... William R. King	13
15	James Buchanan	March 4, 1857 - March 3, 1861	.... John C. Breckinridge	14
16	Abraham Lincoln	March 4, 1861 - March 3, 1865	...... Hannibal Hamlin	15
	Abraham Lincoln*	March 4, 1865 - April 15, 1865	.... Andrew Johnson	16
17	Andrew Johnson	April 15, 1865 - March 3, 1869		
18	Ulysses S. Grant	March 4, 1869 - March 3, 1873	.... Schuyler Colfax	17
	Ulysses S. Grant	March 4, 1873 - March 3, 1877	.... Henry Wilson	18
19	Rutherford B. Hayes	March 4, 1877 - March 3, 1881	... William A. Wheeler	19
20	James A. Garfield*	March 4, 1881 - Sept. 19, 1881	..... Chester A. Arthur	20
21	Chester A. Arthur	Sept. 20, 1881 - March 3, 1885		
22	Grover Cleveland ../......	March 4, 1885 - March 3, 1889	... Thomas A. Hendricks	21
23	Benjamin Harrison	March 4, 1889 - March 3, 1893	.... Levi P. Morton	22
24	Grover Cleveland	March 4, 1893 - March 3, 1897	..... Adlai E. Stevenson	23
25	William McKinley	March 4, 1897 - March 3, 1901	.... Garret A. Hobart	24
	William McKinley*	March 4, 1901 - Sept. 14, 1901	..... Theodore Roosevelt	25
26	Theodore Roosevelt	Sept. 14, 1901 - March 3, 1905		
	Theodore Roosevelt	March 4, 1905 - March 3, 1909	... Charles W. Fairbanks	26
27	William H. Taft	March 4, 1909 - March 3, 1913	..... James S. Sherman	27
28	Woodrow Wilson	March 4, 1913 - March 3, 1921	....Thomas R. Marshall	28
29	Warren G. Harding*	March 4, 1921 - Aug. 2, 1923	.... Calvin Coolidge	29
30	Calvin Coolidge	Aug. 3, 1923 - March 3, 1925		
	Calvin Coolidge	March 4, 1925 - March 3, 1929	......Charles G. Dawes	30
31	Herbert C. Hoover	March 4, 1929 - March 3, 1933	.... Charles Curtis	31
32	Franklin D. Roosevelt ...	March 4, 1933 - Jan. 20, 1941	.... John N. Garner	32
	Franklin D. Roosevelt ...	Jan. 20, 1941 - Jan. 20, 1945	...... Henry A. Wallace	33
	Franklin D. Roosevelt* ...	Jan. 20, 1945 - April 12, 1945	...... Harry S. Truman	34
33	Harry S. Truman	April 12, 1945 - Jan. 20, 1949		
	Harry S. Truman	Jan. 20, 1949 - Jan. 20, 1953	......Alben W. Barkley	35
34	Dwight D. Eisenhower....	Jan. 20, 1953 - Jan. 20, 1961	......Richard M. Nixon	36
35	John F. Kennedy*	Jan. 20, 1961 - Nov. 22, 1963	.....Lyndon B. Johnson	37
36	Lyndon B. Johnson	Nov. 22, 1963 - Jan. 20, 1965		
	Lyndon B. Johnson	Jan. 20, 1965 - Jan. 20, 1969	....Hubert H. Humphrey	38
37	Richard M. Nixon........	Jan. 20, 1969 - Jan. 20, 1973	.........Sprio T. Agnew	39
	Richard M. Nixon*.......	Jan. 20, 1973 - Aug. 9, 1974	.... Gerald R. Ford	40
38	Gerald R. Ford	Aug. 9, 1974 - Jan. 20, 1977	... Nelson A. Rockefeller	41
39	James E. Carter	Jan. 20, 1977 - Jan. 20, 1981	.... Walter Mondale	42
40	Ronald Reagan	Jan. 20, 1981 - Jan. 20, 1985	.... George Bush	43
	Ronald Reagan	Jan. 20, 1985 -	.... George Bush	

Order of Presidential Succession

1. The Vice President
2. Speaker of the House
3. President pro tempore of the Senate
4. Secretary of State
5. Secretary of the Treasury
6. Secretary of Defense
7. Attorney General
8. Secretary of the Interior
9. Secretary of Agriculture
10. Secretary of Commerce
11. Secretary of Labor
12. Secretary of Health, Education, & Welfare
13. Secretary of Housing and Urban Development
14. Secretary of Transportation

Index

Please note: The index which follows contains **topic** numbers, not page numbers. The index also lists first those entries which give a basic explanation or definition. For more information on using the index, see Handbook page *iii* .

A

COMPLEX sentence, 101, 386-387
COMPOSITION, 453, 443-452
COMPOUND
    Direct object, 94
    Modifier, 183
    Noun, 7
    Number, 176, 140
    Predicate, 91, 384
    Sentence, 100, 385
    Subject, 87, 92, 384
    Word, 211
COMPOUND-complex sentence, 102
COMPUTERS, 892-895
COMPUTER terms, 893-895
CONCLUDING paragraph, 449
CONCRETE, 752
CONCRETE noun, 4
CONCRETE poetry, 519
CONFLICT, 753
CONJUNCTION, 75-79
CONJUNCTIVE adverb, 166
CONNOTATION, 754, 362
CONSONANCE, 496
CONSTITUTION, U.S., 896
CONTEXT, 755
CONTEXT clues, 713-716
Continual/continuous, 254
CONTRACTIONS, 204
CONTRAST, 598
    Arrangement by, 342
CONTRAST couplet, 520
CONTRAST paragraph, 632
CONVERSION table, 891
COORDINATE conjunctions, 76
COPYRIGHT, 676
Cord/chord, 250
CORRECTION symbols, back cover
CORRELATIVE conjunctions, 77
Council/counsel, 255
COUPLET, 497
Course/coarse, 252
Creak/creek, 256
Cymbal/symbol, 257

D

DACTYLIC, 501
DAGGER, 216

DANGLING modifier, 398
DASH, 172-174
DATES,
    Holidays, 846
    Punctuation of, 153
DECIMAL/fraction table, 891
DECLARATIVE sentences, 103
DEDUCTIVE reasoning, 453
Deer/dear, 258
DEFINE, 599
DEFINITION,
    Guidelines for writing, 457
DEFINITION poetry, 521
DEMONSTRATIVE pronoun, 27
DENOTATION, 756
DENOUEMENT, 757
DEPENDENT clause, 97
DESCRIBE, 600
DESCRIPTION, 453, 758
Desert/dessert, 259
DETAILS, 453
    Arranging, 342
    Kinds of, 425
DEWEY decimal system, 668-669
DIAGONAL, 215
DIALOGUE, 759
    Guidelines for punctuating,
    544, 190-197
    Using, 543-544
DICTION, 760
DICTIONARY, use of, 686-697
    Prefixes, 719
    Roots, 721
    Sample page, 697
    Suffixes, 720
DIDACTIC, 767
Die/dye, 260
DIERESIS, 216
DIMETER, 516
DIRECT object, 46, 93
DIRECT quotation,
    Punctuation of, 190-197, 544
DISCUSS, 601
DIVISIBILITY tests, 872
DOCUMENTATION, in classroom
    report, 471
DOUBLE negative, 405
DRAMA, 768
DRAMATIC monologue, 769
DREAM poetry, 522
Dye/die, 260

E

EDITOR, letter to, 568-569
Effect/affect, 219
ELEGY, 498
ELLIPSIS, 147-149
EMANCIPATION Proclamation, 899
Emigrate/immigrate, 274
EMPATHY, 770
EMPHASIS, 453
END rhyme, 499
EPIC, 500
EPIGRAM, 771
EPITAPH, 772
EPITHET, 773
ESSAY, literary term, 453, 774
ESSAY, the whole composition, 443-452
    Checklist for revising and proofreading, 452
    Planning and writing the composition, 444
    Sample student essay, 451
ESSAY test, 592-613
ETYMOLOGY, 692
EVALUATE, 602
EVALUATING, 640-644
EVENT,
    Guidelines for describing, 458
EVIDENCE, using, 646-658
EXAGGERATION, 775
Except/accept, 218
EXCLAMATION point, 188-189
EXCLAMATORY sentence, 106
EXPLAIN, 603
EXPOSITION, 453, 776, 534
EXTENDED definition, 453

F

FACT vs. opinion, 647
Faint/feign/feint, 261
FALLING action, 777, 537
FARCE, 778
Farther/further, 262
FEMININE gender, 8
Fewer/less, 263

FIGURATIVE language, 453, 366-369, 779
FIGURE of speech, 780
FILL in the blanks test, 735
Fir/fur, 264
Flair/flare, 265
FLASHBACK, 781
FOCUS, 453
FOOT, 501
FOOTNOTING (Giving Credit), 471
For/fore/four, 266
FOREIGN words, punctuation of, 200
FORESHADOWING, 782
FOREWORD, 677
FORM, 453, 783
FORMING an opinion, 648
FRACTION, punctuation, 177
FRACTION to decimal table, 891
FRAGMENT sentence, 372
FREE verse, 502
FREE WRITING, 453, 350
FRIENDLY letter, 546-554
    Form, 548
    Model, 547
Further/farther, 262
FUSED sentence, 374
FUTURE perfect tense, 42
FUTURE tense, 38

G

GENDER, 8
GENERALIZATION, 453
GENERALIZING, 626-637
GENRE, 784
GERUND, 53
GLOSSARY, 681
Good/well, 267
GOTHIC novel, 785
GRAMMAR, 1-106, 453
GUIDELINES,
    Free writing, 350
    Listening skills, 725
    Note-taking skills, 722-723
    Selecting a topic, 351-352
    Study-reading, 709
    Taking a test, 730
    Writing assignments, 726
GUIDELINES for writing,
    Business letter, 575-579

LIMITING the subject, 453
LINKING verb, 50
LIST, in essay tests, 605
LIST poetry, 524
LISTENING skills, 724-725
LITERAL, 453
LITERARY terms, 736-832
LOADED words, 453
LOCAL color, 788
LOCATION, arrangement by, 342
LOGIC, 453
Loose/lose/loss, 285
LYRIC, 506

M

Maid/made, 286
Mail/male, 287
Main/mane, 288
MALAPROPISM, 789
MAPS, 849-857
    Index to world maps, 855
    Latitude and longitude, 854
    Legend, 852
    Map scale, 853
MASCULINE gender, 8
MATCHING test, 733
MATH SKILLS,
    Decimals, 879-881
    Fractions, 866-878
    Prime numbers, 862
    Solving word problems, 882-889
MATHEMATICS, symbols, 858
    Table of
    Multiplication/division, 865
    Table of
    Weights/measure, 890-891
May/can, 244
MEANING, dictionary, 696
MEASURES, weights, 890-891
Meat/meet, 289
MELODRAMA, 790
MEMORY, reading, 705
MEMORY, writing, 425
MEMORY techniques, 705-708, 729
Metal/meddle/medal/mettle, 290
METAPHOR, 368, 484
METEOROLOGY symbols, 846
METER, 507
METHODS of arrangement, 342
METRIC system, 891

Miner/minor, 291
MISPLACED modifier, 398-400
MODIFIER, 453
MODIFIERS, misplaced, 398-400
MONOMETER, 516
MOOD,
    Literary term, 791
MORAL, 792
Moral/morale, 292
Morning/mourning, 293
MOTIF, 793
MULTIPLE choice test, 734
MULTIPLICATION/division table,
    865
MYTH, 794

N

NAME poetry, 525
NARRATION, 453, 796
NARRATIVE, model, 347
NARRATOR, 795
NEGATIVE, double, 405
NEUTER gender, 8
New/knew, 277
No/know, 278
NOMINATIVE case, 9
NONRESTRICTIVE phrase/clause,
    164
NOTE cards, 466
NOTE-TAKING skills, 722-723
NOUN, 2-9
    Collective, 5
    Common, 3
    Compound, 7
    Concrete, 4
    Plurals of, 123-130
    Possessives, 207-211
    Proper, 3
NOVEL, 797
NUMBER,
    Compound, 176, 140
    Noun, 6
    Pronoun, 13
    Punctuation of, 135-140, 152,
    169, 176-177, 201, 205-206
NUMBER, shift in, 402, 389-397
NUMBER, verbs, 30
Number/amount, 227
NUMBERS, use of, 135-140
NUMERALS, Roman, 891

ROOT,
    List of, 721
RUN-ON sentence, 374

S

SALUTATION, 562
SARCASM, 818
SATIRE, 819
Scene/seen, 308
Seam/seem, 309
SELECTING a topic, 351
    Sample topics, 352
Sell/cell, 248
Semiannual, 228
SEMICOLON, 165-167
SENSORY writing, 425
Sent/scent/cent, 249
SENTENCE, 81-97
    Levels, 427-428
    Types, 98-106
    Writing effectively, 370-406
SENTENCE arrangement, 342
SENTENCE combining, 381-387
SENTENCE variety, 411-417
SEPTET, 514
SESTET, 514
SETTING, 820
Sew/so/sow, 310
SHAKESPEAREAN sonnet, 513
SHAPES, commonly used, 846
SHIFT in:
    Number, 404
SHORT story, 530-545
    Characteristics of, 531-537
    Checklist, 542
    Model, 538
    Model plan, 539
    Writing the short story, 530,
    540-544
Sight/cite/site, 311
SIGNS, hand, 846
SIGNS, plural of, 206
SIMILE, 367, 483
SIMPLE predicate, 89
SIMPLE sentence, 99
SIMPLE subject, 85
SINGULAR, see "Number" and
    "Plurals"
Sit/set, 312

Site/sight/cite, 311
SLANG, 764
SLAPSTICK, 821
SLICE of life, 822
SOCIAL note, 555
Sole/soul, 313
SOLILOQUY, 823
Some/sum, 314
SONNET, 513
Sore/soar, 315
SPECIFIC details, outlining, 446
SPEECH skills, 833-845
SPELLING,
    Commonly misspelled, 142
    Dictionary, 687
    Numbers, 135-140
    Plurals of words, 123-130
    Possessives, 19, 207-213
    Rules, 141
SPONDAIC, 501
SPONTANEOUS writing, 453, 350
SQ3R, 699
STANZA, 514
STATE, 610
STATES, U.S.,
    Abbreviations, 132
Stationary/stationery, 316
Steal/steel, 317
STEREOTYPE, 824
STREAM of consciousness, 825
STRUCTURE, 826
STUDY skills, 698-709
STUDY-READING guidelines, 709
STYLE, 827
STYLE, writing with, 354-420
    Improving through revising,
    357-420
    Using a natural style, 355-356
SUBJECT,
    Of a sentence, 84-87
    Shift in, 404
    Understood, 83
SUBJECTIVE writing, 453
SUBORDINATE conjunction, 78,
    387
SUBSTANDARD language, 405-406
SUCCESSION to the Presidency, 901
SUFFIX,
    List of, 720
Sum/some, 314
SUMMARIZE, 611, 624
SUMMARY, writing the, 624

303